Twayne's English Authors Series

Sylvia E. Bowman, *Editor*

INDIANA UNIVERSITY

Thomas De Quincey

(TEAS) 83

Thomas De Quincey

By JUDSON S. LYON

State University College
New Paltz, New York

Twayne Publishers, Inc.　::　New York

To Peg

THOMAS DE QUINCEY

Preface

In the last thirty-five years the life and works of Thomas De Quincey have begun to receive the close scholarly study they usually were denied in the past. The result has been a gradual revaluation of the man and his writings, which has proceeded quietly on several different fronts. Estimates of the influence of opium, the effects of psychological factors and interests, the quality of his scholarship and thought, and the relation of his works to their sources have all been sharply altered. The purpose of this book is to reconsider De Quincey in the light of the principal results of this revaluation and to present him, in a balanced account and estimate, as he appears today.

Since the autobiographical writings now seem the cornerstone of De Quincey's achievement and since they are the principal source of information about the most interesting parts of his life, the first section of this book is devoted to a retelling of his life story as it is preserved in his writings and in independent records. Thus it may serve in part as an introduction to De Quincey's autobiographical works, preserving some of the emphases and colors he imparted in recounting the passages of his own life. While this biographical section does not pretend to factual completeness, it does resolve some of the contradictions and confusions about matters of fact to be found in previous biographies; and it treats some aspects of De Quincey's life from the fresh perspective of present-day information and outlooks.

The next section of the book is devoted to a critical review of De Quincey's works. After brief comments on the problem of the classification of the works, the various types are considered roughly in the order of their importance. First come the autobiographical works, including the largely autobiographical *Confessions,* and then the *Suspiria,* also partly autobiographical. Next come the biographies, literary reminiscences, and character sketches. Subsequent chapters treat the literary criticism, theoretical and practical; and the history, fiction, and semi-fiction. Categories of lesser extent or importance—such as humorous writings, and studies of politics, economics, religion, philosophy, education, language, and science—are grouped together in a chapter on miscellaneous works. Most of his works are touched upon, and attempts are made at fresh interpretations and estimates of the more important ones. Sources are discussed where they seem significant.

An analytical description and an evaluation of De Quincey's style follow. In the concluding chapter I summarize what seem to me the salient characteristics of the man and his work, and I outline the history of his reputation and influence to the present time. In the bibliography I have listed the most important basic works for the study of De Quincey; more specific references will be found in the notes.

I am deeply indebted to my predecessors, in more ways than I can acknowledge adequately in footnotes. Among past De Quincey scholars, I am most keenly conscious of my debts to David Masson and Horace A. Eaton; and, among more recent scholars, to Albert Goodman, John E. Jordan, Elizabeth W. Schneider, and René Wellek. I am indebted to the trustees of Dove Cottage for information and photographs based on materials in their custody, and acknowledgment is also made to the Manchester Public Libraries Committee for permission to reproduce a likeness of De Quincey from material in their possession. I have also been assisted by a grant from the Research Foundation of the State University of New York. Finally, I wish to express gratitude of a more personal sort to Miss Clare Craig, the great-granddaughter of De Quincey, for her kind interest and assistance; to John E. Jordan, Professor of English at the University of California at Berkeley, and M. J. Harkin, Language and Literature Librarian of the Manchester Public Library, for generous responses to appeals for incidental assistance; and to my wife, who typed the first draft and whose encouragement and criticism have been indispensable.

JUDSON S. LYON

State University College
New Paltz, New York

Contents

THOMAS DE QUINCEY

by
JUDSON S. LYON

The aim of this book is to present Thomas De Quincey and his works as they appear in the light of modern information. De Quincey has been undergoing a gradual reevaluation in the past few decades. This book brings together the results of that reevaluation and arrives at a fresh critical estimate.

The principal facts of De Quincey's life are presented in the new perspective created by the correction of mistaken notions about the causes and effects of opium-addiction and about the quality of De Quincey's scholarship. The sources of De Quincey's unusual character are shown to lie not in opium but in psychological pressures created by early experiences.

De Quincey's total output as a writer is reviewed and re-assessed. His writings based on his own experience and observation emerge as his principal achievement. To clarify the nature of his most original creation, *Suspira de Profundis*, the scattered fragments of this unfinished work are analyzed as a whole for the first time. The achievement of this book is a fresh view of this strange and gifted writer, in all his oddity and power, his humor and compassion.

Chronology

1785   Thomas De Quincey born on August 15, in Manchester, England.

1790   Sister Jane died.

1791   Family moved to Greenhay, new home outside Manchester.

1792   Sister Elizabeth died.

1793   Father died.

1793–   Studied with Reverend Samuel Hall.
1796

1796   Greenhay sold. Family moved to Bath.

1796–   At Bath Grammar School, until accidentally injured.
1799   Brother William died.

1799   First read Wordsworth's poetry.

1799–   Attended school in Winkfield, Wiltshire.
1800

1800   Visited Ireland with Lord Westport in summer; spent autumn visiting Lady Carbery at Laxton, Northamptonshire.

1800–   At Manchester Grammar School. Vacations in Everton,
1802   near Liverpool.

1801   Mother moved to the Priory, Chester.

1802   De Quincey ran away from Manchester Grammar School. Vagrancy in Wales and London. Met Ann.

1803   Reconciled with guardians in March. Went to Everton, where he kept diary. First wrote to Wordsworth. Entered Worcester College, Oxford, in December.

1804–   Student at Oxford. Vacations in London, Bath, Everton,
1808   and Lake Country.

1804   De Quincey, visiting London, first took opium, for facial neuralgia. Met Charles Lamb this year or the next.

1806   De Quincey reached majority and received inheritance.

1807   Met Coleridge in August, and Wordsworth and Southey in November. Gave anonymous gift of three hundred pounds to Coleridge.

1808   Left Oxford abruptly in May before completing examinations.

1808–   November–February, living with Wordsworths at Allan
1809   Bank. Met John Wilson.

1809   In London, saw Wordsworth's *The Convention of Cintra* through press. Leased Dove Cottage, Grasmere.

1810–   Grasmere; London; and Wrington, Somerset.
1811

1812   Went to London to study law. After Catherine Wordsworth's death in June, serious illness and long convalescence.

1813   De Quincey became a confirmed opium addict.

1813–   Grasmere, London, and Wrington. Gradual estrangement
1816   from Wordsworth. First visited Edinburgh. Fortune exhausted. Deep narcosis.

1816   Birth of son William, November 9.

1817   Married Margaret Simpson, country girl, Grasmere, February 15.

1818–   Deep narcosis, and debts. Political activity. Editor of
1819   *The Westmorland Gazette.*

1820   Visited Edinburgh and arranged to write for *Blackwood's,* but arrangement soon failed.

1821   In London, published *The Confessions of an English Opium-Eater* in *The London Magazine* in September and October.

1821–   London and Grasmere; published many articles in Lon-
1825   don periodicals.

1822   *Confessions* published in book form.

1823–   Deep narcosis.
1824

1824   Translation of *Walladmor* published.

1826   Went to Edinburgh, and began writing for *Blackwood's.*

1826–   Edinburgh and Grasmere. Acquaintance with Carlyle.
1829   Contributed regularly to *Edinburgh Saturday Post* and *Edinburgh Evening Gazette,* 1827–28.

1830   Settled permanently in Edinburgh with family (wife and seven children).

1832	Novel *Klosterheim* published. Began publishing articles in *Tait's*. Eighth and last child born. Son Julius died. De Quincey twice imprisoned for debt.
1833–1839	De Quincey bankrupt, forced to flee creditors and to take refuge from debts in "Holyrood" sanctuary.
1834–1840	Autobiographical Sketches and Reminiscences appeared in *Tait's*.
1835	Eldest son William died.
1837	De Quincey's wife died.
1840	Family moved to Mavis Bush Cottage, Lasswade.
1841–1843	De Quincey lived in Glasgow. Newspaper work.
1842	Son Horace died in China.
1844	Last serious opium crisis. *Logic of Political Economy* published.
1845–1849	*Suspiria de Profundis* appeared in *Blackwood's*.
1846	De Quincey's mother died.
1847	De Quincey in Glasgow again. Financial worries ended.
1848	End of opium struggles.
1849	Last contributions to *Blackwood's*.
1850	Began publishing in *Hogg's Instructor*.
1851	Last contribution to *Tait's*. American collected edition began appearing.
1853	First volume of Edinburgh collected edition published.
1854	De Quincey moved back to Edinburgh.
1857	Visited daughter in Ireland.
1859	De Quincey died in Edinburgh, December 8, aged 74.

CHAPTER 1

De Quincey's Life

I *Introduction*

THOMAS DE QUINCEY might well have lived and died
mute and inglorious, or perhaps known only as the author of
a few careful works of erudite antiquarianism or a few strange
flights of exquisite fantasy. Throughout most of his seventy-four
years he was deeply committed to the life of the mind, and for
various complex reasons he greatly preferred to live and study in
quiet solitude. There was no reason for him to rush into print. His
family circumstances assured him of a university education and a
financial competence; he found writing painful and exhausting,
and he had no strong appetite for fame. Nearly everything about
him seemed to indicate that his would be the quiet and obscure
life of a gentleman scholar; and, as late as his thirty-sixth year,
such was the life he might have seemed to have led, for he had
entered upon no gainful career and had written and published
hardly a word.

However, a few quirks of character and a few turns of fate had
already made his course far from quiet; and they now decreed
that he was to be anything but unproductive. For suddenly, mid-
point in his life, he was forced by a multitude of personal problems, including sheer poverty, to turn his talents to the uncongenial work of a journalistic hack. And such he remained, desperate
and harried, poverty-stricken and ill, for most of the remaining
years of his life.

The product of these labors amounts to fourteen volumes—over
six thousand closely printed pages—in the standard collected edition of his works, which is far from complete. All but a handful of
the hundreds of works he produced were designed for the periodical press, and first appeared there; but they were rescued from
the fate of the purely ephemeral by the fact that their author was
instinctively a conscious, a fastidious, artist—one of the supreme

stylists of English prose; and he therefore often wrote far better than his immediate purposes required. In variety, his writings are matched by those of few other English authors; they range over history, biography, autobiography, criticism, fiction, fantasy, politics, economics, science, religion, philosophy, and education. Thus the accidents which led this brilliant, busy mind to devote its life energies to journalistic writing also decreed that posterity should be left a valuable legacy of prose.

The life of Thomas De Quincey spanned a period that brought great changes to England. Born on the eve of the French Revolution, he grew up during the Napoleonic Wars; lived and worked on through the great period of legislative reforms in the early Victorian Age; and, after a flourishing and productive Indian summer in the mid-Victorian era of expanding empire and the triumphs of Tennyson and Dickens, died in the year of the *Origin of Species* (1859). The story of his life is similarly varied. His childhood was comparatively happy, and full of brilliant promise. In his youth and early manhood he developed as a literary prodigy, he became associated with several of the leading writers of the time, but he plunged into erratic and crippling misadventures. His middle and later years were spent in an almost monastic seclusion, poverty, and industry, alleviated only by the concerns—happy and tragic —of his large family of a wife and eight children.

II　*Birth and Childhood*

De Quincey was born on August 15, 1785, in the industrial city of Manchester in the western Midlands. His father was known as Thomas Quincey, for the "De" had apparently been dropped from the name in previous generations of the family. This Thomas Quincey, the son of a Leicestershire squire, and heir to a modest fortune of six thousand pounds, had been a successful linen draper and was now engaged in foreign and wholesale trade. A man with a deep reverence for learning and the owner of an extensive library, he also had some pretensions as an author; for he had already written and published a book describing travels in the Midlands. The mother, Elizabeth Penson Quincey, was the daughter of an army officer who had been attached to the king's household. Her two brothers were serving abroad in the Indian service.

During their twelve years of married life, this young couple had eight children, four boys and four girls. Two of them died in childhood, and a third at the age of fifteen. Only two—Thomas and a sister Jane—lived to advanced age. Thomas was the second son, and the fourth child, in the family.[1] Since his father was generally away from home, traveling abroad on business or seeking relief for an ominous lung infection, and since his elder brother William was also usually away, the child Thomas found himself the pampered darling of a populous female household. In addition to his mother and his three sisters, with whom he lived and slept, there were various female servants and friends of the family. Since the child was tiny and weak, suffering a chronic ague from his second through his fourth year, as well as such common childhood complaints as whooping cough, he was fondly and indulgently nursed. During his infancy the family lived in a rustic cottage on the outskirts of Manchester called "The Farm"; but, when he was about six they moved into a mansion called "Greenhay," which they had built about a mile out of the city.[2]

The happiness of De Quincey's childhood home was frequently marred by tragedies. His maternal grandmother, who joined the household for the duration of her final illness, died when he was four and a half. About the same time his sister Jane, aged three and a half, fell sick and died; he was still too young to be fully aware of the event, although he later professed to remember the rumored cruelty of a servant to the dying girl. His closest companion, and probably the person to whom he was most deeply attached, was his eldest sister Elizabeth; in his seventh year she was suddenly stricken with hydrocephalus, probably tubercular in origin, and died after some days of suffering. This time the boy was more fully aware of what was happening and experienced a shattering anguish. The day after her death, De Quincey later recorded (I, 38),[3] he stole secretly to her death chamber; and, standing there, an urchin of six, in the presence of her corpse, with sunlight blazing through the open window and a strange wind rising, he fell into a trance that brought him an apocalyptic vision, one so vast and impressive that he remembered it clearly for the rest of his life. Elizabeth's death may well have persisted as a powerful influence, conscious and subconscious, on De Quincey's later years; for her shadowy figure and her final agony reappear in countless guises in his dreams and writings.

Another tragedy befell the family a year later, 1793. The father, unsuccessful in his long search for health, was brought home dying of tuberculosis. He was almost a total stranger to his son Thomas, since he had been abroad—in Portugal, Madeira, and the West Indies—for much of the child's young life. The father's return was a deeply impressive event for the small boy; for, kept awake and waiting, with his sisters, a brother, and the servants, through a long evening on the front lawn at Greenhay, aware that his unfamiliar father was coming home to die, he finally saw the coach approaching at a funereal pace, bearing the dying man, propped up on a mass of pillows. The experience was to linger in the son's dreams for the rest of his life. During the following weeks, as his father wasted away, the quiet and delicate boy was permitted to spend much of his time at the bedside; and, when death came to the delirious man on July 18, young Thomas was present.

The father was only thirty-nine when he died; his death placed a heavy burden of responsibility on his young widow. The previous deaths of Jane and Elizabeth left her now with five surviving children: the eldest, William; a daughter, Mary; Thomas, aged seven; a younger son, Richard, always called "Pink" in the family, about four; and another daughter, about two, named Jane after the one who had died. Soon after her husband's death, Mrs. Quincey bore her last child, a son, whom she named Henry. For the support of herself and these six children, Mrs. Quincey was left in an elaborate and thoughtful will a modest fortune with an income of about one thousand six hundred pounds a year. She was made a guardian, along with four of her husband's trusted friends, of the children.

An intelligent and pious woman, Mrs. Quincey took a conscientious view of her responsibilities. She felt an anxious concern for her children and loyally did her best throughout a long life to guide them and to provide for them. She encouraged them in the cultivation of their intellects, and she instilled in them a strong sense of decorum in dress and manners. However, she had a few characteristics which were tragically to thwart her best efforts. She was austerely systematic and authoritative, lacking in humor and sympathetic understanding, and inhibited from communicating the affection which she certainly felt. De Quincey later recalled a daily ritual, one which was unfailingly repeated for years, that gives a telling glimpse of her character. Every morning all her children—for a time six of them—were carefully dressed and groomed; marched into her dressing room, where each in turn was submitted to her detailed inspection; and then sprinkled with lavender water and milk of roses, kissed on the forehead, and dismissed.[4] Her manner with her children, despite her good intentions, may well have been the principal cause of the later rebelliousness of two of her sons, Thomas and "Pink."

For reasons unknown, Mrs. Quincey and her children restored the "De" to their name after her husband's death. Throughout her life she was at home in higher social strata than her husband's background and circumstances could have opened to her; perhaps she felt that the "De" enhanced the dignity of her name. However, after a few years she dropped it again and persisted in addressing her children without it. Nevertheless, her sons continued to use it throughout their lives; and her daughters did so occasionally.[5]

For the boy Thomas, his father's death brought a succession of changes in his way of life. His brother William, a clever and mischievous boy about four years older than he, was almost as much a stranger at Greenhay as the father had been. He had lived for a time abroad with his father, and had subsequently been placed in a boarding school, perhaps partly because he was found unmanageable at home. Thus, in his absence, Thomas, a shy and delicate child, had been accustomed to solitude and to a peaceful life among his sisters and the younger children. Although he had received no formal education, he had learned to read and had devoured many of the books in the excellent nursery library. From early childhood he had been much given to dreaming and reverie, and he also had developed a hypersensitivity to the opinions of others. When William suddenly rejoined the household, his arrival wrought a violent revolution in the quiet tenor of Thomas' life. A bright and unruly boy of about eleven, with all the cocksure arrogance and combativeness that the ordeal of a public school could inculcate, William quickly established his authority over his younger brothers and sisters. Thomas completely submitted to his awesome and contemptuous domination, and life suddenly became full of activity, adventure, and conflict.

III *School Days*

The two boys were now sent daily for tutoring to the home of one of their guardians, the Reverend Samuel Hall, who lived in

Salford, about two miles from Greenhay. This arrangement continued for the next three years, and Mr. Hall and his household became a major influence on the development of Thomas. In some respects an able and conscientious man, the tutor gave his pupils a firm grounding in the Classics, especially Latin. De Quincey became an accomplished Latinist before he was eleven. Among the exacting requirements his tutor made of Thomas was a weekly summary of his own Sunday sermon, to be presented accurately and from memory. De Quincey later looked back on this practice as valuable intellectual training. What has not been sufficiently recognized, however, is the possibility that such close attention to Mr. Hall's pulpit rhetoric—however commonplace that may have been—continued over a period of three years at this impressionable age, may well have had a permanent influence on De Quincey's sense of the syntax and cadence of the English language. Many years later, Mr. Hall appeared in retrospect to De Quincey as dreadfully dull and limited, but he seems to have done his best for the boy, and certainly his efforts were not all wasted. De Quincey's later judgment may have been colored by the fact that Hall had meanwhile served as the principal spokesman for his guardians over a period when they bungled their responsibilities toward him so badly that they became a symbol for him of all the evils of guardianship.

As the young brothers walked each day the two miles to Hall's home in Salford and back, their route took them past a cotton factory by a bridge, where their neat grooming and aristocratic attire soon aroused the attention and ridicule of the boys who worked in the factory. Insults were exchanged, challenges issued, and hostilities begun, to be renewed almost daily as the boys passed the factory at quitting time on their way home. The fertile imagination of William soon inflated the daily encounter into a full-scale war, with all the planning, protocol, and danger of the most elaborate historic battles. Thomas, as his brother's inferior in military rank, was subjected to rigorous discipline, and on a few occasions suffered the ignominy of capture, once being humiliated by kisses from the factory girls before his release.

William's restless fancies and bold adventurousness filled Thomas' life with excitement and terror. William composed treatises and delivered lectures to his audience of brothers and sisters on a vast variety of subjects, including philosophy and necro-

mancy; he tried to devise means of flying and of walking on ceil-
ings; he published a semi-weekly home gazette containing unflattering accounts of Thomas' military conduct; and he composed a
tragic drama and organized his sisters and brothers to produce it.
He created two imaginary kingdoms, one—"Tygrosylvania"—
ruled by himself, and the other—"Gombroon"—by Thomas; these
became so real to the younger brother that he suffered dreadful
anguish at the succession of pressures and humiliations his kingdom experienced at the hands of his brother's. For Thomas, life
with William was a succession of frightening trials. He was repeatedly dared into ascending to terrifying heights on a tall swing
at the home of one of their guardians. He was even challenged to
mount a vicious horse, which he declined to do.

During this period Thomas was once again a witness to the
pathetic sufferings of some innocent young girls. His tutor, Mr.
Hall, had twin daughters about twelve to fourteen years of age,
who were deaf mutes and who had also been disfigured by disease. Their mother, apparently a proud and foolish woman, regarded them as idiots, looked on them with angry humiliation,
and treated them harshly as menial servants. Young Thomas saw
these pathetic creatures almost daily; and, coming to suspect that
they were far more intelligent and sensitive than others considered
them, he secretly developed a strong bond of mutual affection
with them. Suddenly, only a week after one of their most touching
encounters, he learned to his grief that both girls had died of scar-
let fever (I, 105).

The De Quincey family itself was soon to be bereft once again.
Thomas' domineering brother and fellow student William was not
flourishing in his studies. De Quincey says of him, "Books he de-
tested, one and all, excepting only such as he happened to write
himself" (I, 61). No doubt he was also found difficult and disrup-
tive in the hitherto quiet life at Greenhay. Since he had shown
signs of an unusual gift for drawing, some of his works were
shown to a distinguished academician of the time, a Mr. de
Loutherbourg, who was impressed and accepted William as a
pupil, to board with him at his home in Hammersmith. And so this
powerful and frightening force which had so dominated the life
of little Thomas was abruptly withdrawn. The day of William's
departure was appropriately marked for the family by a close
encounter with a mad dog, a terrifying and unforgettable experi-

ence for Thomas. And he never saw William again, for within two years the boy contracted typhus fever and died at de Louther-bourg's house.[6] De Quincey looked back on him later with at least an admixture of affection, for he named his own first child William.

Emancipated from the harrowing leadership of William, Thomas continued his daily trips to Reverend Hall and was now joined by his younger brother "Pink." However, the idyllic Green-hay period was drawing to a close. Too expensive for the widow to maintain, Greenhay was sold at auction on Thomas' eleventh birthday. Mrs. Quincey then moved her family to Bath, which was to remain their principal home for five years.

Here Thomas was entered in the Bath Grammar School, where he studied for about two years. The boy's remarkable talents for scholarship had begun to assert themselves. His accomplishments in Latin under Mr. Hall soon made it apparent that he was in advance even of the older boys at Bath. He was already capable not only of reading the *De Imitatione Christi* but even of taking delight in laughing at Thomas à Kempis' Latinity. Unfortunately, De Quincey's Latin versification was displayed as a model to the whole school, which naturally exposed him to the resentment and threats of his schoolmates. But, when he reacted with pride and redoubled efforts, he gradually won respect and friendships.

De Quincey prospered at the Bath Grammar School. He was enjoying his first experience of broad acquaintance and intellec-tual competition with his contemporaries; and Mr. Morgan, the headmaster of the school, was wise enough to recognize his bril-liance and to encourage him. Thomas' shaky foundation in Greek was soon strengthened, and he made such rapid progress in that language that he developed the ability not only to write Greek verse in the classical meters but also to converse easily in Greek. Socially, he was apparently normal and happy during this period; he even seems to have been taking dancing lessons. In short, he was emerging as a lively boy of unusual gifts; and he was gaining his first sense of independence and confidence.

However, after a little more than two years, a misfortune inter-vened. Near the end of January, 1799, during a recitation in class, one of the lower masters of the school, aiming a disciplinary cane at the shoulder of a boy standing beside Thomas, missed his tar-get and accidentally struck Thomas a sharp blow on the head. The resulting injury sent him home to bed, where his mother's physician ordered him kept completely quiet and inactive for three weeks, after which he underwent a long convalescence. During his illness, his mother read him Ariosto's *Orlando Furioso* and many other books; and he continued reading himself. His mother's growing evangelical zeal kept him supplied with weighty and improving works, and at the same time he was steadily extending the knowledge of English literature he had begun to acquire in his father's library at Greenhay. He now read Milton's *Paradise Lost* for the first time (I, 160). He also became acquainted with at least some of the contents of an obscure little volume of anonymous verse recently published in nearby Bristol —the *Lyrical Ballads* of Wordsworth and Coleridge. To the boy De Quincey this new poetry came as a revelation; he later described his first acquaintance with it as "the greatest event in the unfolding of my own mind" (II, 138). Wordsworth and Coleridge, when he learned that they were the poets, became his heroes.

This period of close contact with his mother tended to confirm her influence on the formation of his character. Because she was a woman of exquisitely gracious manners and sober morality, deeply religious, and conservative in politics, Thomas developed at an early age a confirmed religious faith, a strict sense of decorum, a charming graciousness of manner, and a political conservatism that almost never wavered in later life.

While he was recovering from the accident, he also made a new friend; he met the young Lord Westport. The only son of Lord Altamont, this boy was to be his traveling companion a year later. The earliest letter of De Quincey to survive dates from this period (March 12, 1799), and it gives us a refreshing glimpse into his mind. Addressed to his sister Mary, then in Bristol, it is full of playful humor and mock pedantry; it is remarkably well written for a boy of thirteen and a half, and it reveals a happy ebullience of spirit.[7]

He was expecting to return to his school after Easter, and the masters were so anxious to have their star pupil return that they visited his home and urged his mother to send him. However, she was disquieted by their praising Thomas within his own hearing, which she considered conducive to pride and therefore detrimental to character. Perhaps she had already observed the first signs of an ominous development in his character which was ultimately to bring crucial disasters to his life. His intellectual precocity, particularly his brilliant linguistic aptitude, was becoming more apparent, to him as well as to his teachers, and was tending to inflate his ego. Since she also had doubts of the desirability of some of his associations at the Bath school, she quietly resolved not to send him back. In the meantime, he studied at home with the tutors who were teaching his brothers and sisters.

In the autumn Thomas was sent, with his younger brothers, to a small academy in Winkfield, Wiltshire, a school run by the vicar, the Reverend Edward Spencer, a man of great piety but limited learning. Here the boy, who found himself much in advance of the other students, lacked the challenge and competition he had faced at Bath. Consequently, he was freer to pursue his own interests. He assisted in the editing of a weekly school paper, along with some boys named Grinfield; and he wrote a good deal of verse and prose for the paper. Toward the end of the school year, in June, 1800, he submitted a translation of an ode of Horace[8] in a national contest, and won third prize; the first prize was awarded to Leigh Hunt, who had recently been "first deputy Grecian" at Christ's Hospital School and who was nearly a year older than he. This accomplishment won De Quincey the applause of the school and probably enhanced his rising estimate of his own powers.

However, the year at Winkfield was largely wasted, in terms of educational challenge and intellectual development, as Thomas himself fully realized. Since he was always the undisputed leader academically, and since he found no sympathetic encouragement and no competition or honors to stimulate him, he fell into a sort of intellectual torpor and inertia, which left him frustrated and rebellious at the end of the year, determined not to return to Winkfield. This failure of his school to rise to the needs of its precocious, extraordinarily gifted student probably contributed also to his later misfortunes.

IV *Ireland and Laxton*

During the spring, De Quincey had been invited by Lord Westport's tutor, on behalf of the boy's father Lord Altamont, to serve as companion to Lord Westport on a summer trip to Ireland, an opportunity he was happy to accept. The trip is well documented because Thomas described it in a series of long let-

ters, which have survived. In July, when he traveled to Eton to
join Westport, he visited the ballroom and gardens at Frogmore,
where the queen was giving a fête. He saw the queen and the
princesses; and one day, while he and Westport were playing in
the gardens, he was suddenly confronted by King George III,
who engaged the boys in conversation. His majesty quizzed young
Thomas briefly about his family, asking whether they had come
from France with the Huguenots upon the revocation of the Edict
of Nantes. The boy replied proudly that his family had been in
England since the Norman Conquest, as he had learned from the
Metrical Chronicle of Robert of Gloucester, an answer which appeared to please the king (I, 168). De Quincey saw the king three
more times during this visit to Eton.

Before departing for Ireland, the boys and Westport's tutor
paid a brief visit to Westport's grandmother at Porters, near London, a trip which took them through the city. For the first time,
Thomas found himself in what he later called "the nation of London." The boys elected to spend their few hours in the city visiting
St. Paul's. There the Whispering Gallery especially impressed
Thomas—so much so that it brought on him, as he stood beneath
the great dome, one of his memorable visionary daydreams; in it,
he saw the power of the gallery to magnify a whisper into a shout
as an emblem of the fatality which hangs upon human choices, a
thought which recurred to him just two years later when he stood
upon the threshold of the most fateful decision of his own life
(III, 295). At Porters, he found himself briefly in the society of
literary adults and heard his own attainments recognized and
warmly praised—an experience that was becoming dangerously
familiar.

On July 18 the boys set out for Ireland, traveling across North
Wales. There De Quincey first saw mountains, with a delight that
he continued to feel for them all his life. As it happened, the boys
joined Lord Altamont in Dublin at a historic moment. They were
present as visitors in the Irish Parliament at its final meetings—on
the first of August, when the Union Act was passed; and again on
the second of August, when twenty-eight peers, including Lord
Altamont, were elected to the English Parliament. De Quincey was introduced to Lord Cornwallis, who had recently suppressed the Irish rebellion and was now serving as Lord Lieuten-

ant. He also witnessed the splendid ceremony of the Installation of the Knights of St. Patrick, one of those being installed on this occasion being his host, Lord Altamont.

From Dublin, the boys traveled to the Westport estates in Mayo, on the west coast, going partly by canal boat. The trip gave De Quincey a memorable glimpse into the life of the old Irish nobility and gentry. During the following weeks at Westport, the boys lived a regular, studious life. De Quincey's mind and personality were developing rapidly at this time, and he took a lively interest in the recent events of the rebellion in that area. He was exposed to the pleasures of high society and enjoyed some personal success. He apparently made a strong and favorable impression on his companion's father, for Lord Altamont subsequently entered into an extended correspondence with the boy, which he continued as long as De Quincey responded.

As the summer passed, Mrs. Quincey wrote Thomas and reopened the difficult question of the choice of a school, suggesting Eton as a possibility. Thomas replied with great warmth that he objected to Eton because of the immorality and rigid conformity he had heard prevailed there. He ruled out all private schools on the basis of his very unsatisfactory experience at Winkfield. Since, therefore, a public school seemed indicated, why not Bath again? But Mrs. Quincey was adamant on this point, and the question was left unresolved.

Finally, on September 8 the boys left Westport and returned to England. De Quincey, instructed by a letter from his mother, parted from Lord Westport at Birmingham, and proceeded to join his sister Mary, who was visiting at Laxton, the seat of Lord Carbery in Northamptonshire, where he was to await a decision about his education. Here followed another delightful and flattering interlude. Lady Carbery was an old friend of the De Quincey family. Years before, as a young girl, she had made a favorite plaything of the infant Thomas. Now a beautiful and accomplished young woman, she gave this bright lad of fifteen, her former protégé, a warm welcome. Under the influence of De Quincey's mother, Lady Carbery had developed strong intellectual and religious interests. Discovering the boy's remarkable attainments, she adopted him as a fellow student, consultant, and guide in her theological and philosophical studies; and she also undertook to learn Greek from him. Calling him her "admirable Crichton," she made intellectual demands upon him which stimulated the most rapid development of his powers that he had ever experienced. In return for his scholarly assistance, Lady Carbery provided him with instructors in horsemanship, shooting, and athletics. He had access to a fine library, and he found himself accepted as an intellectual equal by Lady Carbery and her circle.

But this idyllic life could not last. By the ninth of November his immediate future had been settled, for his guardians registered him in the Manchester Grammar School, and there he was sent before the end of the year (1800). It was intended that he should remain there for three years, in order to qualify for one of the school's grants of forty guineas a year for four years at Brasenose College, Oxford; for his guardians felt that his annual income under his father's will was insufficient to maintain him at the university.

V *Crisis*

De Quincey must have established residence at the Manchester School with great reluctance. His previous dislike for private schools had by now developed into a settled contempt for all schools and for all regimented study because, as he tells us, "a premature development of my whole mind was rushing in like a cataract, forcing new channels for itself and for the new tastes which it introduced . . ." (I, 317). He soon learned to despise the aging, deliberate headmaster, Mr. Charles Lawson, because De Quincey unfortunately discovered himself to be already superior to his teacher in some areas of study. Although he found congenial intellectual interests among his schoolmates, he did not develop close friendships and was much alone. He had access to the Manchester library, and for a time he tried piano lessons.

In the summer of 1801 he spent the vacation with his family in the seaside town of Everton, north of Liverpool, which was to become a second home to him in the next few years. The family lodged in a cottage owned by a Mrs. Best. Across the street lived a banker—Mr. Clarke—to whom Mrs. Quincey introduced Thomas. Mr. Clarke was a widely traveled man of strong literary interests; he had a fine library, to which he gave Thomas access; and he introduced the boy to his literary friends in Liverpool, the first literary coterie the boy had encountered, including such persons as Dr. Currie, the editor and biographer of Burns, and a Mr.

Shepherd, an authority on Italian literature. De Quincey found himself at ease in the give-and-take of literary conversation with these men. (He later wrote an unflattering description of the group which gave offense to some of its members.) Mr. Clarke, who was studying Greek, arranged to meet young De Quincey every morning before sunrise to read Greek with him. Thus the precocious youth, now reaching his sixteenth birthday, once again had the flattering but unsettling experience of being accepted as an intellectual equal, or even as a superior, by men of experience, many years his seniors.

Toward the end of August, De Quincey returned to school, increasingly restless and dissatisfied. Lady Carbery alleviated his unhappiness a little by enlisting the aid of a distinguished Manchester clergyman, the Reverend John Clowes, rector of St. Mary's, a disciple of Swedenborg. The elderly scholar received the boy in his home, conversed with him about literature, made him gifts of books, and entertained him by playing the organ and singing for him.

Another pleasant distraction was the appearance of Lady Carbery herself and her Laxton circle in Manchester for several months in the fall. He had not seen her since his unhappy departure from Laxton at the end of the previous year, but he had maintained a correspondence with her on literary subjects. She had now come to Manchester to be near an old friend and former protectress, who was in her final illness. De Quincey was permitted to spend his evenings with her, and he quickly renewed their relationship of the previous year, helped her with her study of Greek, and received from her in return some instruction in Hebrew. He tried to interest her in Coleridge's "Ancient Mariner," but was unsuccessful because she was insensitive to this new poetry which had so deeply impressed him. When she brought all her friends to the school's Christmas festival to hear De Quincey recite some Latin verses, he was humiliated by what he considered the enforced childishness of the ceremony. After Christmas, she and her friends finally left Manchester; and De Quincey, thrown back on the intolerable drudgery of his school life, was more unhappy and rebellious than ever before.

De Quincey's psychological condition was now approaching a crisis which was to alter forever the direction of his life. His awareness of his own expanding powers, and the society of accomplished and admiring adults which he had repeatedly enjoyed in the last few years had encouraged him to think of himself as a prodigy, destined for great achievements. The dull routine of school life and the plodding deliberateness of Mr. Lawson deadened all his waking hours and left him no free time for his own intellectual pursuits, or for refreshing walks and recreation. He now regarded his fellow students as contemptibly boyish. The ugliness of industrial Manchester also contributed to his growing depression. His desperate impatience and unhappiness began to affect his health, and he unfortunately submitted to the ministrations of an ancient apothecary, who gave him two doses of a violent medicine which only increased his illness, and which he later called "tiger-drenches" (III, 275).

In the meantime, De Quincey's mother had grown dissatisfied with Bath as a residence, and had purchased, in October, 1801, an ancient and charming house called "St. John's Priory" in Chester, only forty miles from her son at Manchester, and this residence she now occupied. From there she paid her son a visit in early February (1802). At the moment of her departure, the dam broke; Thomas poured out his unhappiness to her, imploring her to let him leave the school. Apparently unaware of the crisis that had been developing in her son, she was shocked and horrified by his outburst. She proceeded to write him a series of thoughtful letters, in which she warned him against the dangers of overestimating his own powers, and sought to persuade him of his continuing need for educational discipline. Her moralizing tone left him untouched, and he responded by repeating his desperate appeal and then by listing in formal, legal style six reasons for his dissatisfaction.

But no decision was taken at once, and for the next few months a sort of armed truce prevailed. De Quincey took a vacation for most of May and June, but did not go to the "Priory," because of his mother's displeasure, and stayed instead with Mrs. Best at Everton.[9] Apparently he developed a confidential friendship with her during this vacation. However, since no alternative had been agreed upon by late June, he was forced to return to school, feeling sick and depressed.

Now a momentous resolution formed in the boy's mind: he must run away from Manchester. Since he had only about two guineas in ready cash, he wrote to Lady Carbery asking for a loan of five pounds; and she, with generous loyalty, sent him ten pounds, although she did not know his purpose. At first he planned to go to the Lake Country, which he had long yearned to visit and which had now been adorned by the added attraction of Wordsworth's poetry and his presence. However, out of consideration for his mother, he resolved instead to flee to the mountains of North Wales, for the route lay through Chester and the region would be closer to her new home there. He made the necessary arrangements, even to leaving gratuities for the servants with a fellow student; and he engaged a friendly groom to take his trunk to the carrier. In order to mislead any potential pursuers, he prepared a few clues to suggest that he had gone towards the Lakes.

With everything ready by the middle of July, he finally set a date for his departure; and his final day at Manchester arrived. At this point a curious and mysterious event occurred. De Quincey received in the mail a letter in French, containing a draft for about forty guineas. He immediately realized that it was not intended for him but for some French émigré of the same name in Chester. The error which brought this draft into his hands at this moment increased his anxiety, lest somehow it should color his impending act. Since he could find no opportunity to return the letter to the post office that day, he decided he must take it with him and attempt to dispose of it in Chester.

VI *Flight*

The following day (probably July 18), he arose in the darkness of early dawn and completed his packing. As he lingered for a few tearful moments in his room, his experience of two years before in the Whispering Gallery of St. Paul's in London rose in his mind and suggested that the step he was about to take might have most fateful consequences for his later life. Nevertheless, after a final farewell to the familiar objects in his room, he opened the door; crept silently down the stairs, past the door to Mr. Lawson's rooms; and summoned the groom to bring down his trunk. De Quincey stood anxiously at the foot of the stairs as the man struggled carefully down with the heavy burden on his shoulders. Suddenly the groom slipped and lost his hold, and the trunk bounced down and crashed against the very door to Mr. Lawson's room. Despite their danger, the absurdity of the situation suddenly struck them both; and they burst into laughter. But the commo-

tion failed to arouse Mr. Lawson, and they were able to set off in
the dawn on their separate ways—the groom with the trunk to the
carrier, and young De Quincey afoot on the road to Chester, with
a little bundle of necessaries and with nine guineas left in his
pocket.

Thus passed what De Quincey later considered the turning
point of his whole life, the headstrong mistake from which all his
subsequent misfortunes flowed. He came to lay the blame in three
quarters: on his own impulsive wrong-headedness, on Mr. Lawson's tyrannical rigorousness, and on the venal apothecary who
gave him the "tiger-drenches" that so injured his health (III,
272–73). But other causes may be surmised. Perhaps the real underlying cause was De Quincey's own intellectual precocity. His
mother's influence had led him early into intellectual pursuits; and
his unusual aptitudes, especially for languages, reinforced by his
capacious and retentive memory, had carried him far beyond his
contemporaries. Apart from the Bath Grammar School, his teachers had failed to recognize his remarkable gifts and to adjust their
demands to his capacities. At the same time, his brilliance had
won him access to the society of admiring adults, which in turn
had awakened a pride in his own attainments, a confidence that
he was equipped for distinguished achievements, and a contemptuous disdain for his fellow students and the whole academic routine. Perhaps Lady Carbery and his mother were at fault in not
recognizing soon enough the seriousness of his symptoms; certainly, his mother took the wrong approach when she did.

Whatever the causes, De Quincey had now embarked on an
eight-month adventure which was to be the most singular episode
in his long life. At the time of his departure from school, he was
sixteen years old, less than a month from his seventeenth birthday.
He was small for his age, probably under five feet in height, of
slight build, with delicate features, a prominent lower lip, and a
high brow. Though always inclined to shyness, he was probably
fortified by a sense of his own intellectual superiority and, perhaps, by a bit of schoolboy's arrogance.

De Quincey made the forty-mile trip to Chester in two days,
stopping overnight at a wayside inn. He was passed unrecognized
on the road by Mr. Lawson's messenger, who was rushing to
Chester with the news of his disappearance. The torpor and melancholy of the past months fell from De Quincey as he walked

through the sunny countryside, and his spirits rose to dizzy heights. The morning after he reached Chester, he turned his efforts to disposing of the misdirected letter and its forty-guinea note, which he had brought with him. He did not want to keep it any longer than necessary, lest he be suspected of intending to steal the money. On the other hand, he could not take it directly to the post office, for fear of being apprehended as a runaway and perhaps as a thief. Walking on the bank of the Dee River to consider the problem, he fell into conversation with a woman he met there; and he persuaded her to take the letter to the post office.[10]

Now, in order to reassure his mother before proceeding to Wales, he decided to try to contact his sister Mary, who he felt would be sympathetic. However, Mary, misled by her brother's false clues, had already left by coach in an effort to overtake him in the Lake Country. Unknown to De Quincey, his uncle, Colonel Thomas Penson, had recently returned from Bengal on leave and was living with his sister, De Quincey's mother, at the Priory. When the boy attempted to communicate with his sister through the household servants, he was identified and apprehended, much to his surprise, by his uncle.

Haled before his mother's uncompromising wrath, Thomas felt all hope was lost. However, he found an unexpected ally in his uncle. Colonel Penson, a robust man of action, found the boy's impulse to escape from books to an outdoor life among the Welsh mountains perfectly reasonable and supported his plan. Mrs. Quincey, sternly disapproving, but realizing the hopelessness of getting her son to return to school in Manchester, finally offered him two alternatives: to remain at the Priory, or to carry out his plan for a walking tour in Wales, provided he could do so on an allowance of a guinea a week and no more. She was worried about the possible unsettling effects of his rebellion on his younger brothers, should he appear to have won freedom too pleasantly. De Quincey, who seized upon the alternative of the tour, was soon on his way to Wales.

VII *Wales and London*

He proceeded across North Wales, stopping at first at the homes of family friends when the opportunity offered. Arriving in Bangor, he rented a room and remained for some weeks. From there he wandered south into Carnarvonshire, lodging at inns. He walked eight to fifteen miles a day and his health flourished. However, the cost of staying at inns was far greater than his weekly guinea could support; and, when his reserve funds were exhausted, he began sleeping in the open on hillsides and in pastures. Although he carried no coat, he devised a tiny tent from a piece of canvas and used this to shelter him for some weeks. There must have been nights when he suffered from the cold and dampness; for, during the late summer and early fall, he spent nine out of fourteen nights in the open; the rest, in inns and workers' cottages.

He proceeded down the west coast as far as Cardiganshire, and then turned eastward and inland through Montgomeryshire. As he wandered on, he stopped occasionally for a few days in particularly congenial inns or private homes. He struck up lively acquaintances with the innkeepers, cottagers, itinerant lawyers, and tourists he encountered. Among the travelers he met was a young German lieutenant in the British Navy, named De Haren, who gave him his first lessons in German and introduced him to German literature, including the work of De Quincey's future favorite, Jean Paul Richter. De Quincey sometimes served as a scribe for the less literate persons he stayed with. He enjoyed his peripatetic life and the respect his manners and his unusual conversational powers often won him. However, he missed the ready access to books he had always enjoyed. Furthermore, as autumn wore on and the nights became colder, the time approached when he would have to abandon his vagabond, outdoor life and reach a decision on his immediate future. The obvious course was to return to the Priory at Chester and to work out a plan with his mother, which is undoubtedly what she expected him to do. However, he was probably afraid that his return and subsequent plans would involve intervention by his guardians, and that the inevitable result would be his return to the odious school routine at Manchester.

An attractive alternative now occurred to him. He had learned that in London it was possible for minor heirs to borrow money against their inheritances by signing notes, which would be due with interest upon their coming of age. This course would mean sacrificing his weekly allowance of a guinea, severing all but the most tenuous ties to his mother, and fending for himself in "the nation of London." He must have hesitated, with some misgivings, over the decision. However, he probably yearned to keep the new-found health and freedom he had so much enjoyed in the past few months and to avoid returning to his mother's settled disapproval and to the strangling drudgery at Lawson's school. Perhaps there were also other, hidden, motives that impelled him and of which we do not know.

In any event, he finally decided to go to London. Having borrowed twelve guineas from two of his lawyer acquaintances, he proceeded to Shrewsbury. There at the inn he faced his last misgivings, thinking once again of the omen of the Whispering Gallery. Finally, at two o'clock in the morning, he took the London mail coach, which, twenty-eight hours later, set him down in London at six o'clock on a late November morning (1802).

He did not arrive without a plan. He had secured in advance the address of a likely money lender, a Jew named Dell, and had written him letters describing his circumstances (III, 350). De Quincey had calculated that he could live in London for fifty pounds a year; and he hoped, therefore, to borrow two hundred pounds to maintain him for the four years remaining until he reached his majority and came into his inheritance.

On the morning of his arrival, when he presented himself in the office of Mr. Dell, he was informed that Mr. Dell never dealt directly with clients, but only through his agent, a Mr. Brunell, to whom De Quincey was now referred. Mr. Brunell, who also sometimes went by the name of Brown, proved to be a disreputable lawyer. He informed the boy that, while it was perhaps possible to grant such a loan, his identity would have to be established, and various preliminary arrangements would have to be made, and these would take some time. De Quincey produced letters from his friend Lord Westport (now Lord Altamont) and from others as supporting evidence; but he was still told he had to wait. He took cheap lodgings and eked out a slender living with his small store of guineas for several weeks, until his money was exhausted. Then perhaps he slept outdoors for a time.[11] Apparently his diet was reduced for many weeks to scraps of bread from the breakfast table of Mr. Brunell, from whom he was at first concealing his desperate circumstances. He was approaching starvation, and his health was declining. Finally, he was forced to reveal his condition to Mr. Brunell, who gave him permission to sleep in the building in which he maintained his office—a tall, shabby house in Greek Street, empty of furnishings apart from a table and a few chairs, cold, and infested with rats.

When De Quincey moved in, he found a little girl about ten years old living alone, working as a menial servant to Mr. Brunell. She was pale and half starved, terrified of the rats and of imagined ghosts in the empty, echoing house. Of her parentage she knew nothing. With this pathetic creature De Quincey shared the long, cold winter nights. They slept on the floor, with a pillow of law papers and only an old coat and some rags for bedding, often clinging to each other for warmth. When Mr. Brunell arrived irregularly for business, De Quincey was obliged to leave, spending his days walking through the streets, resting in doorways and parks, and taking shelter under porticoes, until he could return at twilight. His weakness increased, and he was becoming ill.

In his cold, lonely wanderings he grew acquainted with the underworld life of the metropolis and particularly with the prostitutes. Like them, he was harassed by the watchmen and exposed to other dangers; they often made common cause with him in his defense. One in particular, Ann, about a year younger than he, who frequented Oxford Street, became his close companion for weeks. They exchanged confidences and offered each other what help and encouragement they could. On one occasion, when he was walking with her, De Quincey's weakness and hunger caused him to faint. Reacting quickly, she ran to procure him a cordial of spiced wine, paying for it out of her own slender purse. This drink restored him at a moment when, he ever afterwards believed, he might otherwise have died.

During his wanderings, De Quincey had kept in occasional touch with his friend Mrs. Best of Everton. Through her, about the end of the year, he had contacted his guardian Mr. Hall, to sound him out about future possibilities; and Mr. Hall had replied.[12] But nothing had come of these overtures. De Quincey was afraid to apply directly to his family for help because he foresaw return to school in Manchester as the price. He failed to seek employment because it had not occurred to him that this was a possibility, nor did he know how to proceed. Finally, in late February or early March, he was recognized by a family friend on the street. After explaining his situation to this man, he extracted a promise not to betray him; and the next day he received a gift of ten pounds.

Part of this he paid to Mr. Dell and Mr. Brunell, who now finally agreed to lend him the money he wanted, provided he could get a friend to guarantee the loan. With this purpose in mind, eight or nine days after receiving the ten pounds, De Quincey took leave of Ann, having arranged to meet her upon his return, and traveled by coach to Eton. There he persuaded a former acquaintance to secure his note under certain conditions.

De Quincey returned eagerly to London, only to meet additional disappointments. The money lenders were not satisfied with the conditions, so more delays were in prospect. But worse, Ann failed to meet him at the appointed time and place. He searched for her frantically in her usual haunts and in the neighborhood where she lived, but he was unable to learn what had become of her. At this low ebb in his fortunes, about the third week in March (1803), something made possible a reconciliation with his family and his guardians, and about the middle of March he left London to return at last to the Priory.[13] His guardians must have given him assurance that he would not be forced to return to school in Manchester.

It had been almost exactly eight months since De Quincey had run away. About half of this time had been spent wandering in Wales, the other half in London. De Quincey later attributed his subsequent ill health, the opium addiction which resulted from it, and hence most of the misfortunes of his adult life to the exposure and privation he suffered during those months. Although he wrote a great deal about this period, he left much unsaid; and the sufferings he did describe in the *Confessions,* he later assured his readers, were less than a thousandth part of what he had actually undergone during these months in Wales and London (II, 55). His separation from Ann he long regarded as the heaviest affliction of his life (III, 375). Her pathetic figure joined his two dead sisters, Mr. Hall's deaf-mute daughters, and perhaps his little house-mate at Mr. Brunell's—the suffering girls and the female pariahs who were peopling his memory, his dreams, and his imagination.

VIII   *Everton and the* Diary

De Quincey remained at the Priory for only a short time; one can surmise what sort of reception he was given there and how he reacted to it. By March 23 he was in Everton once again, living by himself at Mrs. Best's.[14] Perhaps at his own request he was sent there to rest and restore his health. He remained there until the second of August. During this period he kept a diary and note-book, which happily have survived and which afford revealing glimpses into his activities and his state of mind during these last months of his seventeenth year. One striking fact is that the diary contains no reference to his recent ordeal in Wales and London, or to the loss of Ann, which seems strange because of his later view of their profound effects. Perhaps the memories were too painful and had to be suppressed. Another possibility is that some of his sufferings and his relation with Ann were later products of a literary imagination that elaborated on a slender factual basis.

The young man who appears in the diary is one groping toward self-understanding, emotionally a little unstable, but already com-mitted to a literary life. De Quincey apparently did not revive his acquaintance with Mr. Clarke, his daily companion of the summer of 1801, or with his literary coterie; for Mr. Clarke is mentioned only once in the diary. Perhaps by prior agreement with his guar-dians, De Quincey dined daily with a Mr. Cragg, a merchant con-nected with his family. Since the two had little in common, there were some sharp disagreements between them. De Quincey spent much of his time in the family and circle of Mr. James Wright, a Liverpool bookseller. He visited them almost daily, walking and talking with them, reading aloud to them, and using their library. Apparently he was once again enjoying the companionship and respect of his elders.

At the same time he seems—surprisingly—to have patronized a local prostitute, if one may judge by one passage in the diary entry for June 4: ". . . go to the same fat whore's as I was at the last time;—give her ls. and a cambrick hand-kerchief;—go home miserable . . ." (*Diary*, 194). This entry seems surprising be-cause of his protestations about the purity of his relationship with Ann only a few months before (III, 359). Despite his delicacy and sensitivity, he was also not too weak or timid to defend him-self against annoyances; once, when he had been harassed by a drunkard who appeared to him "a pest and disgrace to humanity," he wrote: "I was just on point of hittg. him a dab on his disgustg. face when a gentleman (coming up) alarmed him and saved me the trouble . . ." (*Diary*, 155).

But De Quincey's main preoccupations during these months at Everton were with literature and with himself. He had clearly decided to become a writer, and had set his heart particularly on poetry. On May 26 he made lists of works he had considered writing, including three poems, two pathetic tales, three dramas, four essays, two biographies, and "many different travels and voyages." [15] He collected phrases, words, and alternate spellings. He recorded a series of fancies which foreshadowed the great dream visions he was to write near the end of his career. Some of the imagery and occasional flashes of rhetoric suggest the future style beginning to take shape. He spent the evening of May 20 working out the plot for a projected Arabian drama. When he listed the "sources of Happiness," he placed poetry at the head of the list.

He was reading a great deal, drawing on at least three local libraries, and was beginning to exercise his critical faculties. He compiled a list of great English poets, including—after Spenser, Shakespeare, and Milton—Thomson, Collins, Chatterton, Beattie, Burns, Southey, Coleridge, and then climactically, at the end with three exclamation marks, William Wordsworth. Among his readings at this time, popular Gothic novels and sentimental romances bulked large. On May 21 he mentioned having read "Charlotte Smith's metrical works—particularly 'an ode to the poppy,'" a poem which praises the power of the poppy to alleviate the pains of disease, soothe the soul, and balm the broken heart (*Diary*, 234).

De Quincey's mind was increasingly occupied with Wordsworth and Coleridge. In the interval since his first acquaintance in 1799 with "We Are Seven," he had read the rest of the *Lyrical Ballads*, including the two-volume second edition of 1800; and he had also learned all he could about the two poets. His reactions show how strong the impact of this new poetry could be upon a young mind at the time. De Quincey later claimed credit for being one of the very first to recognize the greatness of Wordsworth and Coleridge; and while he perhaps exaggerated his uniqueness —he was only thirteen when *Lyrical Ballads* was published—he certainly discerned the value and importance of Wordsworth's and Coleridge's work early, and long before it was widely established in public favor.

By the time of the Everton diary, De Quincey's admiration had developed into hero worship. On May 1 he wrote in his diary, "I affirm . . . that there is no good pastoral in the world but Wordsworth's 'Brothers'; and that enchantg composition has more pathos (ah ! *what* pathos!) than poetry in it" (154). And on June 1: "I walk home thinking of *Coleridge;*—am in transports of love and admiration for him . . . —I begin to think him the greatest man that has ever appeared . . ." (191–92). De Quincey's passionate regard for Wordsworth led him to seek the poet's friendship. On May 13 and May 31 (1803), he wrote drafts of a long letter introducing himself to the poet, and on the latter date he sent a copy of the second draft to Wordsworth, through the poet's publishers in London.

The letter, which has survived,[16] is careful and dignified in style, but full of hyperbolical praise of Wordsworth, sentimental effusiveness, and abject self-abasement. Nevertheless, Wordsworth, touched by the obvious sincerity of the young man's tribute, replied in a friendly and thoughtful manner; but he wisely checked De Quincey's ardor by saying that friendship was not his to give; it had to grow gradually through long association. Thus began a correspondence which continued intermittently until the two men finally met four years later; thus also began the first of De Quincey's cultivated literary acquaintanceships, which were to give his life much of its color and direction. His idolization of Wordsworth and Coleridge drew him into their circles like a magnet. His attitude toward them, as he later admitted, "was literally in no respect short of a religious feeling" (III, 41). For the next dozen years he actually submerged his own individual identity in his worship of these men and in his efforts to serve them. But he was inevitably doomed to gradual disillusionment, since these poets were only human, as he was to discover.

De Quincey was also exercising his critical faculties in other directions during this Everton period. The diary records a few judgments which already suggest some of his lifetime biases and his love of shocking irreverence and absolutism of statement. He was systematically reading Cowper's translation of the *Iliad,* a book at a sitting, and confirming his view that "the wretched drivellings of that old dotard *Homer*" were greatly inferior to Virgil (*Diary,* 176). He delighted in shocking his host Mr. Cragg, a great admirer of the *Odyssey:* "I said that I could not bear it; and, as a reason, observed that, independent of the insipidity of the story, there was no character in it: 'What? not Telemachus?' said C. 'No,' said I coolly . . ." (*Diary,* 179). He was also already priming his guns for Dr. Johnson; he wrote of Dr. Johnson's dictum that poetry is not translatable: "This dogma is the only true one on this subject (to the best of my recollection) the bear ever growled forth" (*Diary*, 158).

But, interspersed among these flashes of arrogance, one finds unmistakable signs of youthful perplexity, sensitivity, and close self-examination. Several times he recorded feeling miserable, once because his want of skill in French had been exposed. On May 28 he wrote, "I amuse the ladies by saying that I wish there was some road down to hell by which I might descend for a short time . . . to save myself from a state of apathy . . . talk of the clouds which hang thick and heavy on my brain . . ." (*Diary*, 184). He had the acuity to recognize that his leading characteristic was "*Facility of impression.* My hopes and fears are alternately raised and quelled by the minutest—the most trivial circumstances—the slightest words" (*Diary*, 153). His lists of projected works and of the sources of happiness suggest a mind casting about for its true direction; he was troubled by a feeling of aimlessness.

His absorption in society, in literature, and in himself was complete enough to render him almost oblivious to the exciting public events of the day. England declared war on France again in mid-May, and nearby Liverpool responded with fervent activity, but De Quincey hardly noticed it in his diary.

IX   *Oxford*

On August 2, 1803, he returned to the Priory; and, after long hesitation and delay, in mid-December he finally went to Oxford. He was never to live at the Priory again, for in June his mother had written him that she was obliged to sell it, and she finally left it a few days after her son's departure for Oxford. Her problems with Thomas had recently been compounded by her younger son Richard. "Pink" had come under the rod of a violent schoolmaster. A proud and sensitive boy, though only fourteen, he had reacted by running away, not to be heard from for years. Mrs. Quincey's fears that he might emulate Thomas' rebellion of a year and a half before must have seemed to her to have been tragically confirmed, but De Quincey was later assured that his example had exercised no influence over his brother's flight (III, 314).

When Thomas reached Oxford by the Birmingham coach on a

stormy night in late December, he took lodgings at an inn. Apparently no advance arrangements had been made for his admission to any particular college. He had settled notions of what the proper college should offer, including a chapel with a good organ and a fine musical service. However, after a few days' hesitation he finally entered himself at Worcester College—the chapel had no organ and no musical service—because his funds were depleted, the initial fee was less, and Worcester had the reputation of a relaxed discipline. Apparently he was approaching life at Oxford with wariness about the irksome schoolboy restraints he had suffered in the past. At the university he hoped to remain free to follow his own intellectual bent.

During the four and a half years he remained an active student at Oxford, De Quincey's life was solitary, restless, and studious. Probably his meager allowance cut him off from the strenuous social life of his fellow students. He himself attributed his morbid solitariness to the effects of his sufferings in Wales and London a year before (II, 55), and also to the fact that he found his fellow students ignorant and uninterested in the subject of his greatest enthusiasm, English literature. He made few friends, and he stayed away from the frequent wine parties.

When he had been there only about three months, he had already adopted a negative opinion of college and university life. He wrote Wordsworth on March 31 (1804): ". . . it is singularly barren (as far as my short residence there will permit me to judge) of either virtue or talents or knowledge; so that the intemperance I see practiced, coming unrecommended by any great qualifications, is doubly disgusting to me. . . . from the great aversion I have to a college life, I shall pass no more of my time there than is absolutely necessary; and, for that reason as well as for the little attraction I have found in the society, I have lived almost alone since my entrance; and, until I see something greater or better, I shall continue to do so." [17] Apparently his self-imposed isolation continued, for he later wrote: "for the first two years of my residence at Oxford, I compute that I did not utter one hundred words" (II, 61). One of his most notorious contemporaries at Oxford was John Wilson of Magdalen, a handsome, athletic, and prodigal young man; but De Quincey never heard of him there. In his sole encounter with his first tutor, De Quincey adopted a condescending attitude toward the man's learning and taste; and, since he felt his judgment confirmed by the tutor's remarks, he never sought him out thereafter.

His restlessness appeared in his changes of rooms and residences, in his dissatisfaction with his choice of college, and in his frequent travels away from Oxford. When he wrote Wordsworth on March 14, 1804, he was already living outside of Oxford at Littlemoor. He also found it necessary to go to London, either during Easter vacation or in the fall. He had run out of money; and, to avoid the embarrassment of pleading with his mother and his guardians for more, he had decided to try once again to borrow from Mr. Dell. This time he was more successful, and borrowed two hundred and fifty pounds, at 17½ per cent interest, to be repaid upon his coming of age (III, 365).

X *First Opium*

It was probably during this first visit to London from the university that he was introduced to opium. Rising from bed one night with a sudden toothache and thinking it might have been caused by his having omitted his daily practice of washing his head, he plunged his head in cold water and went to sleep with it wet. He awoke the next morning with excruciating rheumatic pains of the head and face, and these continued for three weeks. Then, on a rainy Sunday afternoon, a friend he met on the street suggested opium as a remedy for his sufferings. Little was known about the properties—and particularly the addictive powers—of the drug at that time; it was considered both an effective anodyne and a widely useful medicine; and, consequently, it was available in common drug stores. On his way home, De Quincey entered the shop of a druggist on Oxford Street, near the Pantheon, and there bought his first opium. Back at his lodgings, he tried his first dose, and the results astonished and delighted him. Not only were his pains relieved, but a whole new world of pleasant sensations opened to him. Thus began his experiments with opium, which were to continue intermittently and secretly for the next nine years, until he became thoroughly addicted in 1813.

During the nine-year period of his early experimentation with opium, he took it both to relieve the discomforts of minor ailments and for the pleasurable sensations it afforded. He sometimes planned opium debauches in advance, using them to enhance his pleasure in concerts and operas, which were a favorite recreation for him, or to prepare himself to enjoy his long solitary walks through the streets of London to observe the life around him. His dreaming tendency revived during his years at Oxford, bringing him the magnificent and terrifying visions he described much later in "Levana and Our Ladies of Sorrow" (XIII, 362–69). He realized that his tendency toward dreaming was not wholly the product of opium, for he had experienced many strange and memorable dreams since early childhood (I, 32). But he attributed to opium the power to revive the dreaming faculty and to affect the quality and intensity of dreams (XIII, 335).

For several generations this view of De Quincey's, supported by Coleridge's account of his experience, gained wide currency. However, expert opinion today holds that opium has no intrinsic powers either to induce dreams in nondreamers, or to increase the frequency or to alter the character of dreams in dreamers. Its only effect on dreams is probably to reduce the addict for longer periods than usual to states approaching sleep, and thus to provide additional opportunities for dreams.[18] The true source of dreams lies elsewhere, in the psychological makeup and condition of the individual.

De Quincey often visited London while he was at Oxford, for a time sharing lodgings there with a fellow student. He spent his vacations in his old haunts at Everton, or visiting his mother at her various residences, or traveling to the Lake Country. And he did not confine his absences from Oxford to the vacation periods, but wandered off whenever the spirit moved him. He also made plans to travel to Germany, and even thought of moving to a sylvan retreat in Canada (II, 108).

Nevertheless, he was not one to shirk his studies. He apparently worked hard in his solitude, mainly on independent projects. He read Greek daily. At one point he was studying the *Parmenides* closely. He became acquainted with a young German named Schwartzburg, who helped him with the study of German, in which he soon became proficient, and with Hebrew. But above all he plunged into philosophy; metaphysics and psychology became his principal interests. Scholastic logic was the one subject in the formal curriculum that seems to have engaged his attention;

he studied it closely, and thus cultivated the acute sense of logical system and discrimination which characterizes much of his later work.

De Quincey now began to aspire to philosophy as a life's work, hoping he might bring great benefits to mankind through his endeavors. He had abandoned poetry as a vocation, concluding that he did not have sufficient talent to gain more than a temporary notoriety. He became aware of the recent flowering of philosophy in Germany, and particularly of Immanuel Kant's work; and it was to study the Transcendental philosophy firsthand that he undertook to learn the German language. Although he approached Kant with great enthusiasm, his first reading of him seemed to suggest that his philosophy came into conflict with the Christian religion; and, since De Quincey was a firm believer, he was deeply disillusioned in Kant and sadly shaken in his own attitudes. In fact, he later called this initial encounter with Kant one of the capital disappointments of his life (II, 107). His interest in the language, literature, and philosophy of Germany was unusual at this time, when there was little known about German culture in England—further evidence of the independence of his intellectual curiosity and energy.

He was also reading in contemporary British literature, even though he found no interest in it among his fellow students. In addition to his idols Wordsworth and Coleridge, he read works by Southey, Landor, and Lamb; and he found them admirable, though their authors were still little known. Having already initiated his acquaintance with Wordsworth, he now hoped to meet Coleridge; and, since he had heard that Lamb was a friend of Coleridge and lived in London, he decided to try to meet Lamb first. About the end of his first year at Oxford, in late 1804 or early 1805, having obtained a letter of introduction from a friend, he sought Lamb at his desk in the India House. De Quincey later recreated the scene of their meeting, in all its oddity and eccentricity, with a delightful Dickensian flourish, in his fine essay on Lamb (III, 38 ff.).

Lamb invited the young man to his home for tea at seven that evening. There he met Lamb's sister Mary. He soon turned the conversation to the real subject of his interest, Coleridge. To his dismay, he could learn nothing from Lamb, who chose to mystify his questioner with playful ridicule of Coleridge, Wordsworth, and even "The Ancient Mariner." So shocked was the ardent young disciple that he actually covered his ears to shut out Lamb's heresies. Lamb's motives in thus ruffling his young caller can only be guessed, but perhaps he was piqued on perceiving that De Quincey had come to him for the sake of Coleridge, not for himself. The kind efforts of Mary Lamb to soothe De Quincey's wounded feelings and to answer his questions about Coleridge did not entirely pacify him, and for about four years he made no other efforts to cultivate Lamb's acquaintance.

The following summer (1805), while vacationing at Everton, De Quincey summoned up courage to make a trip into the Lake Country to meet Wordsworth. However, when he reached Coniston, his courage failed; and he turned back. During this trip he was once again examining his own motives. He wrote out a list of the twelve "Constituents of Happiness," which contains several goals he was to continue striving for in later life; and some he was to attain. Among his objectives were a capacity for thinking; an interest in human life and human nature; a fixed residence in a place of beauty; solitude and society; books; a great intellectual project; health and vigor; mastery of passions and appetites; comtemplation; freedom from worldly care and business; the education of a child; and respectable personal appearance.

The following summer (1806) he was at Everton again, and again he walked into the Lake Country to seek Wordsworth. This time he actually reached the side of Hammerscar, across the lake from Grasmere, before the sense of his own inadequacy stopped him and turned him back.

On August 15, 1806, he came of age and received his inheritance of two thousand six hundred pounds from his father's estate. About six hundred pounds of this sum he had to pay at once to retire his various debts. The remainder was gradually to disappear, for he was not careful with money. He had become an enthusiastic book collector, and spent large sums on the accumulation of a personal library as long as his funds lasted.

In the meantime, his health had declined during these Oxford years. He was convinced that he had symptoms of tuberculosis, the disease that had killed his father. He also had a recurrent liver complaint, and he developed severe stomach pains which he attributed to the effects of his weeks of suffering during his vagabondage. He continued to use opium intermittently to allay these pains, and sometimes he took it simply for the hours of peace and pleasure it brought him.

XI *Coleridge and Wordsworth*

In the summer of 1807, De Quincey finally tracked Coleridge down. Vacationing in the Bristol area, De Quincey was engaged in some research on a legendary young Oxford student of remarkable gifts; and it led him to Joseph Cottle, Coleridge's friend and publisher. Cottle told De Quincey that Coleridge had returned to England and was visiting his friend Thomas Poole in Nether Stowey. De Quincey went there at once; but, finding Coleridge temporarily away, he was detained a few days by Poole, who expected Coleridge's return. Finally, De Quincey sought Coleridge where he was staying, in Bridgewater. Coleridge had reached a painful juncture in his own affairs at this moment; for, having returned the previous year from Malta, where he had gone in an unsuccessful search for health and stability, he was now a confirmed opium addict. Moreover, he had finally recognized his incompatibility with his wife and was now trying to arrange a separation from her.

De Quincey found Coleridge standing lost in reverie in the gateway of the home where he was staying. After observing him for a while, De Quincey presented himself; and he was cordially invited inside for refreshments and asked to stay for dinner and the evening. He had brought a gift for Coleridge, a copy of a rare pamphlet by the philosopher David Hartley. Then, for the first time, he heard the great flood of Coleridge's eloquent conversation, which continued throughout the evening. According to De Quincey's later account, Coleridge spoke with horror, this first evening of their acquaintance, of his enslavement by opium and warned his new young friend against forming such a habit (II, 162). Finally, departing at ten o'clock at night, De Quincey returned to Bristol in a state of exaltation.

He was concerned about Coleridge's obviously troubled condition, and was anxious to be of some assistance. Learning from Cottle two days later that Coleridge was in some financial need, De Quincey generously (and perhaps a little recklessly) tried to make him an anonymous gift of five hundred pounds through Cottle, who persuaded him to reduce the amount to three hundred pounds. This amount was subsequently sent to Coleridge, who accepted it with the stipulation that he would regard it as a loan, to be repaid in two years. De Quincey did not reveal himself as Coleridge's benefactor until many years later.

In the following weeks De Quincey lingered off and on in the Bristol area to cultivate the acquaintance of the Coleridge family —including the poet's wife and three fascinating children—and he was back there in October, deferring his return to Oxford. Coleridge had now accepted an appointment to lecture during the winter at the Royal Institution in London, and he had to find a means of returning his family to their home at Keswick in the Lake Country so he himself could proceed to London. When young De Quincey generously offered himself as an escort, his proffer was gratefully accepted. Thus, toward the end of October, De Quincey, Mrs. Coleridge, and the three children departed for the North by post chaise. After pausing for a week in Liverpool on the way, they proceeded into the Lake Country. Then, about four o'clock on November 4 (1807), De Quincey, after alighting from the chaise to climb a hill and then running ahead down the other side with the little boys, suddenly found himself at the gate of Dove Cottage in Grasmere—and face to face with the man he most revered, the man of all men past and present he most wanted to meet—William Wordsworth.

At first incapacitated by tension, De Quincey gradually relaxed in the simple warmth and dignity of the crowded little household; and he fell under the spell of the poet's solemn and majestic conversation. He slept in Dove Cottage that night, in the bedroom with Wordsworth's eldest son. Mrs. Coleridge, having asked Wordsworth's sister Dorothy not to mention her marital trouble to De Quincey, proceeded to Keswick the next day, after inviting De Quincey to visit her there. De Quincey stayed at Grasmere for two days and nights, once enjoying a long walk around Grasmere and Rydal Water in the rain with Wordsworth and Dorothy.

Then, on the third morning, a family excursion having been suggested to escort him on his way to Keswick, he, to his utter amazement, was loaded into an ordinary horse-cart with the whole Wordsworth family, except the children, for a trip up over Kirkstone Pass to Patterdale. The next day, as he traveled alone with Wordsworth beside Ullswater, Wordsworth read him the introduction to "The White Doe of Rylstone." Then came a visit at Greta Hall in Keswick, where De Quincey first met

Southey, another luminary in his literary heaven. De Quincey was more than a little shocked to hear these admired writers speak disrespectfully of the royal family; for, as he once put it, he "had been bred up in a frenzied horror of jacobinism" (II, 322). He returned to Grasmere with Wordsworth, and then on November 12 he rushed back to Oxford, almost too belatedly to save the Michaelmas term. As the coach bore him along Windermere, he had a strange premonition that his future life would be closely associated with this region (II, 354).

His meeting with his great idol had proved deeply impressive and satisfying; however, he had found Wordsworth a little self-sufficient and remote; and he was to make Dorothy his principal link with the Wordsworth family. Her first impression of him she recorded thus: "He is a remarkable and very interesting young man; very diminutive in person, which, to strangers, makes him appear insignificant; and so modest, and so very shy, that even now I wonder how he had ever the courage to address himself to my brother by letter." [19]

Back at Oxford, De Quincey became ill; but by Christmas time he was well enough to go to London, perhaps drawn there by Coleridge's presence and by the prospect of hearing him lecture. In London he grew ill again, troubled with pains of the head. He was using opium moderately and intermittently at the time. Coleridge, who was living uncomfortably in the offices of the *Courier* in the Strand, was ill and discouraged, deep in the toils of opium, trying to pull himself together sufficiently to give his lectures. There De Quincey visited him almost daily. Apparently he even helped Coleridge with his work. At the *Courier* offices he met Coleridge's friend Sir Humphry Davy. Also about this time he introduced himself to the famous eccentric traveler and author "Walking" Stewart, of whom he later wrote a delightful sketch (III, 93–120). He kept in touch with his new friends at Grasmere by letter, and he saw Wordsworth, who was in London on a visit, in late February.

When De Quincey finally returned to Oxford about March 5 (1808), he plunged into some of the most concentrated studying he had ever done. Despite his frequent and extended absences from the university, and his solitary ways while in residence, he had developed a small circle of friends; and his occasional required performances had established for him a reputation for unusual genius and learning. He had maintained his attitude of indifference to academic routine and rewards, perhaps encouraged by Wordsworth's views;[20] but, when it was now suggested that he read for honors, he accepted the challenge. In order to give himself as much time as possible, he had his name listed under Q instead of D. He read strenuously during the spring months; for example, in a single week he went through thirty-three Greek tragedies. Finally, in May, he presented himself for examination. On the first day he performed so brilliantly that one of his examiners was reported to have said to a Worcester man, "You have sent us today the cleverest man I ever met with; if his *vivâ voce* examination tomorrow correspond with what he has done in writing, he will carry everything before him" (II, 79 n.).

But De Quincey never appeared for the second part of his examination. He had taken the first part on a Saturday, and apparently on Sunday he packed his bags and left the university, without notice or explanation. He never returned, though he remained enrolled and continued to hold his rooms for two and a half more years. This sudden disappearance has some of the same mystery as his flight from Manchester and his vagrancy in London. His later explanation was that he had been looking forward with pleasure to the second day's examination because he had been told that it would be conducted in Greek and he felt well prepared; but, when this arrangement was suddenly changed, in his contempt for the examination and the examiners he determined not to face them (II, 81 n.). Other possibilities are that he felt ill prepared, or that he had incapacitated himself with opium.

Thus De Quincey terminated his years of formal education and launched himself into the world of independent adulthood. He was without plans for earning a livelihood, apparently still relying on his inheritance to support him. After two or three months in London, part of the time sick again, De Quincey paid what was to be his final visit to Everton, and then returned to Grasmere, where he took up residence with the Wordsworths by November 1 (1808). Wordsworth and his family had left Dove Cottage and were now living temporarily at Allan Bank, a large new house; but it was cold, damp, and smoky. Enhancing the attractions of this abode was Coleridge, who was also living there and working, with Sara Hutchinson's help, on the arrangements for the new periodical *The Friend,* which he was preparing to publish. Here De Quincey remained for nearly four months.

Now fully accepted as a member of the household, he shared in all its pleasures and anxieties. He slept with little John Wordsworth, who adored him. Only two months before his arrival, Wordsworth's daughter Catherine had been born; and the infant immediately became a great favorite of De Quincey's. He half playfully exacted a promise from the parents that he should be given sole responsibility for the girl's education, perhaps remembering that one of his "Constituents of Happiness" was "the education of a child." The Wordsworths evidently felt close enough to him to mention their doubts of Coleridge's ability to carry out his plans for *The Friend.*

De Quincey met many of Wordsworth's friends and admirers. Wordsworth introduced him to John Wilson,[21] the brilliant young man whom De Quincey had failed to meet while they were fellow undergraduates at Oxford. The two had much in common, and soon became friends. Wilson, like De Quincey, was an admirer of Wordsworth, and had been drawn to the Lakes by his attraction. He was to become the closest friend De Quincey would ever know; but they formed a strange pair—Wilson about six feet tall, athletic, handsome, and self-confident; De Quincey barely over five feet, delicate, and shy. Before De Quincey left, they went on a walking trip together; and they must have drawn many amused glances along the way. De Quincey also met the ill-fated Charles Lloyd and his young wife, blissfully gay in their early married life—their misfortunes still lying ahead of them.

Wordsworth was occupied throughout the winter with the composition of his great pamphlet attacking the Convention of Cintra. De Quincey, who hitherto had felt little or no interest in public affairs, began to share Wordsworth's interest and became deeply involved in study of the political aspects of the Peninsular War. Wordsworth was anxious to publish his pamphlet before public interest in the subject had died; and, when De Quincey offered to go to London to see it through the press while Wordsworth at Grasmere finished the writing to be done, Wordsworth gratefully accepted his offer—an eloquent indication of the trust he already placed in his young disciple. Before leaving Grasmere, however, De Quincey arrived at the momentous decision to make his permanent home there. He applied for a lease on Dove Cottage, now vacant, and accepted Dorothy Wordsworth's kind offer to oversee its refurnishing during his absence. He set out for London on February 20 (1809).

After he had arrived in London, De Quincey devoted most of his time for nearly three months to his duties in seeing *The Convention of Cintra* through the press. He took his work very seriously, urging the printers on, reading the proofs, meticulously revising the punctuation, and making other slight corrections. At Wordsworth's request, he wrote a Postscript, to be appended anonymously to the work, dealing with the letters of Sir John Moore—a fairly extensive essay, it was De Quincey's first known prose work to be published. Unfortunately, the printing proceeded slowly; various delays were encountered; and, since Wordsworth was increasingly anxious to have his pamphlet published quickly, some tensions developed. De Quincey placed the blame on a compositor who was often drunk and absent.

However, Daniel Stuart, editor of the *Courier,* who was helping with the supervision, heard from the printer, and wrote to Coleridge, that De Quincey's fastidiousness about details caused the delays. Coleridge, who was beginning to adopt a condescending coolness toward De Quincey, replied, "I both respect and have affection for Mr. De Quincey, but saw too much of his turn of mind, anxious yet dilatory, confused over accuracy, and at once systematic and labyrinthine, not fully to understand how great a plague he might easily be to a London printer; his natural tediousness made yet greater by his zeal and fear of not discharging his trust . . ." (*E,* 158). Apparently, Coleridge told Wordsworth what he had heard; and De Quincey sensed the resultant urgency in Wordsworth's letters. Now growing less content to be a mere appendage or satellite of his two former heroes, De Quincey was beginning to aspire toward being accepted as an equal—as a man whose intellectual powers entitled him to respect. In this aspiration he received little encouragement from Wordsworth and Coleridge. Nevertheless, after nearly three months of very hard work, he finally saw *The Convention of Cintra* published; Wordsworth was pleased; and the tensions were for a while relaxed.

Most of what little time De Quincey could spare from his editing duties was also devoted to the interests of his Lake friends. He sent them long letters full of details about the pamphlet and the latest news of the war. He looked for presents for the children, and he even purchased a patented smoke-dispenser for Allan Bank. He spent many hours searching the bookstalls for interesting purchases and was unhappy to discover that the Wordsworths were not interested in what he found. When Dorothy suggested that he write an answer to an attack on Wordsworth by the critic Jeffrey, De Quincey embraced the idea; but he never completed the article. He apparently also considered establishing a press at Grasmere to help Wordsworth and Coleridge with their work.

Meanwhile, he was living an extremely solitary life, spending nearly all his evenings alone because his few friends were out of town and he could not bring himself to tell his name to casual coffee-house acquaintances. He was very lonely, and in April his health declined once again. He complained of a recurrence of his old facial pains, for which he took laudanum; and he suffered for a time with toothache.

Dorothy had written him that the preparation of Dove Cottage was nearly complete; but, instead of rushing back to Grasmere after the publication of the pamphlet, De Quincey lingered in London. His reasons were two: he had collected two or three hundred books which had to be packed and sent to Grasmere, and his long-lost brother "Pink" had turned up, physically wasted and nervously ill, after about six years of fantastic adventures and hardships. After staying in London through June in hopes of seeing him, De Quincey joined his mother in the southwest of England to await him there.

Mrs. Quincey had meanwhile been building, with the financial help of her brother, a new villa in the valley of Wrington, about twelve miles from Bristol in Somersetshire. She had named it Westhay, perhaps with reference to her former home, Greenhay; and the house was just being finished when De Quincey arrived. One of the attractions of the area for Mrs. Quincey was the proximity of Barley Wood, the home of Hannah More, the famous evangelical author, now a close friend of Mrs. Quincey and one of the principal influences on her views. This formidable lady, who soon called to meet De Quincey, was interested in part because he had somehow gained the advance reputation of an infidel philosopher. De Quincey later wrote a delightful description of her and of their meeting, which, he said, "laid a solid foundation for mutual dislike" (XIV, 115). He was to see her often during his subsequent visits to Somerset.

While in London, De Quincey had worked to promote the sale of Coleridge's *The Friend,* and he continued his efforts in Somersetshire, as well as defending the work against criticism. Meanwhile, he was making tentative plans to travel to Spain and to the Levant with his new friend John Wilson. "Pink" finally arrived about September 10, and for a few weeks the whole family was once again united, for the first time in many years. Apparently bygones were forgotten, and a reasonably happy relationship prevailed.

XII *Grasmere and London*

In the meantime, Dove Cottage had long been ready, and De Quincey finally left Westhay after the middle of October to return to Grasmere and take possession. Though his first lease was only for six years, he was to rent Dove Cottage until 1834, about twenty-five years, and to spend a major portion of his middle life there. De Quincey's library, which arrived in twenty-nine boxes, was now very extensive; and in the next few years it was to grow to a total of about five thousand volumes (III, 409). Coleridge, who found the books useful, borrowed as many as five hundred at a time.

De Quincey's next few years were mainly devoted to reading and social life. Since his funds were not yet exhausted, he at first felt no need to enter a profession; nor did he have any clear and immediate plans of writing for publication. He read widely, undertook Danish for a time, and returned to the study of German philosophy—particularly Kant's. The great ambition to become an intellectual benefactor of mankind, which had displaced his youthful poetic ambitions at Oxford, now led him to project a comprehensive philosophical work to be called *De Emendatione Humani Intellectus.* But, like so many of the great plans of the English Romantic writers, this one was also to remain unfulfilled.

As relaxation from his studies, De Quincey resumed walking, covering long distances alone through the varied scenery of the Lakes, often at night, when he enjoyed glimpsing the life of the cottagers through their lighted windows. He visited London and Westhay for varying periods, and in the autumn of 1811 his mother and his two sisters visited him for a month at Grasmere, for the first time seeing his home and meeting his friends. He was still indulging in opium moderately and intermittently, but his health was excellent; in fact, he reported that he had never felt better than he did in the spring of 1812.

His friendship with Wordsworth and his circle deepened. He developed a very close relationship with little Catherine Wordsworth, and he served as godfather to Wordsworth's son William in 1810. Although from the first De Quincey had found Southey a little cold—too absorbed in his own work to be cordially friendly —he saw more of him now; and Southey considered him one of the best-informed young men he had ever met. He was also enjoying the society of Wilson and Lloyd. Wilson lived nine miles away at his estate Elleray on Windermere. He kept a fleet of boats on the lake, and he was an avid horseman and athlete, as well as a heroic drinker. Lloyd and his lovely wife lived near at hand, and De Quincey was often in their home as an intimate friend.

However, the clouds were beginning to close in on this sunny prospect. By the end of 1811, the ladies of the Wordsworth household began to show signs of coolness. Sara Hutchinson started referring to him as "Peter Quince" and criticizing him for absorption in himself and his books. He had begun to realize that his dwindling inheritance was no longer sufficient to support him and that he must find a means of supplementing it. He chose the legal profession; and, at the end of March, 1812, he went to London to enter himself at the Middle Temple to study law. But his commitment to this profession was at best half-hearted, if one may judge by the impression of the diarist Henry Crabb Robinson, who met him in London at this time: "his person is small, his complexion fair, and his air and manner those of a sickly, enfeebled man. . . . His views in studying the law will never, I think, be realized. He has a small independent fortune, and the only thing he wants is a magnificent library; this he is willing to purchase by giving for it a few years close attention to the law. But he is resolved on no account to put himself under a special pleader, nor will he live more than six months during the year in London. I represented to him that I feared *nothing* could be expected from the law *so* studied." [22]

But all study was interrupted in early June by a letter from Dorothy Wordsworth informing him that his beloved Catherine, who had been partially crippled by an illness two years before, had suddenly died. Wordsworth was in London, and De Quincey saw him off for Wales, where Mrs. Wordsworth was visiting. Little Kate's death shook De Quincey with surprising force; to Crabb Robinson, it seemed that his grief was greater than her father's. De Quincey believed he had had premonitions of her death; and, since she had taken on a symbolic aura in his imagination, her death unsettled him deeply, as if he had been possessed by a nympholepsy. He returned to Grasmere about two weeks after hearing the sad news, and there he surrendered to a paroxysm of grief for several weeks, throwing himself nightly on her grave and sometimes even spending the entire night there. Occasionally, he had hallucinatory visions of the child (II, 443–44). Suddenly, toward the end of August, he fell ill with a strange malady, which he considered nervous and which made even breathing painful. He went to Liverpool, Birmingham, Bristol, Bath, and Clifton in search of medical advice; but in November his illness finally passed, leaving him purged of his grief as well. It has been suggested that his illness may have been "a mild yet nontheless [sic] positive case of infantile paralysis, from which he completely recovered"; the symptoms and duration correspond, and he could have contracted the disease from Wordsworth's children.[23] However, it seems possible that the psychic traumas of his earlier experiences of beloved girls' sufferings and deaths contributed something to his reaction.

He went to the baths of Ilfracombe, Devonshire, to convalesce; and there, in December, he heard from Wordsworth of the death of his child Thomas, another sad blow. In January, De Quincey finally returned to Grasmere, to remain there for the rest of the winter and the early spring. During this period he was developing a friendship with the family of a John Simpson, a respectable landed farmer who lived in a cottage, called the "Nab," on Rydal Water. One of Simpson's children, Margaret, then a girl of seventeen, later became De Quincey's wife.

XIII *Opium Addiction*

The following summer (1813) marked a great watershed in De Quincey's life; he then, at the end of his twenty-eighth year, finally became thoroughly addicted to opium, as he was to continue to be, with only a few brief intervals, for the remaining forty-six years of his life. He had returned to London in May to take up his legal studies again. His financial predicament had grown worse. During the spring his wealthy friend Wilson had lost his fortune and had appealed to De Quincey for a loan of two hundred pounds, which De Quincey could ill afford, but which he nevertheless promptly and loyally gave to Wilson. During the summer De Quincey experienced, perhaps partly as an aftermath of his illness the previous fall, a recurrence of the terrible sufferings he had undergone in London during his vagrancy over ten years before: "a most appalling irritation of the stomach . . . accompanied by a revival of the old dreams" (III, 398).

Opium seemed the only recourse because of its tested medicinal powers, and De Quincey continued to believe in them to the end of his life. He always felt that opium had saved him from tuberculosis and had cured or controlled other ailments; he was also convinced that his failure to free himself of the habit in later life was due to chronic ailments which required the drug as a medicine, an anodyne, or a tranquilizer. However, it seems probable that many of the symptoms which caused him to resort to opium were really themselves the results of it. The withdrawal symptoms which follow a dose of it were little understood in De Quincey's day, but are now known to begin to occur eight hours after each dose and to take forms easily mistaken for symptoms of unrelated ailments. Thus, much of De Quincey's supposedly therapeutic self-dosage, even during the first nine years of allegedly nonaddictive indulgence, may really have been forced upon him by the effects of the drug.

Addiction resulting from such medical applications was far from uncommon at the time. All persons are potentially subject to addiction, and three weeks' regular use is normally sufficient to fasten the habit. Among De Quincey's distinguished contemporaries who are known to have been addicted are Coleridge, George Crabbe, William Wilberforce, Isaac Milner (Dean of Carlyle), and a Mr. Addington (an under-secretary of state); no doubt there were countless others, both distinguished and obscure, whose addiction remained hidden (III, 212 n.). It is often possible for addicts, by holding themselves to the minimum sustaining dosage, to function effectively in daily life, their habit unsuspected by their associates. They can even live long and productive lives, for opium used in moderation has intrinsically little or no deleterious effect upon health.

It is quite possible that, as De Quincey always contended and as some medical men have subsequently believed, opium actually saved him from invalidism and made his literary output possible. He never regretted having taken opium; such remorse as he expressed was only for his excesses. One physician has speculated that the physical disorder which led De Quincey into the opium habit was a severe inflammation of the gastric nerves accompanied by gastric ulcer.[24] Another has blamed the trouble on "reflex ocular neurosis," resulting from an uncorrected myopic astigmatism, which manifests itself as digestive problems in men.[25] At least one of the surviving portraits and a photograph of De Quincey in later life seem to show a marked divergency (a "cast" or strabismus) of the eyes, a symptom of such disorders; he did speak of having to read with one eye for a time in later life; and people who had met him sometimes remarked on a sort of squint.

However, the medical excuse for addiction, taken by itself, is probably insufficient—in De Quincey's case and many others—as he himself acknowledged (III, 229–31). The true cause of De Quincey's addiction probably lay much deeper, in a basic psychological debility which rendered him incapable of dealing directly with the shocks and stresses of reality, an unconscious need to regress toward the warm comforts of infancy and childhood. He later described himself as a "eudaemonist" (III, 399), a searcher for happiness; and he certainly displayed throughout his life an inability to confront painful realities and to assume responsibilities. His early precocity, his mother's exacting standards, and his own tendency toward idealizing hero-worship had led him to entertain unrealistic expectations of himself and the world, and the buffets of reality were too painful to be borne.

It is also possible that he nursed forbidden desires of an oedipal nature, requiring a retreat into a fantasy world where they could be dealt with symbolically. (It is interesting to observe that De Quincey specifically mentions Oedipus in describing his dreams in the *Confessions*, and at the most terrible climax he mentions "the incestuous mother," an allusion to Milton's character "Sin" [III, 434, 446].)[26] That psychological problems of some sort were involved is confirmed by the fact that De Quincey includes intense pleasure among his first reactions to opium, and it is now believed that only psychopaths derive pleasure from opiates.[27] In short, opium offered him a release and a refuge; and he was unopposed by fears of the ill effects of opium, for these were still little understood. Moreover, he was uninhibited by moral disapproval of the habit, for that view did not become general until later on in the Victorian Age, although Coleridge already suffered from it in his own mind.

Nevertheless, De Quincey's addiction must not be reduced to mere escapism, a means of running away from adult responsibility. He found in it also a means of running *toward* something positive. The dreams which he believed opium revived and shaped for him seemed to him somehow to be connected with a higher or deeper order of reality; they became in a sense his intimations of immortality.

Whatever the causes, De Quincey recognized in 1813 his dependence on opium; and, while he tried for a time to conceal the habit from friends and relatives, he at first did little to control it. He normally took his opium in the form of laudanum, a solution of the drug in alcohol, which he sometimes diluted with water; for the rest of his life he was never long without a supply of this concoction. Although opium was comparatively cheap in his day, it seemed expensive to him (III, 382). During his periods of higher consumption, he must have been spending two or three guineas a week on the drug, which surely added to the stress of his poverty.

During the next three years (1813–15) De Quincey divided his time among Grasmere, London, and Somersetshire, giving some attention to his legal studies, developing new acquaintances, and sinking deeper into the toils of opium. In London, he renewed his associations with Crabb Robinson, Lamb, and Coleridge. He introduced his brother "Pink" to Lamb, and the two liked each other (III, 57). "Pink" appears to have been influenced by De Quincey to settle in the Lake Country, for he acquired property there in 1814 and held it for two years until his departure from England in 1816, a journey from which he never returned.[28] In Somerset, De Quincey was introduced to the great actress Mrs. Siddons in the home of Hannah More (II, 446–54). In Grasmere, he saw less of his previous friends. The coolness between him and the Wordsworths gradually increased. Wilson, after his financial collapse, had gone to Edinburgh to study law and returned to Elleray only for the holidays. And disaster had overtaken the Lloyds, for Charles gradually lost his sanity and had to be confined to a lunatic asylum; he was to escape and descend upon De Quincey for a nightmarish moment about 1818 (II, 396).

In the fall of 1815, De Quincey was persuaded by Wilson to visit Edinburgh for the first time. There he met Sir William Hamilton, John Gibson Lockhart, and many others of the most distinguished writers, scholars, and professional men of the time. De Quincey's erudition, his gracious manners, and his conversational eloquence created a strong impression. Meanwhile, in Westmorland his friendship with the Simpson family—and particularly with Margaret—was growing. When Wilson dropped in at Dove Cottage late one Saturday night in the autumn of 1814 and, finding De Quincey absent, went to sleep in his bed, he was awakened at three by De Quincey, just returning from the Nab. De Quincey's attachment to Margaret Simpson, which was beginning to be noised abroad, was looked on with disfavor by his friends. The rumors even reached his mother at Westhay, and she wrote on September 9, 1815, to express her concern and to admonish him.

During this same period, from 1813 to 1815, De Quincey's consumption of opium gradually rose to between eight thousand drops of laudanum, or three hundred and twenty grains of opium, and twelve thousand drops of laudanum, or four hundred and eighty grains of opium, a day—an amount which left him sick and incapacitated much of the time (III, 401, 419). He often stayed in bed until noon, and he grew untidy in his dress and personal cleanliness. Even his customary studies in literature and philosophy were abandoned. This period was the first of the few of deep intoxication which were to punctuate his life. He never exceeded the rate of consumption he now indulged in; and, while it was considerably less than Coleridge's maximum, it was enough to render De Quincey an invalid. It has been pointed out that the alcohol solvent in the quantity of laudanum he took in his periods of maximum consumption may have contributed to his invalidism.[29]

Hitherto he had kept his addiction a secret, but it now gradually became known. In October, 1814, Wordsworth and his wife called on De Quincey when he was ill; and Mrs. Wordsworth rec-

ognized the symptoms of opium-eating. Since the Wordsworths
had long suffered from the results of the same habit in Coleridge,
they could not take a hopeful or indulgent view of their discovery;
and, although they tried to be helpful, a cooling of their relationship with De Quincey was inevitable. Soon Dorothy was refusing
to speak with him, and Mary Wordsworth even to meet with him.
Their disapproval of his growing connection with Margaret Simpson did not improve their attitude. He in turn grew incensed with
them; for long periods they did not meet.

During De Quincey's trip to Edinburgh in 1815, Lockhart recorded seeing him openly eating opium tablets from a snuffbox
after dinner at Sir William Hamilton's while the other guests
drank their half-bottle apiece.[30] Crabb Robinson, calling on him at
Dove Cottage on September 5, 1816, recorded his impressions in
his diary: "He has been very much an invalid, and his appearance
bespoke ill-health. He was very dirty and even squalid. . . . It
appears that he has taken to opium, and, like Coleridge, seriously
injured his health."[31] He was also reported to be doing some
heavy drinking with Wilson at this time; but he was ordinarily a
temperate drinker.

In 1815 he paid what was to prove to be his last visit for three
years to his mother at Westhay. He was making one more effort at
the law in London; but now, with the last penny of his fortune
gone, he had to abandon that course, though his intention of ultimately becoming a lawyer lingered in his mind for a while.[32] At
last he was faced with the poverty which was to harass him for
the next thirty years. He returned to Grasmere in a defeated and
hopeless state, one relieved only temporarily by the satisfaction
which his flattering reception in Edinburgh afforded him in the
fall of 1815.

XIV *Marriage*

Apparently De Quincey increasingly sought consolation in the
company of the Simpsons, and his affair with Margaret ripened
into love. Perhaps as a result of this affection, at some point during 1816 he pulled himself together and sharply reduced his consumption of opium (III, 401). He soon found his spirits greatly
improved, and he discovered with pleasure that he was even
equal to reading Kant once again. This pleasant renascence was to

last for a year, until about the middle of 1817; and he later called this period the happiest year of his life.

On November 9, 1816, Margaret Simpson bore De Quincey a son, who was baptized "William Penson, illegitimate son of Margaret Simpson, Nab." Since the child was named after De Quincey's elder brother and his mother's family, he apparently made no secret of his paternity. However, for reasons unknown he delayed marrying Margaret until February 15, 1817, when the ceremony took place in the parish church in Grasmere in the presence of her father and a few others. Wordsworth's son William later said that he had been present, but whether other members of the Wordsworth family were is not known. Certainly, they considered the marriage beneath De Quincey; for "Peggy" was the mere daughter of a farmer; she had little education, while he was a gentleman and an intellectual. The Wordsworth family now regarded De Quincey as a ruined man, and the suspension of all intercourse between them continued by mutual consent. But De Quincey apparently never wavered in his love for Margaret, remaining deeply and happily devoted to her until her death. Although she was almost eleven years his junior and greatly inferior in learning, she made him a loyal, sympathetic, and long-suffering wife. In the *Confessions* he paid an eloquent tribute to Margaret (III, 377), and he left a charming picture of the happiness of their first months of married life in Dove Cottage (III, 409).

However, by the middle of 1817 he had fallen again into the abyss of opium; and there he remained for about three and a half years. During this period of desperation and instability, his reveries and dreams became more distressing than ever before (III, 434). At first his intellectual energy died completely, but in 1818 it was temporarily revived by a birth of interest in economics and politics. Wilson had sent him a copy of Ricardo's *Principles of Political Economy and Taxation* (1817), and reading it awakened a passionate interest which lasted the rest of his life. At the same time, he became interested in Westmorland politics.

XV The Westmorland Gazette

In the spring of 1818, Henry Brougham, the Whig, came into Westmorland and offered himself as a candidate for Parliament in the Kendal election, opposing the local Tory candidate Colonel C.

H. Lowther, whose family had long dominated Westmorland politics. Brougham's campaign was brisk and hard-hitting. To safe conservatives such as Wordsworth had now become and such as De Quincey had always been, Brougham seemed a dangerous radical; they became deeply agitated over the campaign, and their common interest drew them together again. Wordsworth was publishing articles supporting the Lowthers in the *Kendal Chronicle;* but, since that paper was leaning toward the Whigs, the Lowthers established their own paper, *The Westmorland Gazette.* In the meantime, De Quincey wrote an article, "Close Comments upon a Straggling Speech"—a response to an address of Brougham's and an answer to his attacks on Wordsworth and Wordsworth's articles—and he composed and published it in close collaboration with Wordsworth. De Quincey's paper appeared as a pamphlet about mid-April, and he thus emerged as a party polemicist in his first publication since the note to Wordsworth's *Convention of Cintra.* "Close Comments" is also his first known independent essay to be published. It is a sharp, eloquent, and sometimes humorous work.[33]

When the man first chosen as editor of *The Westmorland Gazette* did not work out well, De Quincey—emboldened by his recent collaboration with Wordsworth—wrote to the poet on April 14 to propose himself as editor. Wordsworth apparently cooperated, for De Quincey was appointed the second editor, beginning with the issue of July 18, 1818, and continuing into November, 1819. He did not move to Kendal; instead, he appointed a resident assistant to whom he paid much of his salary of one hundred and sixty pounds, while he himself continued to live in Dove Cottage. There his family had now been increased by the birth of his first daughter, Margaret, on June 5, 1818.

As editor of *The Westmorland Gazette,* a four-page weekly paper, De Quincey at first threw himself ardently into the political debate, and he gradually shifted the emphasis of the paper from its other customary contents to his own peculiar interests. The local and London news, farm and household information, the personal column and the market reports disappeared or dwindled; and they were replaced by essays on political, philosophical, and philological subjects, as well as by reports of murder trials, which had developed into a lifelong interest for De Quincey. The directors were forced to ask De Quincey to restore the local news and to reduce direct controversy with the *Kendal Chronicle*. When his absenteeism grew as he relapsed into narcotic lethargy and lingered at home in Grasmere, the directors felt forced to complain; and he finally resigned after sixteen months.

His financial plight had been worsening. His family expenses were increasing, while his income shrank. De Quincey had borrowed from his sister Jane and had also received help from his uncle; in 1819, he also borrowed from Wilson, who raised money on his note and then was embarrassed—and even in danger of imprisonment—when De Quincey failed to pay it in 1820, for he himself was then in financial straits. Wilson was obliged to tell De Quincey he could accept no more such notes from him. As early as 1818, De Quincey himself had been fearful of imprisonment for debt. He had begun to think of writing regularly for magazines as a source of income, and he had received offers from *Blackwood's Edinburgh Magazine* and *The Quarterly Review*, probably by way of Wilson; but for the present he was unable to exert himself. In the meantime, he turned to his uncle and his mother with long explanations and appeals late in 1818, and received additional help from them.

About this time De Quincey, returning from a late summer's trip to Wrington seeking financial aid from his mother, had one of the most memorable experiences of his life. It was his custom to dose himself with opium when he traveled in order to fortify himself against the cold encountered on the outside of the closed coach, where he usually rode. He had done so on this occasion; and, when the coach, rushing through the night a few miles above Manchester, nearly collided with a gig containing a young man and woman, he experienced an apocalyptic terror which he was to elaborate near the end of his life into one of his most magnificent works, "The English Mail-Coach."

All the financial aid De Quincey received from his friends and his family was insufficient. In his weak, drugged, and erratic state, he was still incapable of action. His practical incompetence, which was to turn his subsequent life into one long flight from creditors, was probably partly the addict's indisposition to make decisions and to take action; but it was also partly the result of a deliberate choice. De Quincey had decided early in his career to devote himself to the life of the mind, and he had done so with some awareness that this would require him to neglect ordinary practical affairs. He demonstrated, on a few occasions in his life, that he was capable of shrewd and precise dealing when he turned his mind to it; but, ordinarily, he preferred to evade all such concerns. His ready sympathy made him a generous and charitable man, even when he was in need himself; indeed, he was repeatedly approached by the same beggars, some with borrowed children, taking advantage of his liberality.

It is interesting to observe that De Quincey apparently never turned to religion with complaints or appeals in the years of his greatest sufferings from opium and poverty. In spite of his deep and firm spiritual convictions, nurtured by his mother's ardent piety, he had not adopted her evangelical bias since he found both the doctrine and the manners of the Evangelical clergy abhorrent. He had apparently developed his own religious coloring, that of a moderate High Churchman, but with an independent approach to matters of controversy. He was untroubled by skepticism, for his faith lent him support. But he seems never to have resorted to religion in any spirit of whining remorse or weak-kneed escapism in the face of his sufferings. He was not even a regular churchgoer after boyhood.

In 1819, when Mrs. Quincey's business agent went into bankruptcy, the ill effects were felt on the family finances. Gradually it became apparent to De Quincey that some sort of action was necessary to avoid utter ruin. Thus in 1820 he turned toward Edinburgh in an effort to solve his financial problem. His friend Wilson had been elected to the chair of moral philosophy at the University of Edinburgh, despite comparatively weak qualifications; and he relied heavily on De Quincey for assistance in preparing himself to assume his position without exposing his limitations. Meanwhile, he had been promoting De Quincey's prospects among his publishing associates in Edinburgh. As a result, De Quincey now entered into an agreement with William Blackwood to supply him with a series of articles for his magazine.

Thus began De Quincey's career as a magazine writer, in his thirty-fifth year—the career he was to follow without intermission for the remaining half of his life. It began inauspiciously, for he found himself unable to write quickly or regularly. He wrote only after long hesitation, and then proceeded slowly and laboriously, constantly revising. Already by August, 1820, Blackwood had begun to complain of the delay. About the beginning of December, De Quincey went to Edinburgh to devote himself more determinedly to his work. He was warmly welcomed by his acquaintances of his visit five years before, but his writing still languished for a time. However, he finally, after repeated postponements and interruptions, forced himself to write; and on December 18 he finished his first article for *Blackwood's,* an essay on Schiller. His success stimulated him, and now he was promising early completion of an essay on opium, as well as essays on Jean Paul Richter, Hannah More, Kant, Malthus, and Ricardo. His mind was clearing and he was beginning to sense the financial resources his abilities might open to him as a magazine writer. So elated did he become at his new prospects that he allowed himself some indiscreet and flippant comments on the magazine in a letter to Blackwood on January 8, which offended him and created a coolness between them. But, when De Quincey returned to Grasmere after a few more weeks, he was still planning to write for *Blackwood's.*

XVI   The London Magazine

However, during the spring of 1821, he for some reason turned his ambitions toward London. Some kind of temporary cloud seems to have come over his relation with his best friend Wilson about this time. De Quincey moved his growing family out of the crowded Dove Cottage and into Fox Ghyll, a charming house nearer Ambleside and Rydal; but he left his books in Dove Cottage. In June, he set out alone for London; and there, through the intercession of Wordsworth, Thomas Noon Talfourd, and Lamb, he formed a connection with Taylor and Hessey, the editors of *The London Magazine.* Taking up his residence at 4 York Street, he forced himself to reduce his opium and to work at his writing. He found now as always that the periods of opium withdrawal were the most painful ones associated with his habit; but, when he arrived on the plateau of a reasonable sustaining dose, the pain diminished; and he was able to work productively. He devoted himself throughout the summer to writing his opium article, which now took the form of *The Confessions of an English Opium-Eater.* Published in two parts, anonymously, in the September and October (1821) issues of *The London Magazine,* it created something of a sensation, because of its peculiar subject and because of its remarkable style.

De Quincey thus emerged abruptly on the English literary scene as a mature and accomplished writer; the reading public acknowledged him at once, and from this point on, he was assured of a ready market for almost anything he wrote. His chronic poverty would force him to keep writing for periodicals for most of his remaining years, although at first he had no ambition to do so, and approached the profession with some condescension. De Quincey's talents did not equip him to write most of the ordinary kinds of magazine material, but he found modes congenial to his capabilities. He drew on his personal experience and observation. He exploited his vast reading, concocting articles out of abridgments, redactions, and translations of the works of others—often with inadequate acknowledgment. He wrote with far greater pains than are usually expended on periodical prose. He even wrote out some of his essays in two distinct forms, and then had trouble deciding which to publish. He worked intermittently, always having to struggle against the lassitude produced by opium, and often, like Coleridge, suffering feelings of revulsion from what he was writing before he had completed it.

When De Quincey received forty guineas from Taylor and Hessey for the *Confessions,* he considered it generous pay. The public response was so favorable that he was led to promise a third part, which he never completed. Nevertheless, in the next three years he published about forty-eight articles or separate installments of articles in *The London Magazine,* and these were of widely varied kinds and uneven interest. They included articles on Richter, Herder, Goethe, Malthus, "Walking" Stewart, the Rosicrucians and Freemasons, English history, English and German dictionaries, suicide, education and literature in general, and political economy; translations from Richter, Goethe, and German fiction; a review of a pseudo-Waverly German novel called *Walladmor;* an appendix to the *Confessions;* and one of his most successful critical essays, "On the Knocking at the Gate in Macbeth." Some of these articles appeared in series extending over more than one issue of the magazine. One such series was called "Analects from Richter"; the articles on political economy appeared in a series called "Dialogues of Three Templars"; and the articles on education appeared as a series of "Letters to a Young Man Whose Education Has Been Neglected"—subsequently parodied by Lamb, with De Quincey's approval, in "A Letter to an Old Man Whose Education Has Been Neglected."

After the publication of the *Confessions*, the second work by De Quincey to be published in *The London Magazine*—the article on Richter—appeared in December, 1821. The *Confessions* was republished by Taylor and Hessey in the form of a small book in 1822; the Appendix which De Quincey supplied, dated September 30, to explain the nonappearance of the promised Part III, was the only new piece of writing he published in 1822. However, in 1823 every issue of *The London Magazine* contained something of his, as did nearly every issue in 1824, until it ceased publication after the end of the year. All his articles in *The London Magazine* were anonymous, published under the pseudonyms "The Opium Eater" and "XYZ"; but the author's identity was not long a well-kept secret. He also published a translation from German fiction in *Knight's Quarterly Magazine* in 1824.[34]

De Quincey was in London only intermittently during these years. While there, he was often lonely, depressed, and homesick for Westmorland and his family, now increased by the birth of his third child, Horatio. He had developed a permanent aversion to literary society, which increased his solitariness. He formed a custom of walking daily in Hyde Park and Kensington Gardens, but the children he saw playing there so increased his homesickness that he had to abandon such walks. In 1821 he stayed about seven months, from June to December. He renewed his acquaintance with Robinson and Lamb, finally beginning to understand and appreciate Lamb. He confessed his misery to Lamb and found him and his sister kind and compassionate comforters. His work also brought him in touch with Hazlitt, Hood, and Macaulay. Through monthly dinners given by Taylor and Hessey, he met several other able young writers, but no close friendships resulted. One of these men, Richard Woodhouse, the friend of Keats, was much interested in De Quincey; and he made records of his conversation.

Despite returns on his writings, De Quincey's financial condition continued to be desperate. He was even driven to the resort of writing to ask Coleridge whether he could repay the anonymous gift of 1807, which Coleridge had considered a loan; but he could not repay it. Through most of 1822, De Quincey remained at home in the North, often ill. During July he went through the painful systematic effort at withdrawal of opium he describes in the Appendix (III, 466–72). When he returned to London in December, he stayed there reluctantly and unhappily until August, 1823; then, back at Fox Ghyll in the fall, he sank into narcosis again. He stayed indoors for months at a time, and on at least one occasion he was not at home to Wordsworth himself. His affairs were in a sad state; he was deep in debt, and his creditors were clamorous. He kept trying to return to London, but his mental and physical condition prevented it.

In July, 1824, he finally set out, and after being delayed by illness in Liverpool, reached London in midsummer. Immediately upon his arrival he learned that he had been the subject of a libelous attack in the sensational new *John Bull Magazine,* which savagely criticized his published writings, cast aspersions on his character, charged that he had married his housekeeper, and asked for the dates of his marriage and the birth of his first child. He was terribly hurt and angry. The anonymous author was Dr. William Maginn, but De Quincey did not learn this fact for many years. He repeatedly tried to correct the false impressions the article created.[35] In his current abysmal misery, it gave him a cruel psychological wound.

De Quincey now became involved in an absurd, tiresome piece of literary hack work. As already mentioned, he had written a long review of a three-volume novel called *Walladmor,* published in Berlin, that pretended to be a translation of Sir Walter Scott's latest work, a wild and ridiculous story of adventure in Wales and western England, but was actually a forgery. De Quincey's review, while it exposed the forgery, included a summary of the plot; and his inaccuracy and incoherence suggest that the book had been read—and the review written—in haste and with carelessness. However, Taylor and Hessey were sufficiently impressed by the commercial possibilities of the novel, as De Quincey had described it, to persuade him to translate it into English for them to publish. It must have been in a weak moment that De Quincey agreed to do so, for it proved a long and painful labor with utterly unworthy material that occupied much of his time in the fall of 1824. On closer acquaintance, he found *Walladmor* so insufferably bad that he freely altered it by reducing its length greatly, correcting some of its glaring weaknesses and errors, and elaborating and heightening some scenes. When the work was published toward the end of 1824 in two volumes, it contained De Quincey's playful dedication to the German "translator." Although he later published a humorous account of this episode (XIV, 132–45), it must have been a tedious drudgery and later a source of some embarrassment.

Despite these painful experiences and his ill health, De Quincey formed some valued friendships during this final sojourn in London. His review of an anonymous book on education (XIV, 9–45) caused the author to seek him out. This was Matthew Davenport Hill, son of the headmaster of the famous Hazelwood School, and later the Recorder of Birmingham and a noted law reformer. The two developed a close friendship during De Quincey's last months in London. For a time, De Quincey used Hill's home as his most convenient London address. Another valued new acquaintance was Charles Knight, founder and editor of *Knight's Quarterly Magazine*, who had met De Quincey in connection with his contribution to the magazine. Knight found De Quincey living in misery and squalor, and he invited him to live as his guest in his own home, which De Quincey did for some months. Knight later reported that De Quincey once left his house and lived for a time secretly in miserable lodgings only because he did not know how to negotiate a postdated bank draft for a considerable sum which he had in his possession.[36]

De Quincey was often in financial straits in London—at times he even feared arrest for debt. His position was slightly improved in 1825 by Colonel Penson's final return from India; Penson's assumption of the expenses of Westhay enabled Mrs. Quincey to pay her son's current debts and to grant him the annuity of one hundred pounds that she continued for the rest of her life. In the meantime, the strain of a precarious and separated existence had begun to tell upon De Quincey's wife Margaret, who was developing symptoms of nervous tension and depression in his absence. Fox Ghyll had been sold at auction by the owner, so she and her children had been forced to move in with her parents at Rydal Nab. Meanwhile, her fourth child, Francis, was on the way. In July, De Quincey wrote in distress to his old friend Dorothy Wordsworth and asked for her assistance in comforting his wife.[37]

Since *The London Magazine* and *Knight's Quarterly* were now gone as sources of income, there was little to hold De Quincey in

London. Therefore, in middle or late summer (1825), he finally
returned to Rydal, thus ending his last stay of any length in London. His comings and goings had probably been more frequent
than the records reveal; he later estimated that, if all his periods
of residence in London were added together, they would not
amount to more than a year and a half; but this estimate seems
too low (III, 126).

XVII *Edinburgh and* Blackwood's

De Quincey's hopes now turned back toward Edinburgh. The
coolness with Wilson and Blackwood had thawed while he was in
London. He was again in correspondence with Wilson, and his
contributions were again being solicited for *The Quarterly Review* and *Blackwood's*. Therefore, after about a year at Grasmere,
he began a period of alternate residence in Edinburgh and Grasmere which lasted four years.

With the appearance of the first part of his article on Lessing in
Blackwood's in November, 1826, his first known publication in
that periodical, he began the association which was to bring forth
much of his best work in the next twenty-three years. Since *Blackwood's* was the leading Tory periodical of the time, De Quincey's
inherited political conservatism made him a congenial addition to
the staff. He seems to have been regarded by the editors as their
principal political writer, in addition to his role in contributing
articles of more enduring interest. He was at first paid at the
going rate of ten guineas a sheet, or sixteen pages.

Meanwhile, he found another source of income in newspaper
writing. In 1827 and 1828 De Quincey was a frequent contributor
to the *Edinburgh Saturday Post* and its successor, the *Edinburgh
Evening Post*, of reviews and political commentary.[38] Apparently,
he now made one of his valiant but painful efforts to break free of
the opium habit; and, while he abstained for a few months, he
devoted himself industriously to this regular employment, perhaps partly in an effort to meet the expense of maintaining two
establishments. Nevertheless, his financial position continued to
deteriorate.

Since his marriage, De Quincey's relations with his mother, his
uncle, and his sisters had become more remote and sporadic. Mrs.
Quincey disapproved of his opium-eating, his marriage, and his
financial improvidence; nevertheless, she continued to contribute

to his support and to help him out of difficulties. Uncle Penson had also wearied of De Quincey's problems, although he too contributed regularly to his support; and his sister Jane had also come to regard him unsympathetically. In the meantime, his sister Mary, having married a clergyman, had died in childbirth at the age of thirty-six, about 1821; "Pink" had been killed in Jamaica about 1816; and Henry had died at age twenty-seven in 1820.

During these years of De Quincey's and his family's travels between Rydal and Edinburgh, he and his wife had been intermittently ill; and the psychological strains had been severe. Finally, in 1830, Mrs. De Quincey's condition became critical, and she wrote a letter threatening suicide to De Quincey in Edinburgh. In this crisis, Dorothy Wordsworth's kind offices were again called upon; and she ventured to suggest that it would be best for De Quincey to move his family permanently to Edinburgh, which he did before the end of the year. The attenuated cords binding De Quincey to the Lake Country were thus finally severed; he never saw Wordsworth again.

Meanwhile, his life during his periods in Edinburgh had not been without interest. He had resumed the one intimate male friendship of his life, that with Wilson; and at times he lived with him for periods of some months. One such visit was protracted for about a year. Wilson, who was now flourishing in his double capacity of professor at the University and leading writer for *Blackwood's,* had alluded to the "Opium-Eater" occasionally in his "Noctes Ambrosianae" dialogues; and he introduced him in 1830 as one of the principal speakers. Representing him as a stately, formal, learned, and often eloquent speaker, he occasionally satirized his verboseness and tedious logic-chopping. Wilson's daughter later recalled that, during De Quincey's visits in their home, he usually stayed in bed by day and worked by night; he took his meals alone in his room, and held daily conferences with the cook, who was bewildered by the elaborate formality of the instructions given her by this strange little gentleman.[39] Wilson attempted to wean De Quincey away from his outlandish, oriental vice of opium-eating to the good old English vice of drinking, but without much success.

De Quincey also made a friend of Carlyle in 1827. De Quincey in *The London Magazine* in 1824 had savagely attacked Carlyle's anonymous translation of Goethe's *Wilhelm Meister* (XI, 222 n.), but now Carlyle was becoming established and held no grudge. He was interested and amused by this dreamy and erudite man who had appeared in Edinburgh. His recorded observations of De Quincey are acute and expressed with his usual pungency. "*Eccovi*—," he wrote of his first impression of De Quincey, "this child has been in hell." [40] A pleasant friendship sprang up between them, while the Carlyles were living in Edinburgh. Mrs. Carlyle nursed De Quincey through a serious illness; and, after Carlyle moved to Craigenputtock in 1828, he cordially invited De Quincey to visit him, though it is not known that he ever did so.

De Quincey made a few other acquaintances in Edinburgh, and occasionally he attended dinners, concerts, and the theater. However, he found it necessary to live much apart from his large family of growing children in order to find the quiet essential for study and writing. Furthermore, after a few years his old friendship with Wilson gradually cooled, until the two men were estranged during their later years. On the whole, De Quincey lived in Edinburgh as solitary a life as usual, busy with his books and writing, harassed by family and financial problems.

During these early Edinburgh years (1826–33), De Quincey contributed articles to *Blackwood's* on Lessing (including a translation of the *Laocoon*), Kant, Richard Bentley, Samuel Parr, and Charlemagne, as well as his long historical series entitled "The Caesars," his translations or digests of German articles—"The Last Days of Immanuel Kant" and the "Toilette of the Hebrew Lady," his important article "Rhetoric," and one of his humorous masterpieces, "On Murder Considered as One of the Fine Arts." He also published in the short-lived *Edinburgh Literary Gazette* his first study of Professor Wilson, which appeared in three installments in 1829. In the meantime, he undertook one ambitious independent literary project, the writing of a novel, *Klosterheim*, to which he devoted much of 1831. *Klosterheim*, published by Blackwood in 1832 as an attractive little separate volume, is one of the very few works of De Quincey that did not originally appear in a magazine.

Despite his productiveness, De Quincey's financial problems continued to grow. He sank rapidly into debt, and in 1832 one of his creditors instituted legal proceedings against him. On October 2 he was actually jailed briefly, but was released because of poor health; and he was again arrested on December 14.[41] Early in 1833

he underwent the process of *Cessio Bonorum,* a sort of bankruptcy procedure under Scots law. At that time he acknowledged
a total indebtedness of six hundred and seventeen pounds, seventeen shillings to fifty-one creditors—about half of them in Edinburgh and the rest in the Lake Region and in London. It was
revealed that De Quincey had been supporting an Ambleside gro-
cer, and had paid fifty pounds to help him out of difficulties, and
also that he had lent one hundred and seventy-five pounds to an
old schoolmate. No matter how pressing his own circumstances
became, De Quincey was always liberal in charity. But now he
was forced to mention Coleridge as his debtor for the three-
hundred-pound gift of 1807.

Finally, by November (1833), all recourses having been exhausted, De Quincey and his wife were forced to flee their creditors by taking sanctuary in "Holyrood," the Abbey precincts of
Edinburgh. This was an area six or seven miles in circumference
where refugees from debts might live unmolested by the civil bail-
iffs. They could emerge only on Sundays; and, while living there,
they had to conform to the regulations of the Sanctuary, which
had its own government. The refugees, who were numerous in De
Quincey's time, lived in crowded conditions.

De Quincey was in Holyrood much of the time from 1833 to
1840, but even there he was occasionally in difficulties over debts
incurred within the Sanctuary and sometimes had to flee into hiding in the city to escape them. His various flights to new residences and his periods in hiding from his creditors and the police
meant that he was often forced to leave his books and papers
behind; and these were sometimes lost, impounded, or forgotten,
and sometimes recovered even after years. Another result was that
he had to do much of his writing on the run, without access to his
books, and he was often interrupted in the midst of preparing
articles. Trying circumstances tended to increase his resort to
opium, which in turn made writing more difficult for him.

The year 1833 was a hard one for De Quincey in other ways. In
February, his eighth and last child, Emily, was born. In September, his next to youngest child, Julius, a boy about four years old
on whom De Quincey doted, suddenly contracted a fever and
died. The grief-stricken De Quincey was even harassed by his
creditors at the boy's funeral. Then, about October, John

Simpson, De Quincey's elderly father-in-law, apparently came to live with him in Edinburgh and added to the burden of his responsibilities.

XVIII   Tait's *and* Blackwood's

In 1833, De Quincey found a new outlet for his writings in *Tait's Edinburgh Magazine.* His connection with *Blackwood's* had been somewhat stormy because he was always pressing for loans and advance payments, often failed to produce articles when promised, and turned in work that had to be rejected. *Tait's,* founded in 1832, was a liberal, or even radical, periodical—an unlikely setting for the work of a staunch conservative like De Quincey. Yet he somehow began publishing articles there in 1833; and, when his old associate William Blackwood grew ill and died in 1834, De Quincey stopped publishing in *Blackwood's* altogether for three years. Turning to *Tait's,* he now published in it some of the most interesting work he ever did. After his mischievous but amusing "Recollections of Hannah More" and his translation "Kant on the Age of the Earth" in 1833, he began publishing in 1834 the series of charming autobiographical sketches which were later expanded into his autobiography. He also began in *Tait's* in 1834 the fascinating and controversial reminiscences of his Lake and London acquaintances, starting with Coleridge, who had just died, and going on to Reverend Clowes (the Manchester Swedenborgian), the Liverpool literary coterie of Mr. Clarke, Sir Humphry Davy, William Godwin, Charles Lamb, Wordsworth, Southey, Charles Lloyd, Professor Wilson, "Walking" Stewart, and others. The articles on Coleridge (1834-35) and those on Wordsworth and Southey (1839) deeply offended De Quincey's former friends in the Lake Country by their unvarnished and gossipy frankness; in fact, they put a final seal on his alienation from them.

Tait demonstrated his political tolerance by also publishing in 1835 De Quincey's article "A Tory's account of Toryism, Whiggism, and Radicalism." Two articles on Greek literature and the touching account of the tragic deaths of George and Sarah Green, entitled "Early Memorials of Grasmere," also appeared in the 1830's in *Tait's.* While most of De Quincey's articles in *Blackwood's* had been, like those in *The London Magazine,* anonymous or pseudonymous, his articles in *Tait's* were usually signed with his name. About this time De Quincey also published articles in the *Encyclopaedia Britannica.* Adam Black, the publisher, happened to meet De Quincey one day in 1837 in the custody of the police, on his way to jail for debt. He volunteered to assume responsibility for the debts in return for articles on Shakespeare and Pope, which De Quincey then wrote. De Quincey also supplied articles on Goethe and Schiller for the *Encyclopaedia.*

In addition to financial and health problems, personal tragedies crowded in upon De Quincey during these years. After the death of his child Julius in 1833, he lost Uncle Penson in 1834, the year which also took his old friends Coleridge, Lamb, and William Blackwood. But the most devastating blow of 1834 struck when his eldest son William, now a young man of seventeen and brilliantly promising, was stricken with a dreadful disease, probably meningitis.[42] De Quincey, who had fastened his dearest hopes and affections on this boy, suffered terribly as he watched him fall sick and then become successively deaf and blind before finally succumbing. These family bereavements contributed to the decline of Mrs. De Quincey's health; in 1837 she contracted typhus, and died in Holyrood on August 7, only forty-one years old. She left her husband, now nearly fifty-two, with a family of six children to care for. Her twenty years of married life had been difficult, because of the births and nurture of eight children, the constant financial stress, and the nursing of her husband through the years of his deepest narcosis. She had been a loyal and loving wife to him, and De Quincey was painfully grieved by her death.

De Quincey's connection with *Blackwood's* was restored after the three-year interval with the publication in 1837 of one of his most impressive narrative works, "The Revolt of the Tartars." For the next twelve years he divided his allegiance between *Tait's* and *Blackwood's.* He regularly received more than the usual rate of pay from *Tait's,* as apparently he did also from *Blackwood's* in his later years. In *Blackwood's* appeared his articles on the English language, miracles, casuistry, the philosophy of Roman history, Roman meals, Milton, the Essenes, Greek tragedy, modern superstition, the opium conflict with China in 1840, style, Plato's *Republic,* Homer, Herodotus, pagan oracles, Cicero, modern Greece, Ricardo, Adam Smith, Ceylon, the Secession from the Church of Scotland, Greece under the Romans, and Coleridge and opiumeating. Finally, in 1845 and 1849, when he was in the great Indian summer of his sixties, the uncompleted series "Suspiria de Profundis," with its magnificent dream visions, and the climactic three-part masterpiece "The English Mail-Coach" were published.

In the meantime, during the 1840's he also contributed to *Tait's*, in addition to the works already mentioned, an account of his gradual estrangement from Wordsworth and a criticism of Wordsworth's poetry, as well as varied articles on temperance movements, Godwin, Hazlitt, Shelley, Keats, Landor, Joan of Arc, the Marquess of Wellesley, Christianity as an organ of political movement, astronomy, secret societies, conversation, and Protestantism, and the narrative called "The Spanish Military Nun," among others. His last article in *Blackwood's* appeared in 1849; his final contribution to *Tait's*—four articles on Pope—in 1851. In 1848 he published three articles in the *North British Review*, another Edinburgh quarterly, on Goldsmith, Pope, and Lamb.

After the death of his wife, De Quincey's life continued for a time to be painfully difficult. He engaged lodgings for himself at 42 Lothian Street in Edinburgh, where he worked for a time and where he was later to settle for the last six years of his life. He was almost constantly in flight and in hiding from creditors, and his poverty was so acute at times that his children went hungry and he was even afraid they might starve. At one point, when he sold his shoes and clothing to provide for them, he had to stay indoors, and to work wrapped in a blanket; at other times, he was forced to do his writing in the streets. He often had to live apart from his children, in concealment from his creditors, and was much alone.

He boarded for a few years in the home of his solicitor, a Mr. McIndoe, a violent and vengeful man who later pursued and persecuted him. In his timid and helpless practical incompetence, he was sometimes victimized by his landlords and creditors; and he came to view some of them with a fear approaching delusions of persecution, which made him more furtive and solitary than ever. He had a horror of letting anyone come into possession of his autograph. During one period of fifteen months, he saw no one but Mr. and Mrs. McIndoe and his son Fred. Sometimes he continued to hold leases for long periods on lodgings he had been forced to flee. At his death, he was found to be the nominal tenant of six different lodgings.

However, his difficulties were alleviated by the good sense and efficiency of his children. His eldest daughter, Margaret, about nineteen at the time of her mother's death, quietly took charge of the household and proved a competent manager. In 1840 the children moved out of Edinburgh to the cottage Mavis Bush near Lasswade, seven miles to the south. Here they provided their father with a second home, and he joined them there from time to time throughout his last nineteen years.

Nevertheless, it was at least partly to escape from his creditors that De Quincey now left Edinburgh and moved to Glasgow, where he resided for about two years, from March, 1841, to June, 1843. At first he lived with friends, Professor J. P. Nichol, the astronomer, and then E. Lushington, a professor of Greek. Subsequently De Quincey took lodgings, and one of these he also continued to lease long after he had ceased to occupy it. While he was in Glasgow, he wrote for a local newspaper; and he continued to send articles to Blackwood. He lived a lonely and sickly life, often deeply depressed, though his spirits were occasionally raised by visits from his sons. His old friend Knight also visited him in Glasgow, in 1843, and found him wearing a foot-long beard.

In the meantime, his family had begun to disperse. His oldest surviving son, Horace, went to China as an officer with the Twenty-sixth Cameronians, where he died of malaria in 1842. His second son, Francis, held a commercial position in Manchester for a time; but he then returned to Edinburgh, undertook the study of medicine, and earned his degree in 1849. Paul Frederick, De Quincey's youngest surviving son, went to India as an officer in the Seventieth Queen's Regiment. In January, 1846, when De Quincey's mother died, over ninety years of age, she had never seen her grandchildren. Her correspondence with her son had been less frequent in her last years. She had never been fully reconciled to his marriage, and she doubted that he was providing a proper education for his children. Nevertheless, she loyally contributed to his support until her death. Her death brought a modest increase in De Quincey's income, which, together with his own earnings, at last gradually released him from serious financial want.

For twenty-five years De Quincey had been writing for periodicals under the stress of immediate and acute financial need. He had begun this career reluctantly, and he had continued it only by anguished struggle against his narcotic inertia. Now that the goad of debts no longer pricked him on, he could have ceased writing for the magazines and returned to more congenial pursuits; but he did not. He continued to write for his remaining thirteen years, perhaps because his attitude toward this work had changed and because his habit of life was now too deeply ingrained.

When De Quincey returned from Glasgow to Lasswade in 1843, he began another attempt to reduce his consumption of opium; it had risen once again to a dangerous and debilitating level of about five thousand drops of laudanum a day. He suffered dreadful withdrawal agonies for several months; and, since exercise helped him to bear the discomfort, he resorted to long daily walks. However, the familiarities of persons he encountered in the neighborhood embarrassed him, and he therefore confined his walks for eighteen months to the little garden at Mavis Bush, measuring the circuit of the space and keeping an account of the distances covered by moving ten small stones on the bars of a garden chair as he passed (XIV, 275). In this manner he calculated that he walked a thousand miles in one period of ninety days. After a long struggle and various relapses, he finally succeeded once again in abstaining totally, for about eight weeks, in 1848; and afterwards he returned merely to the minimal sustaining dose, which he seldom exceeded in his last eleven years. His serious troubles with opium were over.

He continued writing throughout this final crisis, and with his disintoxication came a new access of creative energy. His book *The Logic of Political Economy* was published by Blackwood in 1844, and then began the Indian summer already mentioned which produced some of his greatest work, the *Suspiria*. When *Tait's Magazine* changed hands in 1846 and moved to Glasgow, De Quincey was persuaded to return there for a time to help keep it going. He stayed in Glasgow from the beginning of 1847, writing for *Tait's* and its affiliated newspaper, the *North British Daily Mail*, until he left for the last time in November.

XIX   *Last Years: The Collected Edition*

From 1847 to 1854, his sixty-second to his sixty-ninth years, De Quincey lived mainly at Lasswade with his three daughters and his son Francis. Throughout these years he continued his habit of long daily walks, often covering the seven miles to Edinburgh and

back, and normally walking ten to fifteen miles a day. Even in his
seventieth year he was still walking seven miles a day.

The household at Lasswade was a happy one. His daughters
were musical, and he loved to hear them sing and play. And he
had his usual untidy room full of books and papers to work in.
Among other places, he kept his papers in a disused bathtub,
which was filled to the brim (XIII, 251 ff.). In his single-minded
absorption in his reading, he sometimes caught his hair afire at the
lamp and had to be informed of the fact by his daughters. He was
as solitary as ever, reading and writing alone, often doing his
walking at night or through obscure byways in order to avoid
meeting people. He was careless and absent-minded about his appearance, often casually or shabbily clad. So shy, quiet, and even
furtive were his ways that many people forgot about him or
thought he had died.

De Quincey's long connection with *Blackwood's* had now
ended, and he was soon also to cease publishing in *Tait's*. In 1850
he submitted an unsolicited article to a different periodical, *Hogg's
Weekly Instructor;* and, when it was accepted, he offered himself as a staff writer to the Hoggs—and walked twenty miles to
do so. The Hoggs were astonished at the sudden appearance of
this courtly and eloquent little man in his oversized greatcoat and
at seeing him produce from an inner pocket a manuscript, which
he proceeded to dust off carefully page by page with a small
brush produced from the same pocket, before handing it over to
them. They made the most of their good fortune; De Quincey
worked for them alone in his remaining nine years.

In *Hogg's Weekly Instructor* he published articles on such subjects as conversation, the Theban sphinx, Professor Wilson,
French and English manners, language, Sir William Hamilton,
California and the gold-digging mania, and Judas Iscariot among
others, and a few autobiographical sketches. When Hogg's new
periodical, *The Titan,* succeeded the *Weekly Instructor* in 1856,
De Quincey also wrote for it, publishing articles on Aelius Lamia
and the opium question with China as it appeared in 1857.

Despite his personal obscurity, De Quincey's name and his
work were known in England and abroad. He received many letters from admirers of his work, including Charlotte Brontë; several distinguished persons sought him out; and occasionally he

was induced to meet visiting dignitaries. When Emerson was in Edinburgh in 1848, friends brought them together at a dinner in the city. Emerson recorded that De Quincey had walked through the rain and mud from Lasswade and was soaked. He also recorded that De Quincey had recently walked home from a dinner in Edinburgh late at night, instead of taking the coach, because two street girls had robbed him of his eight shillings and his umbrella. A week later Emerson dined at Lasswade, and De Quincey was also induced to attend one of Emerson's lectures.[43] In 1852, De Quincey was visited by Harriet Martineau, the Reverend Francis Jacox, J. R. Findlay, and James T. Fields, all of whom left records of their impressions.

The visit of Fields resulted from the undertaking by his publishing firm, Ticknor and Fields of Boston, to bring out a collected edition of De Quincey's works. After seeking in vain to elicit a response from De Quincey to letters asking his permission, they had proceeded to begin publishing in 1851, with the understanding that they would share the profits with the author. When Fields visited De Quincey at Lasswade in 1852, he presented him with payment for the first seven volumes—an honorable proceeding which won De Quincey's gratitude. He then cooperated with the American editors, providing them with lists of his works. Since he had forgotten many of his writings, the assistance of friends, as well as careful research by the American editors, was necessary.

De Quincey had hitherto considered the task of assembling his scattered works for a collected edition to be impossible, but the American edition showed him otherwise; and he now agreed to Hogg's proposal of a British collected edition. Thus at the age of sixty-seven, De Quincey turned his attention in 1852 to the task which was to occupy most of his time until his death: the gathering together and the arranging and revising of his life's work for Hogg's collected edition, entitled *Selections Grave and Gay from Writings Published and Unpublished,* which began appearing in 1853 and which was completed with the fourteenth volume the year after De Quincey's death. To facilitate working with the printers, De Quincey returned to his old lodgings at 42 Lothian Street in Edinburgh.

He worked hard at the task of editing. He rearranged, expanded, revised, and annotated many of his works. Some he published with little change, but others were largely rewritten. He expended his greatest efforts on the *Confessions* in 1856, working through six shattering months of unrelenting nervous illness (III, 220). The total edition did not have any very clear prior plan of arrangement, nor was it intended to be complete. While working on it under the continuous but kind stimulus of Hogg, De Quincey still found time to compose occasional articles for the magazines, nor had he lost his lifelong capacity for developing vast and unrealistic plans. He talked of undertaking a twelve-volume history of England and actually began work on it.

However, De Quincey's life was gradually contracting in these final years. Death successively took his former friends—Wordsworth, in 1850; Wilson, in 1854; Dorothy Wordsworth, in 1855. Occasionally, De Quincey accepted invitations and attended dinners, theater, or concerts; and he entertained his daughters in Edinburgh. However, the little family circle at Lasswade was gradually dispersing. His son Francis, having completed his medical studies, emigrated to Brazil in 1851. His eldest daughter Margaret married Robert Craig, a Lasswade neighbor, in 1853 and moved to Ireland. In 1854 her two sisters visited her there when De Quincey moved into Edinburgh. On September 25 his first grandchild, Eva Craig, was born in Ireland. The next year Florence, the elder of his two remaining daughters, went to India to marry Colonel Richard Bairdsmith. Emily spent much of 1856 with her sister in Ireland, when De Quincey's second grandchild, John Craig, was born.

In 1857 De Quincey's youngest son, Paul Frederick, returned home on furlough from India; and, with the help of his sister Emily, he took De Quincey, now seventy-two, to Ireland to visit Margaret and to see his grandchildren. The trip, which lasted about two weeks, was a great source of pleasure to De Quincey. In 1858 his third grandchild, Florence Mae Bairdsmith, was born in India. The travels of his children to China and India had awakened his interest in current international events, and he studied for a time the news from those countries closely. He was especially anxious during the Indian Mutiny of 1857 during which Colonel Bairdsmith sustained wounds, but survived after playing a heroic role.

De Quincey relinquished his daily walks during his last four years at 42 Lothian Street in Edinburgh. He lived entirely among his books and a sea of papers, the latter scattered throughout his

rooms, often getting lost in the confusion and even on one occasion catching fire. His landlady, Mrs. Wilson, and her sister, Miss
Stark, took a kind and solicitous interest in the eccentric old man;
and they did much to make his last years peaceful and comfortable. From late May, 1856, to late March, 1857, he left his rooms
only once: to hear a performance by the great soprano Grisi. His
condition during these years is recorded in intermittent volumi-
nous letters to his daughters. He was still having weird dreams, as
he had had since childhood; he was subject to delusions of persecution; and he worried morbidly about his papers.

As his health gradually declined, he found movement increasingly painful; and he suffered from fever. Finally, in the early fall
of 1859, Emily was summoned home from a visit in Ireland by a
note from Hogg. Her father's condition was so poor that in late
October she moved to 42 Lothian Street herself to keep close at-
tendance upon him. On October 22, a physician, Dr. Warburton
Begbie, was summoned; and he cared for De Quincey regularly
until the end. Dr. Begbie, who left an account of his observations
of De Quincey during these last weeks,[44] found the little man, despite his illness, still intellectually alert, eloquent, and winningly
gracious in manner. De Quincey's condition improved temporarily, but then declined again, with recurrent fevers.

On December 4 Emily became alarmed, and she sent the next
day for her sister, Margaret Craig. De Quincey was still able to
recognize Margaret when she came. Finally, on December 8, in
his last conscious moment, he looked at those about him in the
room and said tenderly, "Thank you,—thank you all!" He then
sank into a sleep apparently filled with dreams, for he spoke
aloud, to his mother and a sister—perhaps the beloved Elizabeth
of his childhood—before finally ceasing to breathe.

The doctor could find no specific cause of death; De Quincey's
body was simply worn out. He was buried in St. Cuthbert's
churchyard in Edinburgh, beside the remains of his wife Margaret, who had preceded him by twenty-two years.

XX Conclusion

De Quincey's life had been a lonely, unhealthy, and troubled
one. Despite his arduous literary labors, he had been in serious
financial difficulties for most of his thirty-eight years as a maga-

zine writer. David Masson estimated that De Quincey's earnings during those years could not have exceeded an average of one hundred and fifty pounds a year, or three pounds a week (XIV, 393). He had lived through the deaths not only of his parents but also of his brothers and three sisters, his wife, and three of his sons. He had seen the failure of his lofty early ambitions for himself, and he had lost the friendship of his early idols and companions. The opium habit had partially crippled him for forty-six years; he had alternately succumbed to it, fought it at the cost of great agonies, and held it for periods at relatively less harmful levels.

Nevertheless, he had never yielded to whining self-pity. Many of his troubles he had brought upon himself by his own deliberate choices; but, however much he came to regret some of them, he always acknowledged his own responsibility. But the eccentricity of his life and character were probably also the result of forces he failed to recognize: the lack of affection from his mother, the death of his sister Elizabeth and the sufferings of other girls he had witnessed, the early admiration by adults which his precocious intellectual development had brought him, the failure of his schools to meet his capabilities, and the disillusionment occasioned by the extravagant hero worship of his adolescence and early manhood. He had kept his saving grace of being able to view himself humorously, and he had retained his compassionate love for humankind.

De Quincey had shown heroic recuperative powers in undergoing the agonies of opium withdrawal, and for years he had exercised the moderation which kept him on the minimum sustaining dose. His addiction no longer evokes the contemptuous moral disapprobation it once did, for it is now recognized as a symptom of psychological illness and its total cure as exceedingly rare. His original indulgence is excusable partly on the grounds of the general ignorance of the dangerous properties of opium in his time, its easy availability, and the freedom with which it was prescribed as a medicine or anodyne.

At various points in his life De Quincey could still look back and decide that his earthly experience showed an overbalance of happiness and that he would not have had it otherwise (II, 382; X, 15–16). He probably even took quiet satisfaction in the knowledge that the misfortunes which had shackled him to the periodical press had also rescued him from the fate of a mute, inglorious Milton; for, among the two hundred and fifty or three hundred articles he had published in his lifetime, there were some on which he had lavished a learning, an imaginative genius, and a dedicated artistry which entitled them to live.

CHAPTER 2

Autobiography and Confessions

ALTHOUGH almost all of the immense literary output of De Quincey was originally written for the periodical press, he published four books (apart from the collected editions of his works) during his lifetime; but two of these—*The Confessions of an English Opium-Eater* (1822) and *The Logic of Political Economy* (1844)—were based on previous magazine articles. Only the pseudo-translation of the pseudo-Waverley novel *Walladmor* (1825) and De Quincey's own novel *Klosterheim* (1832) were originally written to be published in book form. He also published elsewhere than in magazines one pamphlet, *Close Comments upon a Straggling Speech;* a note to Wordsworth's *Convention of Cintra* pamphlet; four articles for the *Encyclopaedia Britannica;* and a few other scattered pieces. Apart from these, all the writings of De Quincey, which have filled from eleven to twenty-four volumes in the various collected editions, were originally written for publication in periodicals. David Masson estimated the total number of De Quincey's ascertained contributions to periodicals at two hundred and fifteen (XIV, 392), but subsequent researchers have considerably increased this total.

I *Classification of De Quincey's Works*

So varied are De Quincey's writings that they do not submit to any simple classification, nor do they divide neatly into clear-cut periods of gradual development. Nevertheless, several attempts have been made to classify his works and to demark periods in his career. De Quincey himself divided his works into three types: first, those that have the primary purpose of amusing the reader but which may sometimes rise to "an impassioned interest"; second, those that are addressed primarily to "the understanding as an insulated faculty"; and, third, those that are written in "impassioned prose" (I, 9–14).[1] He applied the term "essay" only to the second of these types, and he considered the third, "impassioned prose," to be the highest and the most original form his writing had taken.

But this classification is of very limited usefulness since many of the finest passages of impassioned prose occur in works which fall in the first two classes, and, conversely, a major part of the two works he mentioned as examples of impassioned prose— *Confessions of an English Opium-Eater* and *Suspiria de Profundis* —falls into the other two classes. His restriction of the term "essay" to the second class seems unnecessarily narrow and arbitrary: he described the essay as addressing itself to the solution of a problem, and he added that, in writing essays, he always sought to make an original contribution to his subject, either by rectifying errors or by correcting injurious limitations of the truth (I, 14). But the term "essay" can surely be broadened to include works which make their primary appeal to other faculties than the "insulated understanding" and which have other aims than solving problems. In short, this classification, like most others, fails to simplify and to do justice to the complex variety of his work.

Similar difficulties obstruct the division of his career into periods. He was a mature man in his thirty-seventh year when he first really emerged as a writer: his intellectual allegiances were already formed, and his style was already mature; and neither underwent marked changes during the years of his active authorship. His soaring fancy, his playful humor, his grand rhetoric, his subtle music, his inverted constructions, and his climactic apostrophes were all present from the first. Perhaps the only perceptible change in his later years is a gradual increase in his tendency toward pedantry and discursiveness.[2]

Nor did his subject matter shift conclusively over the years. For example, his first major work, the *Confessions,* was primarily autobiographical; his mid-career yielded the autobiographical sketches in *Tait's;* and his partly autobiographical *Suspiria* was a product of his later years. Likewise, he wrote literary criticism and articles on economics in all three periods. Only a few broad shifts can be observed in his subject matter: his translations and fictional narratives were mostly products of the early and middle periods; his literary reminiscences, mainly of the middle and late periods.

The external criterion of his magazine affiliations is more clear-

cut, though of limited significance; this divides his career into
three phases: when he was writing primarily for *The London
Magazine* (1821–25), for *Blackwood's* and *Tait's* (1826–49), and
for Hogg's *Instuctor* and *Titan* and the collected edition of his
works (1850–59). In the middle period, the kinds of material he
published in *Blackwood's* and *Tait's* differed. In the former publication appeared mainly his articles on history, economics, philosophy, the classics, and critical theory; in the latter, his literary and
autobiographical reminiscences.

Perhaps the most useful approach to De Quincey's work is by
types, arranged roughly in the order of their importance in his
canon: the autobiographical writings, including the *Confessions;*
the partly autobiographical *Suspiria;* the literary reminiscences, biographies, and character sketches; then the criticism, theoretical
and practical; the history, semi-fiction, and fiction; and, finally, the
many miscellaneous types. Even this classification must involve
some questionable decisions, for many of De Quincey's works
contain features of more than one type.

II *Autobiography*

Like Wordsworth, De Quincey devoted much of his productive
life to writing about himself—to re-creating and evaluating the
experience of his own earlier years, and to recording impressions
of his intercourse with the world around him and within him. Although a strong impulse toward defining and coming to terms
with himself animates much of his work, he probably did not
think of himself specifically as an autobiographer until about his
fiftieth year when he began publishing his autobiographical
sketches in *Tait's.* However, in *The Confessions of an English
Opium-Eater,* and in parts of other works, he had already published a great deal of autobiography; and he was to write much
more afterwards in the *Suspiria de Profundis,* in his Lake and
London reminiscences, and elsewhere. He may never have fully
realized what a large and important proportion of his writings
was in some sense autobiography.

When he began preparing his collected edition in 1852, he decided to devote the first two volumes to an assemblage of his scattered autobiographical sketches, many of which he now drew together into a chronological sequence that covered his life more or
less consecutively down to his entrance at Oxford in 1803. This

collection was not complete; for it did not include the *Confessions,* all the autobiographical *Suspiria,* or many passages in other works about his early life. Likewise, he failed to incorporate the various writings that deal with his life after 1803. If all these other autobiographical writings are considered along with that basic narrative, it becomes apparent that De Quincey wrote more autobiography than any other type of literature and that his autobiographical works include the vast majority of his most original and most memorable writings. Thus De Quincey is in the anomalous position that, while he left no complete and unified autobiography as such, it is first of all as an autobiographer that he continues—and will continue—to be read.

Critical opinion has been divided over De Quincey's stature as an autobiographer. Some would place him in the first rank with Cellini and Rousseau. Others would place him lower, on the grounds that his autobiographical writings are too diffuse, indiscriminate, and abstract, and were never shaped into a coherent whole. Perhaps the judgment depends on whether one measures De Quincey as the author of *an* autobiography or as the author of a series of autobiographical sketches. In the latter role he can hardly be denied an originality and an excellence that have seldom been equaled. And his stature in the more exalted role would be greatly enhanced by a really careful and complete gathering, winnowing, and arrangement of all his autobiographical and quasi-autobiographical writings.

The fact that the *Confessions* came first and that many of his subsequent autobiographical writings were first conceived as supplements to the *Confessions* may have influenced the kind of autobiography he would write. Although he sometimes laid claim to the utmost precision (III, 293 n.), he really did not concern himself greatly with completeness nor with accuracy of detail in presenting the external facts of his life. Nor did he feel any obligation to reveal the intimately personal. He never abandoned a certain dignified restraint in speaking of himself; a few crucial turnings in his strange, long life he never fully described or accounted for. His reticence in the face of conventional taboos was Victorian; he never indulged in merely lurid self-exposure.

Instead, his autobiography is chiefly a series of accounts of the moments of fateful decision, of great emotion, and of deepest insight in his life, interspersed among narrative, expository, and re-

flective sections of less intensity. His angle of approach to the crucial moments is primarily psychological. In both these respects his
autobiography resembles Wordsworth's in *The Prelude*. De Quincey's attitude toward his climactic experiences was intensely curious and analytical, and he believed that his accounts of them
might have permanent value as psychological records (II, 440).
On the other hand, he sometimes viewed his autobiographical
writings as merely entertaining narratives; and he classified them,
apart from the *Confessions* and *Suspiria,* among works proposing
primarily to amuse the reader, though occasionally rising to an
impassioned interest (I, 9). Whatever his aims and attitudes, autobiography elicited from De Quincey much of his best writing
because it offered him sufficient freedom to pursue his special insights and engaged his feelings deeply enough to prevent him
from excessive aimless wandering and tedious word-spinning. He
certainly shows remarkable psychological penetration and a full
intuitive hold on experience.

Since De Quincey himself is our sole informant about many of
the events he narrates in his autobiography, the question of his
credibility arises. Clearly, he is not reliable on dates, ages, and
such numerical details. His inconsistent alternate accounts of a few
events also suggest some factual untrustworthiness. He was at
times probably swayed by the particular literary aim of the moment, and by current literary fashions, to color the events of his
life in the telling. For example, the Romantic cult of genius as an
inborn sensitivity, passionateness, and profundity may have led
him to exaggerate his youthful uniqueness and his early philosophical attainments. It is also possible to question the authentic-
ity of some of the dream visions he recorded, or to ask how much
they were reshaped by conscious artistry. De Quincey's native
tendency toward neurotic dreaming converged with literary
vogues; his writing about dreams probably owes something to the
Gothic novels, to books of Oriental travels, to the current cult of
the dream, and to German Romanticism—especially to the dream
visions of Jean Paul Richter, who did not conceal the artificial
nature of his dreams.[3]

Nevertheless, after these few allowances, it seems probable that
De Quincey's autobiographical writing is basically authentic.
There is abundant evidence that he had an extraordinarily capa-
cious and retentive memory; and, despite his carelessness of de-

tailed accuracy, the truthfulness of many of his accounts that have been questioned has later been vindicated by the publication of supporting documents. In sum, it can be said that, while De Quincey as an autobiographer was capable of the utmost precision and candor, he was not usually concerned with such aims; instead, he devoted his efforts to the communication of feeling and to the suggestion of meaning—to shaping his recollections into the form of art. In his subtle powers of introspective analysis and his awareness of the importance of brief and obscure moments, he is—as Virginia Woolf has pointed out—superior to Scott, Jane Austen, and Byron; in fact, De Quincey is scarcely matched by any one of the nineteenth-century writers of fiction.[4]

His tone in much of his autobiographical writing has a curious detachment and formality, as if a wise and tenderly tolerant older man were narrating in a spirit of good-natured, condescending whimsy the life of a naive and wayward youth. There is a veiled remoteness to the narrative, an almost dreamy aloofness. He often resorts to gentle irony; and some of his finest effects, like the account of his life with his older brother William (I, 56–120), are achieved in the form of mock-heroic. The humor which pervades the autobiography thus enhances the tone of affectionate condescension. At times, as De Quincey himself observed, the tone ascends to more solemn and rhetorical utterance. At other times, it can be flatly, coldly candid, and even tinged with asperity, especially when he treats his relationships with persons about whom he had mixed feelings.

Structurally, the autobiographical writings most often take the form of major scenes loosely strung together. De Quincey at his best is a masterful scene-painter, imbuing his pictures with a mythical intensity of suggestiveness, surrounding them with an aura of fateful portentousness. In a few sentences he creates mysterious living tableaux, credible demi-worlds. It is hard to forget such scenes as his boyhood confrontation with a mad dog on the day of his brother's departure, his final moments in his Manchester schoolroom before his flight, and his first meetings with Lamb, Coleridge, and Wordsworth. To the extent that his autobiographical writings are unified at all by a governing theme, they seem to be bound together by such notions as the fateful consequences of apparently trivial actions (symbolized in the *Confessions* by the Whispering Gallery of St. Paul's), the effects of suffering on a weak physique and a hypersensitive mind, and the relation of waking and dream visions to the underlying realities of life. But interspersed among all the more relevant autobiographical parts —including even those De Quincey organized into a fairly consecutive narrative—are numerous digressions with only tenuous connections to their contexts. Some of these are comparatively brief, and some amount to extensive essays.

III   The Confessions of an English Opium-Eater

The Confessions of an English Opium-Eater, the first major work De Quincey published and the one which won him fame almost overnight, is really primarily a segment of his autobiography. It narrates his life from his schoolboy days to the year after his marriage in 1817. It also includes the first of his dream visions to be published, and some of his theories on the effects of opium.

The *Confessions* falls into three main parts. The first, which is by far the longest, is an autobiographical introduction, tracing De Quincey's life from the time of his father's death through his flight from school and his subsequent adventures in Wales and London. Its professed purpose is to explain the underlying causes which led De Quincey to opium-eating and to provide background for the dreams to be described later. However, the autobiographical narrative it presents has no direct relevance to opium-eating and almost none to dreams. Instead, it is really presented as an autonomous account; and it takes on an independent interest.

The second part, "The Pleasures of Opium," is also autobiographical, continuing the narrative from De Quincey's early university days, when he first took opium, through the period when he became addicted, down to 1816–17, which he considered his happiest year. This section concentrates mainly on his first thirteen years of experience with opium, but it also contains a rebuttal of three common misconceptions of the effects of opium (that it produces intoxication, that the euphoria it produces must be followed by an equal depression, and that it produces torpor) and a narrative of a strange visit De Quincey once had from a wandering Malay. The third part, "The Pains of Opium," is devoted primarily to an account of the deep narcosis which De Quincey entered in the latter half of 1817 and of the dreams which accompanied it.

Thus an autobiographical framework supports the *Confessions;*

and, despite the other elements it contains, the interest of the work remains mainly autobiographical. It overlaps some of his other, later, autobiographical writings; and, like them, it includes informative and reflective passages—typical De Quinceyan excrescences—on many incidental subjects besides the principal one of opium. On the whole, the *Confessions* is of a piece with De Quincey's other autobiographical works. Nevertheless, it was first published as an independent work; and in several respects it deserves to be approached as such.

The *Confessions* has almost always been considered De Quincey's masterpiece, and in ways it merits this rank. The autobiographical narrative has great intrinsic interest, and the sections on opium and dreams are equally interesting in their different ways. There is nothing lurid or sensational such as the title might seem to promise, for the pleasures of opium are not sensual pleasures. The original subtitle of the *Confessions*, "The Life of a Scholar," suggests this stabilizing counterpoise. The character of the young De Quincey revealed through the narrative is appealing, but that of the mature De Quincey revealed through the style and point of view is equally so. Here we find a man learned and earnest, sober and dignified, always committed to telling the truth, but often playful and ironically self-mocking.

The style—easy, fluent, and ductile—is at once spontaneous and artfully polished. It moves gracefully and evenly through the narrative sections; it is crisp and systematic in expository sections; and it rises to ardent eloquence in climactic passages of invocation, apostrophe, and exclamation. It reinforces extreme contrasts, like that between the idyllic summer in Wales and the purgatorial winter in London, or that between the first blissful months of marriage and the years of opium sufferings that followed. All is poise, balance, and artful variation; but these qualities are combined with a tone of headlong intensity and passionate sincerity.

The dream visions which come at the end were something new and remarkable in English literature. They represent an attempt to recreate the living content of dreams and to do so in a language which captures some of the mysterious quality of the dream world through musical and poetic effects. The symbolism seems authentically De Quincey's, and some of the meanings seem transparently obvious in the light of his early experience. There are dancing ladies of the court of Charles II, now all long dead, as De

Quincey is sadly aware. There are dreams of massive, endlessly growing and self-reproducing architecture, like that in a picture by Piranesi once described to De Quincey by Coleridge. There are dreams of clear lakes transformed into weltering seas paved with suffering human faces. There are Asiatic scenes in which De Quincey is scorned, worshiped, sacrificed, and buried. He is horrified by dreadful monsters. In another dream he sees a vision of Catherine Wordsworth's grave, which is transformed into a vision of Jerusalem, where he finds Ann of Oxford Street. Then comes a dream of a cataclysmic battle, which he feels he could decide, if only he could bestir himself, but he cannot, and must bid everlasting farewells to beloved female figures, an effect so dreadful that he awakes resolved to sleep no more, and to renounce opium. Since these astonishing dreams need the reflected light of the *Suspiria* to reveal their full meaning, they are discussed in Chapter 3.

IV   *The Two Versions*

In discussing the *Confessions,* it is important to specify which version is under consideration; for this work has survived in two distinct forms—one, the original version published in *The London Magazine* in 1821 and republished as a book with only a few minor changes the following year; the other, the revised version published in Hogg's collected edition in 1856. There are substantial differences between the two.[5] In revising the *Confessions,* De Quincey more than doubled the length of the work as a whole; and he quadrupled the length of the "Preliminary Confessions," now called Part I. In the original version, this first, most purely autobiographical section constituted almost a half of the total *Confessions;* in the revised version, it constitutes well over two thirds.

The second part was little altered in revision, but it combined what had previously been two separate sections, "The Pleasures of Opium" and "Introduction to the Pains of Opium." In the original version the third section, "The Pains of Opium," began with three brief explanatory notes; in 1856 these were greatly expanded to include an extensive discussion of the physical and medical aspects of opium addiction, which nearly doubled the length of this third part and left the account of opium dreams occupying less than half of it. Thus, in revising the *Confessions,* De Quincey added a great deal of material which is highly interesting and indispensable to a biographer; but the verdict of most critics is that the earlier version is artistically superior. De Quincey himself realized that readers might find it so.[6]

The theme and purpose of the *Confessions* are difficult to fix. De Quincey's own statements about his aim are inconsistent. In some, he stresses the psychological purpose of revealing the mechanism and grandeur of human dreams (III, 233; XIII, 334–35); in others, he stresses the medical purpose of revealing the effects of opium, especially upon dreams (III, 215, 412–13); and in still others, he stresses the moral purpose of warning the opium-eater (III, 209, 448). However, dreams can hardly be the main theme of a work of 225 pages when only sixteen pages are devoted to dreams. The moral motive can hardly underlie a work which leaves a predominantly favorable impression of opium-eating and its effects—De Quincey specifically renounced this theme.[7] In revising the *Confessions,* De Quincey altered some of his statements about the aims of the work, but without troubling to make them consistent; in general, although he added a great deal of medical information, he at the same time shifted the emphasis away from the medical purpose and towards the study of dreams. The end result is increased diffuseness of theme. De Quincey himself once admitted that the true object of the *Confessions* probably lay not in "the naked physiological theme" but in "those parasitical thoughts, feelings, digressions, which climb up with bells and blossoms round about the arid stock." [8]

The structure of the *Confessions* was more tightly organized in the original version. There De Quincey began with three reasons for presenting the autobiographical narrative of the first part, and then he plunged at once into the narrative itself, which he presented with few and brief digressions. In the revised version, however, after first raising the question of how he fell victim to opium, he digressed into a discussion of the medical benefits of opium and into a long comparison of his own and Coleridge's reasons for taking opium—a much weaker beginning. The narrative which follows is interrupted in the revised version by digressions on guardians, on the neglect of English and modern literature in the great public schools of England, on the excellence of seventeenth-century English prose, and on the best choice of literature for schoolboys.

The second part, which was little altered in revision, ends with an exclamatory climactic preparation for the third part, "The Pains of Opium." In the original version this last section began a little anticlimactically with a brief, three-point apology to the reader before plunging into the description of the ill effects and the dreams caused by opium. In the revised version, this anticlimax was greatly increased by the addition of the long treatment of the medical aspects of opium already mentioned, which, far from illustrating the anticipated "pains," actually *defends* opium-eating on the basis of its medicinal efficacy and the possibility of curing addiction. When he finally turned to the "pains" in the revised version, he expanded the brief digression on reading aloud before proceeding to the description of his opium dreams, which remained essentially unaltered. In both versions, the work as a whole leaves an impression of incompleteness because of its ambiguous theme and because it arouses more expectations of accounts of dreadful dreams than it fulfills.

The original *Confessions* received various important accretions, in addition to the revisions already noted, during De Quincey's lifetime. The sense of imbalance—of unfulfilled expectations—which it leaves was soon called to De Quincey's attention; and he responded, as has been noted earlier, in a letter published in *The London Magazine* in December, 1821, admitting the justice of the complaint and promising soon to provide another part in an attempt to make clearer the pains of opium (III, 464–66). Since this additional part was never written, one cannot be certain what he intended it to include; but it was probably to contain additional descriptions of his condition during his deepest narcosis, and especially additional accounts of painful dreams. When the *Confessions* was published in book form in 1822, in lieu of this new part he provided an Appendix in which he corrected the impression left by the original work that he had freed himself entirely from the opium habit and in which he described in detail the process of withdrawal he had since undergone.

CHAPTER 3

Suspiria de Profundis

I *Composition*

MANY years later, in 1845, he finally began in *Blackwood's* a sequel to the *Confessions,* entitled *Suspiria de Profundis* (Sighs from the Depths), which was to have four parts (III, 369). Originally intended to consist of a collection of fantasies and dream visions, perhaps as a belated fulfillment of the promised additional part of the *Confessions,* it was broken off after four installments, in the midst of Part II, and was never resumed. Several of the pieces first published with these installments of *Suspiria,* or intended for inclusion, were dispersed by De Quincey into new contexts in the collected edition, until only six and a few additional stray paragraphs were left from those originally published (XIII, 331–33); of those remaining in manuscript, some disappeared and others were accidentally burned (III, 221).

Nevertheless, De Quincey continued to develop his plans for the *Suspiria,* revising those already written, and composing some new ones, perhaps in preparation for a final version to be included in the collected edition. At one point he made a list of thirty-two pieces of *Suspiria,* of which only about half have survived in any form,[1] and in 1853 he remarked that not more than a third of the *Suspiria* had yet been printed and that the rest would enhance his reputation (I, 14–15). Unfortunately, he died before he completed the final version of *Suspiria,* so it remains fragmentary. However, if all of the published *Suspiria* are reassembled, if those pieces originally intended for *Suspiria* but instead first published in other contexts are added, and finally if the unpublished *Suspiria* found among De Quincey's manuscripts are included,[2] a very impressive body of work results—one which probably affords some notion of what the total work would have been like, if it had ever been completed.

II *The Theory*

The *Suspiria* pieces are unified by two related clusters of ideas
—one theoretical, the other mythical. The former consists of a
body of psychological theory on dreams and waking fantasies, for
De Quincey had more than a dilettante's interest in dreams. He
was aware that he had had from childhood an exceptional capacity for dreaming, and his dreams under the influence of opium at
Oxford and later in his periods of deepest narcosis seemed to him
to have had a special character imparted by the narcotic. All his
life he was interested in the psychology of dreaming, and he developed his own theories, based on his reading and his self-obser-
vation. These he presented in the *Confessions* (III, 433–47) and
in some of the *Suspiria*—most notably in "Dreaming" (XIII,
333–40), "The Palimpsest of the Human Brain" (XIII, 340–49),
and "Vision of Life" (XIII, 350–51).

De Quincey believed that, of all the countless ideas, images,
and feelings which occur in the human mind, none is ever finally
extinguished; all survive and can be brought into harmonious—
and sometimes horrifying—relationship by the synthesizing powers of the human mind. The strong impressions of childhood
are especially important since they store the mind with the basic
materials for assimilation and combination. Suffering is an inevitable part of the process: "Either a human being must suffer and
struggle, as the price of a more searching vision, or his gaze must
be shallow and without intellectual revelation" (XIII, 351). Extreme experiences of joy and suffering, he held, do not achieve
their full dimensions until they are "reverberated" from dreams
(I, 49). These mental records can be revived in strength by the
approach of death, by fever, or by the effects of opium. One's
waking fantasies can recur in dreams, as can the minutest incidents of childhood.

Space and time he found vastly expanded in dreams. De Quincey was interested in the infinite divisibility of space and time as a
clue to the nature of infinity and eternity; the dislocation of the
space and time senses in dreams seemed to him to suggest the
connection of dreams with a higher reality divorced from space
and time. Thus the dreaming faculty became for him "the one
great tube through which man communicates with the shadowy
. . . the magnificent apparatus which forces the infinite into the

chambers of a human brain, and throws dark reflections from eternities below all life upon the mirrors of that mysterious *camera obscura*—the sleeping mind" (XIII, 335).

De Quincey attributed to the dreaming faculty some of the same lofty powers which Wordsworth attributed to the imagination and Coleridge to reason. The fact that De Quincey's own dreams often seemed to parallel the Christian truths he had always accepted probably seemed to him to confirm his theory. He even seems to have granted at least a half-credence to the power of dreams to foretell the future.[3] Since reveries and dreams are usually the products of solitude, De Quincey believed that "No man ever will unfold the capacities of his own intellect who does not at least checker his life with solitude" (XIII, 335). And, since De Quincey also believed that many of these powers of dreaming are either dependent upon or greatly enhanced by opium, he trembled upon the verge of treating opium as a consciousness-expanding drug capable of assisting one to a unified religious view of experience: "It is in the faculty of mental vision, it is in the increased power of dealing with the shadowy and the dark, that the characteristic virtue of opium lies" (V, 211). Even if he had known, as modern investigations reveal, that many of the dream effects which he attributed to opium are also common to non-opium dreams, and therefore must result from psychic forces rather than from drugs, he would probably not have abandoned the rest of his dream theory.

Supporting this dream theory was De Quincey's observation of his own dreams, over which he seems to have commanded total recall throughout his life. The strong impressions his dreams created upon him, and the important symbolic meanings he discerned in them, confirmed his view of their importance, and led him to expend his greatest artistic pains on efforts to re-create them. The materials of his dreams provided him with the symbolic structure for a personal myth, which constitutes the second main cluster of ideas in the *Suspiria*.

III   *The Myth*

The principal concern of this myth, the problem of human suffering and death, usually centers upon a suffering human figure —always female, often an outcast, and sometimes a child. She is identified in some contexts with Ann of Oxford Street and in others with De Quincey's sister Elizabeth. She is shown as undeservedly suffering tragedy, degradation, and ostracism. Her efforts towards hope and restoration are thwarted by some shadowy force of malice. However, after she appears to have been finally destroyed, she is miraculously regenerated in an infinite and eternal dimension; and she undergoes a compensating process of redemption. The overall theme can thus be said to be redemption through suffering. Although De Quincey, a devout Christian, uses a Christian theme, he does not work it out primarily in terms of Christian symbols in the *Suspiria* but in terms of his own psychic symbols.

As has been seen, De Quincey had lived through the sufferings —sometimes fatal—of many beloved girls and young ladies in his early years: his sisters Jane and Elizabeth, the handicapped twin daughters of Reverend Hall, the waif in Mr. Brunell's house, Ann of Oxford Street, and Catherine Wordsworth. The cumulative shock of these experiences to his sensitive and affectionate nature was perhaps traumatic, sufficient to trouble his dreams for the rest of his life with suffering girls and female pariahs, who tend in the *Suspiria* to coalesce into a single symbolic figure that sometimes resembles Elizabeth or Ann. It seems very probable that this figure also has oedipal implications since De Quincey's affection for his sister Elizabeth may well have been a surrogate for thwarted or suppressed mother love, transferred in time to Ann, a still better disguise.[4] In the pariah status of the figure there may also be an element of self-identification, reflecting De Quincey's own sense of rejection by his mother, or his unconscious guilt.

Another kind of human figure which appears in De Quincey's visionary myth is a sort of somber guide, preceptor, or tutelary angel. This figure serves to expose the mind to earthly sufferings and despair as a preparatory discipline to the experience of the highest bliss. This personage embodies the paradox of life's mingled pleasures and pains, fulfillments and catastrophes—an interplay of opposites which leads to understanding and redemption. It appeals and repels, it entices and disciplines. In one vision this type of figure appears in the form of stately women, whose model could have been De Quincey's mother; in another, it is a girl, closer to the Elizabeth-Ann figure; and then there is the "Dark

Interpreter," a mysterious male guide and teacher. The redemptive process is also symbolized by the Battle of Waterloo, which is envisioned as an apocalyptic event.

Although the sufferings and redemptions in De Quincey's dream visions are projected mainly through such personal symbolism, the parallels with Christian symbolism are obvious. The female pariah suggests the Magdalen or the woman taken in adultery, and the sufferings and redemptions parallel the Messianic prophesies and Christ's Passion and Resurrection. The preceptor figures are suggestive of the Virgin Mary, the prophets, or the apostles. There are many incidental biblical parallels as well. De Quincey's deep and steady commitment to Christian orthodoxy may have required this subconscious or half-conscious conforming of his basic dream pattern to Christian tradition.

The various parts of De Quincey's dream theory and its related myth of suffering and redemption appear separately or in combination in the several *Suspiria,* as well as in the *Confessions.* About half of the *Suspiria* are primarily direct treatments of theory in abstract terms, while the other half are mainly concrete illustrations in the form of narrative re-creations of actual reveries and dreams. The *Suspiria* can be sorted into these two categories and arranged so as to illustrate roughly the sequence of ideas in each category.

IV   *The Theoretical* Suspiria

In "The Princess who overlooked one Seed in a Pomegranate" (*PW,* I, 22–23), De Quincey discusses the tendency of apparently insignificant events in childhood to lead to terrible sufferings and sorrows in later life; and he points to his own opium career as an instance. In "Memorial Suspiria" (XIII, 351–59), he asks what man, if he could foresee the tragedies he must face in later life, could face the hour of birth. In "The Dark Interpreter" (*PW,* I, 7–12), he treats the relation of suffering to knowledge and tells of the Dark Interpreter, the shadowy figure who appears in the dreams of profound, introverted, abstracted natures and awakens their awareness to the worlds of human suffering. "Vision of Life" (XIII, 350–51) tells how exposure to the horror of life is essential to an experience of the highest raptures of life, such as came to him unusually early, that is, in his childhood; only by this confluence of opposites does life reveal its deepest secrets. The way soli-

tude can reveal sublime attractions in the grave—even to children, as De Quincey felt it had to him beside his sister's dead
body—is treated in "The Solitude of Childhood" (*PW*, I, 13–15).
"Dreaming" (XIII, 333–40), which was originally the "Introductory Notice" to *Suspiria,* presents his strongest theoretical statement of the apocalyptic function of dreams, and relates the
dreaming to opium. In "The Palimpsest of the Human Brain"
(XIII, 340–49), the mind, with its power to receive and uncon-
sciously preserve countless impressions, which can be recovered
under the stimulus of approaching death, fever, or opium dreams,
is compared to an ancient manuscript on which successive writings
have been effaced but can be recovered. In it, De Quincey approaches an adumbration of the unconscious mind that antici-
pates Freudian psychology, including the relation of the unconscious memory to dreams.

V *The Mythical* Suspiria

In the remaining *Suspiria* the emphasis is less upon abstract
theorizing and more upon concrete illustration in the form of nar-
rations of actual dream visions. These accounts of dream visions,
together with those at the end of the *Confessions,* De Quincey
considered his most original and elevated compositions. It was
probably especially to them that he referred when he spoke of
"modes of impassioned prose ranging under no precedents that I
am aware of in any literature" (I, 14). Although he could perhaps
have acknowledged a debt to the dream fantasies of Jean Paul
Richter, which he had known and admired since youth, and although he is close to Wordsworth in his interest in suffering
women, in the influence of childhood on later experiences, and in
the mysterious depths of the human mind, nonetheless his claims
of originality for these works are not far off the mark.

"The Affliction of Childhood," with its sequels "Dream-Echoes
of These Infant Experiences" and "Dream-Echoes Fifty Years
Later," was first published as part of the *Suspiria,* though De
Quincey later incorporated it in his autobiography (I, 28–54).
"The Affliction" tells how the childhood experience of witnessing
his sister Elizabeth's suffering and death brought to him at her
bedside an apocalyptic vision of upward struggle, dreadful resistance, and an evolving resolution, which in turn was repeatedly
echoed in subsequent visions and dreams; ". . . the faculty of

shaping images in the distance out of slight elements, and group-
ing them after the yearnings of the heart, grew upon me in morbid excess" (I, 46). He beheld the regeneration of suffering children in visions at church and in sleep (I, 46–48); and the same
basic elements recurred in his dreams at Oxford a dozen years
later, and again fifty years after the original event.

A comparable recurrent vision is described in "Who is this
Woman that Beckoneth and Warneth me from the Place where
she is, and in whose Eyes is Woeful Remembrance?" (PW, I,
16–21). In it, he sees a female figure beside a cottage, at once
beckoning him on and warning him off. This vision he later con-
siders a revelation of the future; for, he tells us, he came to meet
that woman at that cottage some five years later. This woman
seems a fusion of his sister Elizabeth and his wife Margaret, and
she seems to symbolize the contrary appeals of love and death.

The mingled repulsion and attraction of death is also symbolized in "The Daughters of Lebanon," which De Quincey appended
to the Confessions in 1822 as an example of the kind of dream
vision by which he planned to complete that work. This female
pariah resembles Ann of Oxford Street. Terrified and reluctant in
the face of death, she is reconciled by a vision in which her dead
sister awaits her in heaven.

In many ways the most important and impressive of the Suspiria is "Levana and Our Ladies of Sorrow" (XIII, 362–69). De
Quincey called this piece the record of a waking vision of his Oxford years which reappeared in his dreams, and he suggested that
it held the key to the Suspiria.[5] Levana is an allegorical representation of the mysterious forces by which life educates the growing
child, deeply and inwardly, especially through grief. Her associates are the three sisters, Our Ladies of Sorrow: Madonna, or
Our Lady of Tears, the first, is the one who weeps for dead
children and who enters the chambers of the sleepless; the second,
Our Lady of Sighs, is the meek and humble visitor of the pariah—
the Jew, the bondsman, the prisoner, the slave, the prostitute, the
innocent outcast; the third, Our Lady of Darkness, is the defier of
God, the mother of lunacy, the suggestress of suicide. The first
captured De Quincey in childhood, made him an idolator of
death, and seasoned him for the second, who in turn will prepare
him for the third. Together, they will educate him to the deeper

truths; they will plague his heart until they unfold the capacities of his spirit and he is regenerated, even before death.

The whole of this vision is clothed in a prose so stately, intense, and musical that it has been regarded by some (including Masson) as the supreme achievement of De Quincey's genius, the most original thing he ever wrote. The prose has a musicality which brings it to the borders of poetry: Saintsbury called it, "for rhythmical *maistria,* hardly inferior to anything of the same length in our literature . . ."; and he said of the description of the third sister, "I do not believe that the piece can be beaten, as a concerted piece, from the purely artistic-rhythmical point of view. . . ." 6

Another of the *Suspiria* which has a weird, haunting strangeness and which touches on the same theme of the mysterious regenerative power of suffering is "Savannah-la-Mar" (XIII 359–61). In this vision a town is smitten by God and submerged beneath the sea, where it is visited by De Quincey and the Dark Interpreter, who explains it as an emblem of God's ways. Since for God there is nothing transitory, he says, there can be nothing that tends to death; and therefore God works by grief indifferently. "Upon the sorrow of an infant he raises oftentimes from human intellects glorious vintages that could not else have been. Less than these fierce plowshares would not have stirred the stubborn soil."

Finally, there is the longest and most elaborately orchestrated of the works originally designed for *Suspiria*—like "Levana" it has been admired by many as De Quincey's masterpiece—: "The English Mail-Coach" (XIII, 270–327). This work is in three parts, each having a profile of rising emotional intensity taken separately; but the three together also ascend toward a climax. Section I, "The Glory of Motion," begins as a low-key historical account of the evolution of the mail coach in England. It includes descriptions of the social attitudes and public functions associated with the mail coach, and is enlivened with humor and anecdote. It rises to a climax in a brief description of dreams De Quincey had, based on a resemblance he saw in a Bath coachman to a crocodile, and on the coachman's beautiful granddaughter Fanny, the two interweaving like rows of ballerinas in De Quincey's dreams.7 There follows, at the end of Part I, a concluding section, subtitled "Going Down with Victory," in which De Quincey, in his best

sharp and swift narrative-pictorial style, describes the departure
of the mail coach from London carrying with it the glorious news
of a victory in the Napoleonic Wars, which spreads joy along the
route, but also bereaves a few women who have lost loved ones. A
superlative piece of social history, it is as alive as anything in
Dickens.

In Section II, "The Vision of Sudden Death," De Quincey begins with abstract reflections on the meanings that sudden death
has for people under various conditions, and on the subconscious
death wish which reveals itself in reactions to threats of sudden
death in dreams. He then turns to a narrative account of the experience which first opened these ideas to him—the near accident he
witnessed in the summer of 1817 or 1818 on the Manchester-to-
Glasgow mail coach. This section begins humorously, but gradually ascends through suspense to a climax at the moment when the
mail coach, hurtling through the night with the coachman asleep
and De Quincey entranced on the box beside him, suddenly confronts in its path a tiny gig containing a young couple. De Quincey sees the vision of sudden death strike them as the coach bears
down on them. They barely escape, and the young woman rises
and sinks in her seat in terror; ". . . the turn of the road carried
the scene out of my eyes in an instant, and swept it into my
dreams forever" (XIII, 318).

Section III, "Dream-Fugue: Founded on the Preceding Theme
of Sudden Death," is one of the most ambitious pieces De Quincey ever wrote. Subdivided into an introduction and a series of
five related visions, it begins with a question about why the image
of "woman bursting her sepulchral bonds" has recurred so power-
fully and persistently in his dreams for forty years. In the first two
sections, the lady of the coach incident reappears in a series of
scenes at sea, where she is exposed to dangers and death while
De Quincey watches. In the third section, he finds a girl fleeing in
panic along a beach and pursues her, only to see her devoured in
quicksands; his grief is interrupted by martial sounds that suggest
some final victory. In the fourth and climactic section, he is carried in a triumphal car to spread the joyous news of *"Waterloo
and Recovered Christendom!"*

Finally, he is borne into a gigantic minster, past sarcophagi covered with battle scenes, until he meets a female child in a frail
carriage, who, it seems, must somehow but dreadfully be "the ran-

som for Waterloo." A miraculous trumpeter sounds the death note; and then De Quincey sees the child, now become a woman, delivered and ascending to salvation. Thus, various elements from his observations and experiences of coach travel, as recounted in the first two sections, are assimilated in the "Dream-Fugue" into the characteristic pattern of his private myth of human suffering and death, symbolized by the usual solitary female figures, followed by the divine compensations in the apocalyptic news of the victory at Waterloo and the final redemption of the suffering woman. The scenes succeed one another with the kaleidoscopic discontinuity of a true dream, and the tone is one of intense imaginative and spiritual exaltation.

But the most striking feature of the "Fugue" is its musicality. Its title, its epigraph from *Paradise Lost,* and its notation (surely half-humorous)—"*Tumultuosissimamente*"—all suggest a musical intent: of shaping the rhythm and tone of the prose to the intense and exalted dreamland passions it conveys. And the themes and images are interwoven with a careful fugue-like intricacy, the language tuned and modulated with the nicest possible musical discrimination. De Quincey's lifelong devotion to music seems to have emboldened him to attempt a close approach to the condition of music in the rhythm, tone, and contrapuntal structure of the "Fugue"; and the result is one of the supremely finished and eloquent passages in English prose.[8] De Quincey revised the original version carefully before sending it to press, and he painstakingly re-tuned the language of "The English Mail-Coach" as a whole for the collected edition, as he planned to do for all the *Suspiria*. In this labor he demonstrated the depth of his conviction that, in "all attempts to clothe in words the visionary scenes derived from the world of dreams, . . . a single false note, a single word in a wrong key, ruins the whole music . . ." (I, 14).

In the dream visions of the *Confessions* and *Suspiria,* De Quincey ranks as the creator of a new literary subgenre; and he remains one of its supreme practitioners. If there are moments of incoherence, sentimentality, and melodrama in them, and if in some respects they derive from the then current literary fashions, on the whole they ring true. They are remarkable testaments from De Quincey's inner mind, projected by a bold and original artistry.

CHAPTER 4

Literary Reminiscences, Biographies, and Character Sketches

I Biographical Theory and Practice

DE QUINCEY devoted much of his literary career to writing accounts of other people: some in the form of reminiscences of persons he had known, others as more or less formal biographies, and a great many as incidental character sketches. Despite his elusive and solitary habits, he had a deep interest in other people and sharp powers of observation and analysis. He enjoyed gathering together the complex and conflicting information about an individual and trying to reach a balanced judgment. He also enjoyed correcting what he considered erroneous public images of persons. One of his principal tendencies as a critic was to examine the biographical evidence for a dominant tendency in an author's mind as a key to understanding his writings. Eccentric characters were especially interesting to him, and he enjoyed trying to capture on paper the flavor of their eccentricities.

In his pronouncements on the subject of biography he showed that he had given some thought to the principles and problems involved in that art. Some kinds of biography he regarded as providing lasting memorials to distinguished persons (III, 159). He mentioned the importance of avoiding bias and of respecting the sensibilities of the living (V, 11–12), and he expressed his distrust of second-hand information (XI, 353). In the brief essay he wrote on biography, he stated that one should not write the lives of persons one hates; and he counseled against recording the human infirmities of distinguished literary men, saying these should be forgotten. On the other hand, he cautioned the biographer against special pleading: "Let him expose the *total* aberrations of the man, and make this exposure salutary to the pathetic wisdom of his readers, not alimentary to their self-conceit, by keeping constantly before their eyes the excellence and splendor of the man's powers in contrast with his continued failures" (*PW*, I, 123). He saw the dangers of obscurantism and distortion in laudatory biography, and he warned against it (VI, 180–85). He also deprecated a biographer's concern with trivial factual data when dealing with the great (IV, 46). Thus his professed philosophy of biography seems weighted toward positive didacticism, scrupulous accuracy, and balanced candor.

His actual practice, however, often seems to have betrayed these principles. He exposed his subjects to unsparing analysis, revealing all the personal crotchets and peccadilloes he had observed in them or heard reported of them. Far from rejecting rumor, he sometimes seems to have taken the malicious gossip's pleasure in purveying it. Nor did he always reject subjects of whom he disapproved; he was capable of waspish savagery and utterly destructive bias. He wrote with such merciless candor of the recently deceased that he deeply pained their surviving friends and families; and he wrote of the living with the same cool detachment, as if they were dead and beyond the embarrassment of his revelations. He was capable of combining the biographical and satirical modes to devastating effect.

De Quincey has been bitterly attacked and roundly condemned for these practices, but there is much to be said in his defense. While his professed biographical principles resembled a combination of Thucydides' objective accuracy with Plutarch's didacticism, his actual practice was closer to that of Herodotus in that De Quincey felt obliged to report all that was said of the person, whether favorable or unfavorable, verifiable or mere current rumor. This practice puts the person in a broad perspective of contemporary attitudes and preserves information of the utmost interest which might otherwise have been lost. His method approaches realism more than panegyric. When he introduces mere scandalous rumor, he often identifies it as such; and sometimes he apologizes for it or qualifies it appropriately (XIV, 112 n.). It is regrettable that the candor is sometimes tinged with petty vindictiveness and blind prejudice, but De Quincey deserves some credit for deviating from the prevailing Victorian practice of converting writers and other distinguished figures into noble and edifying public monuments after death.

Moreover, he certainly made many of his subjects live in the mind of his reader as few others of their biographers have been able to do. The racy, gossipy tone that often prevails makes these works eminently readable; indeed, *Tait's Magazine* never sold better than when De Quincey's literary reminiscences were appearing in it. The details he provides are often indispensable, he shows brilliant insight into the characters of the persons he is discussing, and he has a remarkable capacity for summing persons up in a few sentences which capture the essential qualities in all their complex equilibrium. He preserves records of the hidden sides of their natures and reputations which help to keep his subjects alive to posterity.

De Quincey left comparatively few discrete, formal biographical accounts of single individuals. Most of his biographical writings are mingled with autobiography, criticism, fantasy, history, and various other forms; and his writings on some of the most important of his biographical subjects must be assembled from separate sources, sometimes numerous and widely scattered. Even when he did address himself to a formal biographical effort, he often approached it from the oblique angle of a special thesis which limited or biased his view. Furthermore, he often yielded to his native tendency to explore byways, and the resultant digressions dilute many of his biographical efforts almost beyond recognition as such. Nevertheless, his keen powers of observation, his tenacious memory, his penetrating psychological analysis, and his humorous and mischievous candor make most of his biographical writings well worth the labor of assembling or winnowing. Moreover, these characteristics make some of them delightful and unforgettable.

II   *Literary Reminiscences, etc.*

The most prominent subjects of De Quincey's reminiscences are Wordsworth and Coleridge. His youthful adulation of these two men and his subsequent disillusionment had affected the course of his life in important ways. As a result, he touched upon these two men again and again in his writings, both in major articles about them and incidentally in many briefer passages in works on other subjects. The complexity and ambivalence of his feelings toward both men enriched the accounts he wrote of them; for, while he was anxious to do justice to their very real merits, which, he wished it to be known, he was among the first to recognize, his disillusionment in them and the injuries—real or imagined— which he had received at their hands made it possible for him to analyze them with cool detachment and to record the most personal and unflattering details drawn from his observation and from current gossip.

Apart from his critical essay on Wordsworth's poetry (XI, 294–325), De Quincey wrote two major articles on Wordsworth (II, 299–302; III, 197–206), two articles dealing with Wordsworth and one or two others (II, 303–47), and many articles in which he touched upon Wordsworth, either at some length or in brief passing allusions.[1] The portrait of Wordsworth that emerges from De Quincey's writings about him is delightfully human and realistic. Some allowance must be made for the tinge of malice that occasionally creeps into the picture from De Quincey's sense of personal injury and from the disillusionment of his early hero-worship, but the sidelights he throws on Wordsworth's character and personality are unique and priceless. With the exception of his ruthlessly common-sense strictures on *The Excursion*, De Quincey remained a loyal and helpful partisan of Wordsworth's poetry throughout his life, bestowing much praise, perceptive appreciation, and just criticism upon it. But on Wordsworth the man he exercised his sharp powers of analysis and appraisal, as well as his humorous raconteur's love of revealing anecdote. He made some effort to do justice to the positive traits of Wordsworth's character; for example, he gave him credit for his freedom from ostentation and envy, and acknowledged his skill as a reader of poetry. But he also exposed the poet's limitations and human quirks.

The greatest weakness he found in Wordsworth's character was an excess of pride, which made familiar, friendly intercourse or real human love impossible to him (III, 189). De Quincey found him incapable of listening to explanations or apologies in times of misunderstanding, and insultingly dogmatic in his opinions on scenery—utterly intolerant of the opinions of others (III, 198). Wordsworth also offended De Quincey by his occasional arrogance in human relationships; for example, he once refused to tell De Quincey some news about Charles Lloyd on the grounds that it was fit only for friends of the family—"This to me!—O ye Gods! —to me, who knew by many a hundred conversations how disagreeable Wordsworth was to both Charles Lloyd and to his wife . . ." (II, 389). This view of Wordsworth's proud coldness and insensitivity to the feelings of others probably reflects De Quincey's disappointment over his own failure to achieve a true mutual intimacy with his erstwhile idol. His warning against seeking the love of persons who live too much in the atmosphere of admiration and praise is a pathetic epitaph for his friendship with Wordsworth (XI, 295).

De Quincey also found Wordsworth uncommonly narrow and one-sided intellectually; he was oblivious and unresponsive to ideas beyond the pale of his own established interests (III, 204). De Quincey exposes Wordsworth's intellectual blind spots, as, for example, on De Quincey's pet subject of political economy; and he delights to show him in error about Westmorland architecture.[2] Wordsworth did not read or venerate books sufficiently in the eyes of the bibliophile De Quincey, who, with characteristic hyperbole, estimated that Wordsworth had only read "at the outside twelve volumes 8vo in his whole lifetime" (VI, 106). De Quincey was horrified to see the poet cut the pages of a book with a dirty butter knife (II, 312–17). The contrast between Wordsworth's unfailing good luck in financial affairs and his own hard lot led De Quincey to write one of his most amusing and rueful little *jeux d'esprit* (II, 293). As a counterbalance to the growing Victorian image of Wordsworth as a high-minded, spiritual artist-philosopher, De Quincey called attention to his shrewd sense of business, finding him a hard pursuer of what he considered fair advantages (II, 359). He also recorded personal anecdotes and local legends which show Wordsworth in a ridiculous light (II, 242–43, 429–30). De Quincey's sense of personal injury is overtly revealed in his expression of disappointment that Wordsworth never saw fit to allude to him or Wilson in his works, while he immortalized many persons of far less consequence (II, 419). But, despite all the refractions of De Quincey's picture of Wordsworth through personal prejudice, legend, and gossip, it remains more live, revealing, and convincing than most other accounts.

Some of the same acerb frankness flavors De Quincey's picture of Dorothy Wordsworth—her jerky, nervous way of moving; her stooping walk; her ungraceful, unsexual appearance; her unladylike demeanor; and her lack of ordinary female accomplishments —but, on the whole, he treats her with profound respect and affection (II, 238–39, 293–302). She was a little less charitable to him in a few of her letters, but she served him well many times during his life.

De Quincey also wrote a great deal about Coleridge. In addition to the series of four articles published in *Tait's* soon after Coleridge's death (II, 138–228), he published an article on "Coleridge and Opium-Eating" (V, 179–214) and one treating Coleridge together with Southey and Wordsworth; still another, on "Conversation and S. T. Coleridge," was published posthumously (*PW*, II, 1–60); and De Quincey also left numerous scattered comments on Coleridge. De Quincey's total portrait of Coleridge, as of Wordsworth, shows a real effort to do justice to "this astonishing man," this "sublime old somnambulist." He speaks of Coleridge's merits in the highest terms—"Where is the man who shall equal these things?"—and predicts his future fame (V, 181–83). He calls him an unrivaled psychologist and praises him as a conversationalist (*PW*, II, 14, 16), defending him against the criticism that his conversation lacked sequence. He describes Coleridge's annotations in borrowed books as greatly enhancing the value of them. He also gives him credit for his warm, gentle kindliness. But undercutting such laudatory passages are a host of accusations, criticisms, disagreements, and innuendoes which leave the impression that De Quincey felt a subtly hostile animus against Coleridge.

The most damaging charge De Quincey brought against Coleridge was that of plagiarism. He discovered and published the fact that, despite Coleridge's disclaimer of indebtedness, an extensive passage in his *Biographia Literaria* was a *verbatim* translation from Schelling; and he also alleged that Coleridge was regularly given to unacknowledged minor borrowings from the works of others (II, 142–48). While these charges were sound and important, they seem a little strange coming from such an inveterate borrower as De Quincey. He sought to expose errors in Coleridge's pronouncements on art, drama, and style, and he treated Coleridge's pretensions on political economy with contempt. He accused Coleridge of pronouncing upon books after reading only the first and last pages (IX, 17), and he gave a very unfavorable account of Coleridge as a lecturer and reader aloud (II, 189–90).

He exchanged sordid accusations with Coleridge on the purposes of their first indulgences in opium and on the causes of their subsequent addiction. He described Coleridge as generally unreliable, ill-humored, uncharitable, and proud, and as ludicrously incompetent in business affairs. In human relations he found Cole-

ridge subject to extreme likes and dislikes, a tendency De Quincey
attributed to the effects of opium (V, 195–99). He recorded gossip that Coleridge's marriage had foundered partly because of his
wife's jealousy of Dorothy Wordsworth; and rather astutely he
judged that Coleridge, like Byron, would have quarreled with any
wife (II, 161).

The reasons for the undertone of hostility in De Quincey's remarks on Coleridge can only be guessed. The similarity in their
psychological problems and a sense of rivalry over their common
intellectual interests probably contributed to the antipathy. De
Quincey's youthful hero worship of Coleridge (*Diary,* 191–92)
made disillusionment inevitable, and his desire to be accepted by
Coleridge as an equal was probably painfully rebuffed if De
Quincey sensed the attitude of supercilious condescension which
Coleridge soon adopted toward him. Whatever the source of the
malice which tinges his portrait of Coleridge, the candor of his
revelations horrified many of his contemporaries. Carlyle, dining
with Southey in 1836 or 1837, asked him whether he knew De
Quincey; and he recorded that Southey replied, "Yes, sir, . . .
and if you have an opportunity, I'll thank you to tell him he is
one of the greatest scoundrels living! . . . I have told Hartley
Coleridge . . . that he ought to take a strong cudgel, proceed
straight to Edinburgh, and give De Quincey, publicly in the
streets there, a sound beating—as a calumniator, cowardly spy,
traitor, base betrayer of the hospitable social hearth, for one
thing!" [3]

De Quincey has often been thus condemned for disloyalty and
bad taste in his writings on Coleridge. However, Coleridge's admirable daughter Sara, who took a more balanced view, found De
Quincey's characterization of her father eloquent and discriminating; she rejected the suggestion that De Quincey had been motivated by any real enmity towards him. [4] De Quincey defended
himself against the charge of disloyalty to Coleridge by writing:
"I never had lived in such intercourse with Coleridge as to give
me an opportunity of becoming his friend. To *him* I owed nothing
at all; but to the public, to the body of his own readers, every
writer owes the truth, and especially on a subject so important as
that which was then before me" (II, 227; cf. *PW,* II, 15). A few
discriminating contemporaries saw that, despite the occasional in-
discretion of De Quincey's writing on Coleridge, they, like those

on Wordsworth, were basically accurate; subsequent scholarship has confirmed this view, after making allowances for De Quincey's occasionally careless handling of factual detail and for his hidden animosity toward Coleridge.

De Quincey wrote biographical—or quasi-biographical—accounts and character sketches of many others of his contemporaries. Among the best of these are his accounts of his unfortunate friend Charles Lloyd; of the memorable eccentric "Walking" Stewart; of Charles Lamb, John Wilson, Robert Southey, William Hazlitt, and Hannah More. The reminiscences of Charles Lloyd are deeply sympathetic and affectionate (II, 381–402). The two articles on "Walking" Stewart, published seventeen years apart, reflect De Quincey's delight in eccentric characters and constitute a highly interesting and amusing portrait (III, 92–120).

Charles Lamb is also presented in a warm and playful light, but he is more fully dealt with since De Quincey came to know him better (III, 34–92; V, 215–58). The picture is enlivened by skillfully rendered comic descriptions and anecdotes—Lamb's descending from his stool at India House on their first meeting, tormenting the young worshiper of Wordsworth and Coleridge, being thrice dipped in the sea by mistake because of his stuttering, and falling asleep after dinner. But these are balanced by sober and judicious estimates of Lamb's character and writings. De Quincey was poles apart from Lamb on some subjects, such as politics and the stature of Hazlitt as a thinker; but he was capable of forgiving Lamb such divergences in reaching his final estimate of the man. He defended Lamb against the then current charges of drunkenness and over-tolerance, and he praised him for his unique courtesy, kindness, and hospitality. He found hatred of affectation to be the basic quality of Lamb's character. Despite its critical detachment and its comic moments, and despite its recurrent digressions, De Quincey's portrait of Lamb breathes affection and respect for the man; and it remains one of his finest accounts of a contemporary.

His friend John Wilson, of whom he wrote three sketches, he treated less critically than was his wont; but he left an attractive and at times amusing picture of him. His writings on Southey suggest respect for his character and amiability, although he found him habitually preoccupied and unfriendly. De Quincey's analysis of Hazlitt's character is unsparingly incisive; but, despite his dis-

like for the man, he had a sufficiently sympathetic insight to discern in Hazlitt a hidden need for love, and he recognized his gifts
and sought to do him justice. For De Quincey at his mischievous
and merciless best, one should read his longer essay on Hannah
More (XIV, 94–131), in which he evens an old account with this
evangelical autocrat of the Clapham Sect, or his description of the
marital troubles of the famous educator Andrew Bell (II, 185 n.).

Other contemporaries of whom De Quincey left sketches are Sir
William Hamilton, the Marquess of Wellesley, Sir Humphry
Davy, Edward Irving, James Hogg, Thomas Noon Talfourd, John
Clare, Allan Cunningham, William Godwin, Mrs. Siddons, Richard Watson, and Dr. Samuel Parr. Some, such as the essay on
Hamilton, are too rambling and digressive to be very successful;
others, such as those on Wellesley and Parr, are too tainted with
political bias to command much respect, although the latter
affords some highly entertaining examples of what Masson has
called De Quincey's "mischievous biographico-satirical vein"
(V, 1).

III   *Other Biographical Writings*

Apart from his writings on his contemporaries, De Quincey also
wrote biographical studies of many distinguished literary and political figures of earlier times. These include most of his attempts
at formal biography, as well as numerous biographical sketches
and vignettes incidental to works primarily critical or historical.
Some of them were written as notices of books recently published
by others, some as translations of works by others, some as ency-
clopedia articles, and some as independent original articles. In
general, these biographical writings are more derivative and less
reliable than those on his contemporaries; and they are more subject to the distortions of fixed ideas and thesis fallacies. Nevertheless, some of them are substantial, scholarly, and artful achievements in biography; and most of them offer some interest and
entertainment.

One of De Quincey's most scholarly-seeming biographical
efforts is his study of Richard Bentley, the brilliant and controversial classical scholar of the previous century (1664–1742; IV,
118–236), which was undertaken as a review of a new biography
of Bentley by James Henry Monk, D.D. De Quincey's study, a
spirited defense of Bentley's character and scholarship, deals in

considerable detail with Bentley's works and his turbulent career. The essay, which creates an impression of great scholarly range and authority on the part of De Quincey, has been highly praised. However, it has recently been shown to be really just "a sequence of skillfully drawn and impressively mounted abstracts" from the book under review, which De Quincey disingenuously depreciates, and from Bentley's own work.[5] It is an instructive example of De Quincey's ability to create a clear, interesting, and original-seeming work out of skillfully managed second-hand material.

Among these biographical and partly biographical works must also be included De Quincey's essays on Cicero, the Caesars, Charlemagne, Joan of Arc, Shakespeare, Milton, Pope, Goldsmith, Herder, Goethe, Schiller, and the last days of Kant. The essay on Cicero, somewhat wandering, perverse, and second-hand, is an examination of his public morality, leading to the view that its true sanction was expediency. On Julius Caesar, De Quincey professes to be treating the aspects neglected by other writers; and, after examining Caesar's private life and personal peculiarities, he concludes that Caesar was the greatest of all men of action. He also gives an extended biographical estimate of Augustus, and some narrative and anecdotal attention to Caligula and Nero. The Charlemagne essay is an elaborate comparison with Napoleon that is interesting for the insight it provides into the analytical basis for De Quincey's hostility toward Napoleon, a view in which he differed sharply with his friend Lamb and with Hazlitt. In dealing with Joan of Arc, De Quincey enters combatively into some of the arenas of controversy surrounding her story. After a long and laudatory account of her conduct at her trial, he ends with some of the most rapturously eloquent apostrophe in the entire canon of his work in which he strongly foreshadows her beatification and excoriates the Bishop of Beauvais.

De Quincey recorded that no paper ever cost him so much labor as his essay on Shakespeare; it deals with several of the disputed questions on Shakespeare's life, and offers solutions. A patchy, speculative, and partly derivative performance, it still deserves reading because of its shrewdness and critical insight. In his biographical essay on Milton, the soundness of De Quincey's scholarship is confirmed by the finding of Masson—whose view should certainly bear weight in this instance—that he "shows real familiarity with the materials for Milton's life" (IV, 86). De Quin-

cey answered charges against Milton which he felt were counte-
nanced by Addison and Dr. Johnson; and he used the occasion, as
he used many others, to impugn the character and scholarship of
Dr. Johnson. His extensive study of Pope contains valuable ker-
nels of truth, but is largely borrowed without acknowledgement,[6]
and is partly invalidated by special pleading and hyperbole; and
his treatment of Goldsmith, while it shows some sympathetic insight, is less original and appreciative than he would have one
believe. His biographical writings on Herder, Goethe, and Schiller
are negligible; but his essay on the last days of Kant, although
largely a translation, is artfully written and creates a live and
hauntingly memorable picture of the man—the first to appear in
England.

One of the chief delights in reading De Quincey arises from the
countless amusing and touching sketches of eccentric characters
which waylay the reader here and there throughout his writings.
From full-length studies, like those of "Walking" Stewart and
Hannah More, to mere passing glimpses, like that of a man seen
sitting outdoors at night "mooning himself," De Quincey's works
abound with portraits of odd and unconventional characters. It is
plain that De Quincey, who struck many of his contemporaries as
something of an oddity himself, was a fascinated and sharp-eyed
observer of human eccentrics. To re-create them in his writings,
he called into play the utmost artistry of his gifts for human por-
traiture and whimsical caricature. The brilliant female infidel who
shattered the pious decorum of his mother's dinner table (I,
134–48), the garrulous erudite madman De Quincey encountered
on his travels with Wilson (II, 435–37), the compulsive builder of
a monstrous villa (II, 447–50), and the forsaken bride who secluded herself for twenty years in silence (I, 207) are among the
more memorable in De Quincey's vast gallery of human oddities,
one which has much in common with that of Dickens.

CHAPTER 5

Criticism

D E QUINCEY, a prolific writer of literary criticism, wrote at
least as much as Coleridge and more than Lamb. Sixty-seven
of the articles that Masson included in De Quincey's canon are on
literary subjects or contain substantial critical material, and thirty-
eight are in some sense reviews.[1] A great deal of critical writing
also appears in many of his ostensibly noncritical works. His critical pronouncements touch on at least seventy-seven English authors and thirty-seven foreign authors.

The intense interest in literary criticism in the twentieth century has resulted in a curious anomaly: although the leading
scholars have generally agreed that De Quincey cannot be placed
in the first rank of critics, his critical writings have been more
intensively studied in recent decades than the rest of his canon.
Actually, De Quincey himself did not ordinarily lay claim to much
accomplishment in literary criticism: he disliked writing criticisms
of his contemporaries; he professed to have written only two real
book reviews and never to have written a complete criticism of
any man's work (III, 174; XI, 294). In most of his "reviews," he
gave the book only the most cursory attention and then proceeded
to write an essay of his own on the subject of the book or on some
other topic suggested to him by it; his own name for this kind of
essay was "an excursive review" (X, 81 n.).

It is now felt that De Quincey made few if any important contributions to critical theory and that, as a practical critic, he was
often erratic, prejudiced, and unsystematic, generally an untrustworthy guide. He solemnly parroted commonplaces of the critical
theory of his own and previous ages, and he was sometimes guilty
of wrong-headed quibbling, grotesque facetiousness, polemical
dogmatism, and fantastic misjudgment. He belabored questionable minor matters to the point of tedium, while evading major
considerations; and he seldom troubled to make his views consist-

ent. All these faults, together with his inveterate habit of digression, resulted in the fact that, in the eyes of at least one scholar, De Quincey, "except for one paper on Macbeth, has not one critical composition that is quite satisfactory." [2]

But, despite his faults and limitations as a critic, De Quincey commands attention. In bringing the powers of his unusual intellect, with its curious learning and its wide-ranging powers of association, to bear upon important literary principles, he inevitably cast new light on some of them, at least in flashes. He usually sought out some salient aspect of his subject that he could master and advance. His analytical acuity and his native eloquence enabled him to strike off some memorable formulations of theories that interested him.

As a practical critic he often gained remarkably penetrating and original insights into individual authors, such insights being at times quite at odds with the main drift of critical opinion in his day. He had a great gift for imaginative reconstruction, for reproducing in his own prose the effect of a work under discussion. Some of his criticism is buttressed with solid research; in general, he must rank, therefore, among the most learned of English critics.[3] And it is possible to discern a broad underlying consistency of theory and practice in his critical writings.

Opinions have differed sharply about how De Quincey should be classified as a critic. He has been called an eighteenth-century dogmatist, a preceptist, a formalist, and a categorist; on the other hand, he has been labeled a Romantic, an organicist, an expressionist, and a relativist; and he has even been considered a nineteenth-century historicist and a Victorian moralist. Although there are some grounds for each of these designations, the fact is that De Quincey adopted varied approaches to criticism; and, in sum, he took a very broad, comprehensive view of literature which partly reconciles the divergent opinions and practices found in his critical writings. He is primarily a Romantic critic in his stress on feeling, his capacity for wonder, his Gothicism, and his near-mysticism; but—in his powers of subtle and complex logical analysis, precise discrimination, and ruthless common sense—he proves a less subjective critic than most of his contemporaries. Although there has also been some disagreement about De Quincey's comparative stature as a theoretical and as a practical critic, the best-informed recent opinion has found him more valuable as a practical one.

I   *Theoretical Criticism*

De Quincey devoted few essays primarily to literary theory; the most important are those entitled "Rhetoric," "Style," and "Language" (X, 81–263). However, passages containing reflections and pronouncements on this subject are liberally scattered throughout his works; at one time or another, he touched upon most of its major concerns, though he never gathered up his views into one unified, comprehensive, and consistent statement. In his writings on critical theory, De Quincey was self-confident, and extremely uncharitable to his peers; but his work was almost entirely derivative. Only to Wordsworth, whose theories were his principal source, did he acknowledge his indebtedness; of the critical theories of the important German and English predecessors on whom he drew, and particularly of Coleridge, who also influenced his ideas, he had little to say that was not unflattering. Nevertheless, only by granting his theories broader applications and greater depth and consistency than he ever gave them can De Quincey be shown to be an important original critical theoretician. He stated some critical distinctions and definitions in striking and memorable ways; but, when examined closely, they usually turn out to be commonplace notions in a new garb, to be of limited usefulness, or to have questionable validity. However, his stance on critical theory has considerable historical interest; and his views are intermittently illuminating, challenging, and memorable.

De Quincey's esthetic theory is a composite of mimetic and affective elements. He holds that the fine arts imitate the great impressions of human experience—not directly or factually, which would be "a base *mechanic* mimicry," but instead in another medium, in a different form, or by a different instrument—*"idem in alio"* (X, 368–79). In its grandest, most elevated form, this artistic mimicry captures the *sublime,* the supreme object of the arts in De Quincey's theory—"of all powers which act upon man through his intellectual nature, the very rarest . . ." (X, 400). The sublime is for him a mysterious and awesome force, abstract and quasi-religious, that makes itself felt in the reaction of the mind to mighty objects, more than in the artistic medium itself. It has the power of appealing to the spiritual in man, to the capacity by which man tends to brotherhood.

Thus the highest end of the fine arts is not to evoke pleasure but "the sense of the illimitable incarnated . . ." (XI, 173 n.); through excitation of feeling and expansion of awareness, the arts lead to spiritual enlargement and moral exaltation, and then to a new repose. The experience of the sublime in art is not to be confused with teaching or learning, which is a function of "the *insulated* understanding"; "the fine arts (all of which alike speak through the genial nature of man and his exalted sensibilities), can teach only as nature teaches . . . —viz. by deep impulse, by hieroglyphic suggestion" (XI, 88). Nor is the sublime to be confused with the striking or the pathetic, as in Longinus (X, 300–301). Like many of his contemporaries, De Quincey sometimes treats the sublime as opposed to the beautiful, which he tends to identify with the lovely, the graceful, the elegant. He distinguishes three classes of the sublime—the moral, the ethico-physical, and the dark; and he tends to regard its higher literary projection as a peculiarly English and Christian achievement, best exemplified in Milton.

While the relation of art to the sublime is basically mimetic, the presence of the sublime in art is discernible to the critic primarily in affective manifestations, as psychological responses in the audience or as psychological states in the artist. Thus De Quincey's esthetic theory is preeminently psychological; and he himself explicitly affirmed his conviction that a sound psychology is the basic prerequisite to an absolute or philosophic criticism (XI, 294).

Literature, in the highest sense of the term, De Quincey considered the supreme fine art—deeper, more widespread, and more durable than the other arts (IV, 308–10; X, 47). He called literature a great social organ, its one essential element being "some relation to a general and common interest of man" (XI, 53–54). His further definition of literature took the form of his famous distinction between literature of knowledge and literature of power. This distinction was founded primarily upon his psychological theory, which distinguished between "the *mere* discursive understanding" and "the higher understanding or reason"; literature of knowledge appeals to the former, while literature of power appeals to the latter—"but always *through* affections of pleasure and sympathy" (XI, 54).

To this union of feelings with the higher understanding he applied the biblical term "the understanding heart"; and he declared it, as "the great *intuitive* (or non-discursive) organ, to be the interchangeable formula for man in his highest state of capacity for the infinite" (XI, 56). De Quincey felt that all men have latent within them this capacity for "power," this sympathy with the infinite. As has been seen, he also believed that dreams are "the magnificent apparatus which forces the infinite into the chambers of a human brain" (XIII, 335), which seems to suggest a relation between the unconscious cerebration of dreams and that which underlies the highest literary creativity. It is the role of a great writer to stimulate or enlarge this capacity in others (X, 48). Writings which perform this higher function he called "the literature of power," or "literature proper"; and at times he even suggested that only such works can be called "literature" at all. More commonly, however, he called all other kinds of literature the "literature of knowledge."

The function of literature of knowledge is to teach, but that of literature of power is to move. Only literature of power has the capacity for the sublime, though it is not clear that it always ascends so high, for he included common novels in this category. While he defined literature of power primarily in terms of the mind of the reader, he also ascribed to it an expressive function, in that it bears the stamp of the author's individuality, unlike the literature of knowledge (*PW*, I, 303).

There has been disagreement over the value and originality of this distinction of De Quincey's. He himself mentioned Wordsworth as his source (X, 48 n.), and it is true that similar distinctions can be found in Wordsworth (*Prelude,* VIII, 599–601). But Coleridge is probably another tributary source, Hazlitt and Herder possibly still others, and the idea is not far from the traditional distinction between applied and imaginative literature.[4] The clarity of the distinction is questionable; De Quincey himself was forced to posit an intermediate class of literature that was part knowledge and part power. The vagueness of borderlines between these three classes, together with difficulties of definition, limits the usefulness of De Quincey's formulation.

De Quincey also espoused a number of other critical theories which were in the air in his time.[5] He adopted the developmental view of literary history, seeing literature as having passed through alternating creative and reflective periods and as having been affected by social and economic conditions (X, 200–201). He was also much interested in the critical comparison between ancient and modern literatures or, as he preferred to call them, Pagan and Christian. He found the essential difference between the two to reside in the Christian sense of sin, and on this principle he based his emphatic preference for modern literature and his occasionally violent antipathy to Hellenism. He explored the distinction between genius and talent, describing genius in characteristic Romantic terms as spontaneous, passive, and intuitive, and as expressing the whole man; but he did not carry his investigation far enough to add significantly to the theories of his time. He was much wedded to the law of antagonism in his critical theory, tending to see "polar opposites" almost everywhere—genius and talent, knowledge and power, creation and reflection. This principle of opposition is also involved in his favorite principle of *idem in alio,* the esthetic effect created through the imitation or reproduction of a great object in another medium, establishing similarity in dissimilarity (XI, 195–96 n.). De Quincey saw the validity and importance of Wordsworth's description of style as "the incarnation of thought," with its implication of the inseparability of style and thought (X, 230); but he restricted the principle to the subjective in literature, and elsewhere he treated style as an end in itself (X, 260).

In his theory of genres, he treated poetry as the most ancient and natural form of impassioned utterance. He defined it, in Wordsworthian terms, as "the spontaneous overflow of real unaffected passion, deep, and at the same time original, and also forced into public manifestation of itself from the necessity which cleaves to all passion alike of seeking external sympathy . . ." (I, 194). The passions of poetry he considered grander than those of fiction, "allying themselves with forms more abstract and permanent . . ." (IV, 297). Since he regarded teaching and poetry as antithetical processes, he treated didactic poetry as a contradiction in terms; such poetry could succeed only in spite of its teaching, only by overcoming the resistance of its teaching (XI, 88–97).

A curious fact is that, despite the reverence he professed for poetry, De Quincey gave it limited attention in his criticism. He took very little notice of the magnificent flowering of lyric poetry in his own day. His criticism of poetry is characteristically confined to longer poems. And, despite his strictures on didactic poetry, he tended to examine poetry for its implicit philosophy. Crabb Robinson, after talking with De Quincey in 1815, recorded his impression that De Quincey had the narrowest poetical creed he had ever encountered.[6] One suspects that De Quincey's deep predilection for the majestic, the elaborate, and the sublime led him to the tacit assumption that lyric poetry was a minor form.

De Quincey's theory of prose is extremely one-sided but highly interesting within its limits. He believed the secret of prose style lay in transition and connection—in the way words, phrases, clauses, and particularly sentences are interrelated. He took a strong stand for the superiority of the sustained, elaborate, rhythmic style (III, 51), regarding it as a more versatile instrument than the plain style, as more commensurate with man's profounder or more sublime experiences; without it, in fact, "much truth and beauty must perish in germ . . ." (V, 234). Grand, impassioned subjects, he felt, demand a grand, impassioned style. In speaking of this higher style, he always tried to make it clear that he was not referring to anything stiff, tumid, or bookish. Instead, he had in mind the most artful and tasteful contrivance. As has been noted, he took the position that style and thought are indistinguishable in subjective writing; but he also held that "style has an *absolute* value, . . . quite distinct from the value of the subject about which it is employed . . ."; it "ranks among the fine arts, and is able therefore to yield a separate intellectual pleasure quite apart from the interest of the subject treated" (X, 260).

De Quincey not only believed that the elaborate style is an indispensable medium for the representation of certain higher truths, but he also felt that it has an intrinsic esthetic value—that there is a special "beauty in the balancing and structure of periods," and that there is a special "art by which a succession of periods modify each other" (X, 122). Conversely, he considered the plain, simple style as a meaner, more restricted instrument, incapable of representing the higher forms of human experience, and as intrinsically less interesting and pleasing in itself as an esthetic object. Out of this double view of the elaborate style—as an instrument for conveying the highest truths, and as an independent art form—arose, respectively, De Quincey's theories of impassioned prose and rhetoric.

In his treatment of language and literature as historically evolving phenomena, De Quincey held that poetry was the earlier, more natural form of impassioned utterance; prose, as a later development dependent upon a higher and more complex state of civilization, required great courage of the man who first used it for an impassioned form of truth. Prose could never rival poetry as a vehicle for truth, for "It is such truth only as ascends from the earth, not such as descends from heaven, which can ever assume an unmetrical form" (X, 173). Nevertheless, De Quincey, in writing those passages which he classified as impassioned prose, believed he was creating a new literary form, a kind of prose poetry, which, while it was kept carefully free of regular meter, approached the state of music and poetry. This type of prose, as has been seen, he made the vehicle for some of his dream visions—those glimpses behind the veil of earthly life. It required the most elaborate and fastidious pains in the turning and interweaving of words, phrases, and sentences. Since he considered dreams an access to the infinite, it seems clear that in his impassioned prose he felt he was after all originating a prose medium which could lead man to heavenly truth, through the hieroglyphics of dreams, as well as to the higher earthly truths.

De Quincey's theory of rhetoric involves a peculiar and interesting limitation of the term. He defined rhetoric as "the art of aggrandizing and bringing out into strong relief, by means of various and striking thoughts, some aspect of truth which of itself is supported by no spontaneous feelings, and therefore rests upon artificial aids" (X, 92). By this statement he apparently meant to single out the element of mental play in speaking or writing—the pure delight in embroidering a subject by the utmost manipulation, for its own sake, of ideas, humor, fancy, image, and anecdote; the "eddying about" of thoughts; the conscious and profuse lavishing of ornament for effect (X, 115, 121)—all quite apart from passion and practical purposes of convincing, which he considered the province of eloquence.

This disinterested mind-play—in which he perceived a special sort of intellectual pleasure, perhaps of an inferior order but one as legitimate as any other (X, 101)—is analogous to ceremoniousness in manners and gorgeousness in costume (X, 121). In identifying and describing this component of rhetoric, De Quincey was performing a genuine service, perhaps making his most important original contribution to critical theory. His account of the history of this type of rhetoric is learned and interesting. However, De Quincey was not content to isolate and describe this element of mind-play in rhetoric; unfortunately he went further and attempted to restrict the term "rhetoric" to this meaning, ruling out all the other, traditional applications of the word. The result of this mistaken effort has been the beclouding and the partial discrediting of his theory.

De Quincey touched briefly on the theory of other genres, such as biography, as has been noted. On the novel he made a few theoretical assertions, but his views are too limited to be of great value. His predilection for the mysterious led him to overrate the Gothic novel, and the strain of evangelical prudery that he had inherited in spite of himself from his mother led him to underrate the great realistic tradition then developing in the English novel (III, 206). He prophesied a moral decline for the novel because of its necessity of appealing to popular taste, and he considered it an ephemeral form of literature (IV, 297). Nevertheless, he also declared it sufficiently justified by its idealization of the passion of sexual love (XIV, 370–71); and he surprisingly included even the commonest novel in his category of the literature of power (XI, 57), apparently in contradiction of his view that novels are transient.

II *Practical Criticism*

As a practical critic, De Quincey used a variety of approaches, but he tacitly united them in a basically consistent system. As John E. Jordan has summarized it, "His method, briefly, is to feel an effect, analyze its cause, attempt to make it concrete or to recreate it, and then to trace it back to some precept or reconstruct the age or the individual which produced it." [7] Thus, although De Quincey usually begins by analyzing the effect a work of literature has upon the feelings of a reader (normally himself), he escapes the pitfall of what has been called the "affective fallacy" by looking for the cause of the observed effects in the work itself and in its relation to the laws of its genre; in the author's life and his mind-construct or ruling passion; or, even farther back, in the historical conditions which may have influenced the author. In particular critical studies, he might emphasize one stage or another of this method; but usually, underlying whatever he did, there was, at least implicitly, the affective approach already noted. While nothing in this method was unprecedented, the particular combination of approaches was peculiarly his own. In general, he preferred exploration and explanation as critical activities over judgment. He loved to make broad abstract generalizations about writers, genres, national literatures, and literary periods, and then to support them with extended argument and illustration. He tended to pursue psychogenetic and historical investigations farther than his contemporaries.

At its best, this method enabled De Quincey to perform highly valuable services in exploring, revealing, and adjudging the works of several writers. He was capable of marvelous flashes of insight. He was among the earliest to appreciate Wordsworth and Coleridge; some of his views on their work, particularly on Wordsworth's, remain valid today; and both men demonstrated in their letters great confidence in his critical judgment. De Quincey was able to reach critical evaluations quite at variance with the dominant views of his time: he praised Euripides, Pope, and Donne when it was fashionable to ignore or depreciate them; and he dismissed Byron in spite of his current popularity. His dramatic criticism placed more emphasis on stagecraft than was common in his day. He performed a genuine service in the introduction of German thought and German writers to English readers. He undoubtedly also stimulated interest in many other writers, ancient and modern; provided new insights into some of their works; and contributed to just critical estimates.

However, it must always be borne in mind that De Quincey is not a uniformly reliable or sufficient guide. His range was limited; among modern literatures he concentrated mainly on the English, and even there he left much out of account. He lost touch with recent developments in his later life; for example, he took no notice of the works of Tennyson and Browning. His knowledge of French literature seems to have been very slight. His comparative silence about lyric poetry also restricts the range of his practical criticism, as does his Romantic tendency to overemphasize content and to neglect form.

In addition, the weaknesses of his character, the trying circumstances under which he wrote, and the peculiar set of his mind rendered many of his judgments invalid. The fact that he was writing for a particular periodical press in an era of polemical abuse, extravagant horseplay, and pontifical dogmatism contributed to the occasional warping of his views. The necessity of flight, which repeatedly separated him from his books, and an intermittent slipshod lassitude, perhaps partly induced by opium, interfered with his scholarly precision, encouraged his sometimes slavish dependence on the work of others, and enhanced his native tendency to be discursive, abstract, and diffuse. He often frankly sought the effect of the single surprising, unconventional stroke, without any pretense of comprehensiveness; this practice led to some of his finest successes and to some of his most outrageous aberrations. He also tended to reduce an author's work to the terms of a single mind-construct or master passion, which sometimes produced distorting oversimplifications, especially in the case of earlier writers.

But by far the greatest weakness of his critical writings resulted from his many prejudices. De Quincey was a man of strong convictions, inherited and acquired. Wherever literature impinged on the areas of these convictions, De Quincey's reactions tended to be affected. He could sometimes rise above his prejudices and reach surprisingly tolerant judgments, but more often his outlook was confined as if between rigid blinders, or was discolored beyond all reason. In general, he was more prone to special pleading when his prejudices caused him to disapprove than when they supported his approval. In estimating De Quincey's practical criticism, it is important to take account of the principal prejudices which conditioned it.

His strongest biases were toward whatever was English, Tory, and Christian. Despite his great gift of aptitude for the Classical languages, his many years of close study of Classical history and literature, and some impulse of sympathy for the Classical outlook, the paganism of Classical antiquity provoked in him a strong, narrow Christian reaction. The resultant hostility colored many of his judgments of Classical culture and led him occasionally into absurd special pleading against it. A John-Bullish cultural snobbery infected much of his writing on foreign cultures, ancient or modern, that amounted at times almost to a rabid xenophobia. He was particularly contemptuous of Oriental cultures, especially the Persian and the Chinese; but he also habitually depreciated French and German culture—he was, with few qualifications or intermissions, a lifelong Francophobe.

Within the tradition of English literature, he was generally unsympathetic toward the eighteenth century and favorable to the seventeenth. His Toryism made almost anything that smacked of Whiggery or radicalism anathema; and his High Church leanings, tinged with evangelical prudery, stiffened him against earthy realism or bawdiness. And as has already been noted, his predilections for the mysterious and for the stylistically elaborate tended to close his eyes to the grace and power possible in simple realism and in the plain style.

These handicaps prevent one from turning confidently to De Quincey for balanced, comprehensive surveys and judgments of literary history, authors, or works. He seems to have lacked the measured sureness of vision which enabled Hazlitt's judgments to stand up so well over the years. However, De Quincey's great intellectual gifts, the breadth of his critical system, the brilliant flashes of insight he sometimes had, and the marvelous flexibility and precision of his prose style assure ample awards to the cautious and discriminating reader of his critical writings.

Despite his frank Christian and modern bias against Greek literature, De Quincey felt a strong fascination and challenge in it which again and again drew him back to it and which caused him to devote a major portion of his critical writings to exploring and evaluating it. He prided himself on his Greek scholarship, and once he even went so far as to rate himself the second Greek scholar in the kingdom.[8] He devoted two major essays to broad studies of Greek literature ("A Brief Appraisal of the Greek Literature in its Foremost Pretensions" and "Theory of Greek Tragedy" [X, 289–359]); and many of his other writings contain treatments of Greek literature, from passing generalizations, comparisons, and judgments to specific, detailed analysis. Despite his prejudice and his intermittent inaccuracy, De Quincey's treatment of Greek literature is sometimes stimulating and instructive.

In general, De Quincey argues that Greek literature failed to cultivate style successfully, to achieve the true sublime, and thus to reach the consummation of art. He also finds it deficient in tenderness and the picturesque. The seventeen-year-old boy who could not bear the *Odyssey* and who considered "the wretched drivellings of that old dotard Homer" inferior to Virgil (*Diary*, 176, 179) grew into the mature De Quincey who continued to oppose the inordinate veneration of Homer, finding him inferior to the greatest modern writers and to Chaucer and Milton. Despite his bias and his mistakes, De Quincey's essay on Homer (VI, 7–95) is still worth reading. He argued cogently for the unitary authorship of the *Iliad* and a later date for the *Odyssey;* and, in dealing with some of the other Homeric questions, he managed to avoid the errors prevalent in his time.

Against Socrates, Plato, and Xenophon, De Quincey sustained a virulent and varied attack, motivated partly by moral prejudice. He criticized the *Republic* as vague, visionary, and immoral (VIII, 42–83); he denounced the Socratic method as mean and limited; and he confessed a dislike for all three men based upon his conviction that they were "humbugs" (X, 181). He found Aristotle much more congenial, probably because of his clarity, his logical system, and his comprehensiveness. Herodotus, he felt, was not really a historian, but more a polyhistor or encyclopedist; he admired the universality of Herodotus' accomplishments and the breadth of his scope. De Quincey had a sound understanding of the nature of Herodotus' work, and his defense of its accuracy on some points has been shown to be well founded (VI, 96–138).

To Thucydides, on the other hand, De Quincey's critical reaction was much less sympathetic; he disparaged him with some of his least pardonable flippancy (X, 317–19). He criticized Greek oratory as being too baldly utilitarian—wanting in general interest and in the advantages of collateral information and extrinsic ornament (X, 332)—a view arising directly out of his convictions on the superiority of the elaborate style and on rhetoric as mindplay. Pindar he dismissed on the grounds that his subject matter and his meter had lost their interest for modern times (X, 314–15).

For Greek tragedy De Quincey confessed an almost idolatrous enthusiasm (X, 364). His essay entitled "Theory of Greek Tragedy" is one of his most sustained, objective, and concentrated efforts to penetrate and define a body of literature. He elaborates upon his views in his essay "The Antigone of Sophocles" (X, 371–79). Basically, his theory rests on the contention that Greek tragedy is static—lacking in conflict and action—because it represents life in a purified and ennobled form, idealized and superhuman. He calls it "statuesque" or "sculpturesque," as opposed to the picturesque, an analogy he may have borrowed from the Schlegels.[9] To achieve this effect, he felt, the Greek dramatist consciously and systematically endeavored "to unrealize the scene" (X, 374); and, instead of mimicking life mechanically, he sought to represent it in another form, by a different instrument. Thus Greek tragedy is the most complex example of the basic esthetic principle of *idem in alio* (X, 368–70). This theory provides a valid and helpful insight into one of the leading qualities of Greek tragedy, and De Quincey develops it effectively, even embracing technical theatrical considerations such as costume and the physical form of the theater. However, he characteristically pushes his thesis much too far and seeks to attribute the total characteristic effect of Greek tragedy to this single factor.

De Quincey's admiration of Greek drama was not uniform nor unqualified. He was troubled by a conviction that its presiding power was death, while that of English drama was life; and at one point he declared that Greek drama "shows us the ultimatum of the human mind mutilated and castrated of its infinities, and (what is worse) of its moral infinities"—a view which probably shows his Christian-moral critical bias prevailing again (*PW*, II, 279).

Although De Quincey included the Roman along with the Greek in his general disparagement of pagan culture, wherever the two came into comparison he tended to prefer the Roman. He was forced to concede the superiority of Greek literature (X, 54), but not without reservations: as a boy, he had found Virgil superior to Homer; later on, he found Roman rhetoric superior to the Greek. He wrote very little about Roman literature, but he granted great powers to some of the masters, with serious qualifications. Lucretius struck him as possessed with a self-canceling demonic frenzy, his poem as a "divinity of stormy music sweeping round us in eddies, in order to prove that for us there could be nothing divine . . ." (XI, 379). Horace he called "the exquisite master of the lyre" but the "most shallow of critics" (I, 126). The Romans approached sublimity, he found, not in poetry but in acts and sayings. Perhaps for this reason De Quincey's major writings about Rome are historical rather than critical.

De Quincey's greatest critical efforts were devoted to English literature, which he generally found superior to ancient and to

Continental literature. His coverage of English literature in his criticism is sporadic, and it is weighted by the already mentioned allegiances; but, within its limitations, it is often impressive and serviceable. Much of the earliest English literature he ignored. He had little to say about Chaucer, beyond praising his skill in the picturesque and contending for the intelligibility of his language; perhaps Chaucer's realism and occasional bawdiness made him a little uncongenial to De Quincey's decorous sensibility. He also gave little or no critical attention to Spenser and to other Elizabethans, apart from Shakespeare.

De Quincey venerated Shakespeare more than any other writer; he alluded to him constantly, and always with approval. His overall view approaches bardolatry. Nevertheless, he studied the plays closely and gave to the analysis of Shakespeare's achievement some of his steadiest and most independent thought, with the result that his criticism of Shakespeare stands up well beside that of any of his contemporaries or predecessors. At the end of the biographical essay on Shakespeare he wrote for the *Encyclopaedia Britannica,* he listed what he considered the chief sources of Shakespeare's power: his primacy and supremacy in the portrayal of women and the supernatural, "his teeming fertility of fine thoughts and sentiments," and his skill in adapting dialogue to the representation of forms of life and human passion (IV, 69–79). The emphasis on the supernatural and on feeling in this formulation, taken with the greater emphasis on subject matter than on form, illustrates the Romantic bent of De Quincey's critical method. But he was also capable of keen observation and analysis of detail and technique. This ability led him to interesting discoveries about the quality of the language in the play within the play in *Hamlet* and about a particular stage effect in *Macbeth* (X, 345–47, 389–94).

By general consent, De Quincey's finest single critical piece is "On the Knocking at the Gate in Macbeth." It begins—characteristically—with an observation of the strangely powerful effect produced upon his feelings by the knocking on the gate after the murder scene in *Macbeth.* The cause is sought and is located in the symbolic meaning of this stage effect as a signal of the resumption of ordinary human goings-on, after their horrid suspension during the murders—an opposite reaction which best defines the previous action. This insight seems acute and valid. For such bright moments, as well as for the broad soundness of his observations in general, De Quincey's criticism of Shakespeare remains well worth reading.

Because of his strong stylistic and intellectual affinity for the great English authors of the seventeenth century, De Quincey's criticism, brief as it is, of this period has a special value. His definition of rhetoric as mind-play opened his eyes to an appreciation, rare in his time, of Donne and of the metaphysicals; his observation that "rhetorical" would be a more accurate term for them than "metaphysical" is apt (X, 101). He saw Sir Thomas Browne, Jeremy Taylor, Milton, and the best of their contemporaries as constituting a matchless constellation in the history of elaborate and rhetorical styles.

De Quincey, who wrote five papers on Milton, granted him some of his highest praise. He declared the moral of *Paradise Lost* by far the grandest ever formally illustrated by a poet (XI, 456). In his biographical essay on Milton, he made an interesting comparative judgment of *Paradise Lost* and *Paradise Regained* (IV, 100–102). His principal critical essay on Milton is devoted mainly to the contention that this poet is the chief exemplar of the sublime in literature (X, 395–413). He finds *Paradise Lost*, more than any other human composition, sublime both in conception and execution. This special emphasis on the sublime in Milton was not original with De Quincey; it was axiomatic at the time, as Byron points out in the "Dedication" of *Don Juan* (l. 76). Still, in De Quincey's hands this principle leads to some profound and instructive insight into Milton's work. Unfortunately, it also tends to become a reductive thesis and to narrow De Quincey's view of Milton, which leaves much of Milton's varied achievement out of account and lacks a balanced, comprehensive grasp of any of his work. Yet De Quincey was free of the sentimental hero worship of Milton which afflicted many of his contemporaries; and, within the terms of his special view of Milton, he was incisive and original.

The same intellectual and artistic commitments that endeared seventeenth-century English literature to De Quincey made him, with a few exceptions, insensitive and even hostile to eighteenth-century literature. He wrote of Addison that he "was a master of the humble and unpretending English [that was] demanded, or indeed suffered, by his themes, but for that very reason little familiar with its higher or impassioned movements" (XIV, 156). He credited Addison with an exquisite humor and a delicate pen for the delineation of character, and he defended him against the charge of pedantry—but only in order to establish his dominant view of Addison as "the champion of all that is easy, natural, superficial" (XI, 19–29). He stigmatized much of Addison's work as "rubbish," and he declared him, as a critic, to be "thoughtless and irreflective, . . . an absolute ignoramus as regarded the literature of his own country; and . . . a mere bigot as regarded the antique literature of Pagan Greece or Rome" (IV, 307; XIV, 155).

De Quincey's treatment of Swift is one of the clearest examples of his critical astigmatism, his inability to recognize any merit of a high order in the plain style. He grudgingly allowed that the merit of Swift's style lay in "vernacularity," but he considered this a very small merit, for "grand impassioned subjects insist upon a different treatment; and *there* . . . Jonathan would have broke down irrecoverably," for he had a "rigid incapacity for dealing with the grandeurs of the human spirit" (XI, 14–17).

De Quincey devoted a major critical effort—five papers—to the analysis and appraisal of Alexander Pope, and the result is that he gained some valid insight into the man and his work, appreciating Pope's achievement more justly than did Wordsworth and others of his contemporaries. He praised Pope as the supreme poet in the witty treatment of human manners, "in the sportive and aërial graces of the mock heroic and satiric muse . . ." (IV, 237, 280). He found *The Rape of the Lock* "the most exquisite monument of playful fancy that universal literature offers," and he declared *The Dunciad*, despite its flaws, Pope's greatest work—in fact, the greatest monument of satiric power man has produced (IV, 260, 270). De Quincey sought to combat the prevalent critical clichés on Pope—his Frenchness, his inferior rank, and his superior "correctness"—with some justice. Unfortunately, the virtues of De Quincey's critical appreciation of Pope are partly counterbalanced by characteristic aberrations. He developed the thesis that Pope was basically insincere—that he was unprincipled, shallow, and indolent, not really a satirist at all, but a sort of Romantic manqué, a man of noble and generous nature who had adopted the hypocritical stance of a satirist. De Quincey pushed this questionable thesis to hyperbolical and reductive extremes (XI, 98–155).

To the eighteenth-century novel he tended to raise moral objections, finding some of Smollett's scenes "bestial and degrading," and exclaiming, "How coarse are the ideals of Fielding!—his odious Squire Western, his odious Tom Jones!" (IV, 297). His essay on Goldsmith is largely devoted to biographical and abstract critical questions; although he gives credit to Goldsmith for a humble sort of exquisite genius and professes to be correcting the low estimate of Goldsmith's contemporaries, he actually does little or nothing to enhance his reputation (IV, 288–322).

Although De Quincey never wrote a major critical essay on Dr. Johnson, his works abound with references to him; and most of them sound a note of settled hostility. He ranked Johnson among the four greatest biographers and even gave him the first rank in point of composition, but he also attacked him on various points as a biographer, calling him libelous, defamatory, credulous, superstitious, arrogant, jealous, prejudiced, spiteful, and inaccurate. He accused him of envy and bias in his treatment of Milton, and he offered an extended rebuttal of his views (IV, 104–17). While he conceded that Johnson was a master of conversation, he restricted his mastery to a minor mode of conversation and thereby found him inferior to Burke (V, 53). He impugned Johnson's scholarship in general and pronounced him especially ignorant of philology. Against the charge of indolence he defended Johnson, but he found him deficient in human sympathy. He considered Johnson's style seriously flawed with tautology. As for the famous letter to Lord Chesterfield, De Quincey felt that it was "petulant and boyish at the best, but, at the worst, it bore a more sinister connotation." [10] All in all, De Quincey seldom missed a chance to denigrate Dr. Johnson, a habit which is a little difficult to account for adequately.

De Quincey recorded his views of several other eighteenth-century literary figures. In his history of the Caesars, he paused to dissent from Gibbon's views of the cause and the beginning date of Roman decline. He also criticized Gibbon for failing to distinguish the separate stages of Roman decline, for leaving important omissions, for including only such facts as lent themselves to his scenical mode of treatment, and for often assuming the very knowledge he should have been providing. However, elsewhere De Quincey gave Gibbon high praise for scholarship, though ranking him below Southey in an extended comparison (VI, 361; II, 338). He shared the admiration of his contemporary writers for Chatterton, and he spoke highly of "that fine mystic, Blake the artist" (II, 400). He became obsessively involved in the controversy over the authorship of the sensational "Junius" papers, arguing with passionate persistence for Sir Philip Francis. Sheridan he called "'an absolute *charlatan* . . . a mocking-bird" (X, 112). His highest praise for an eighteenth-century figure was bestowed upon Burke, "the supreme writer of his century, the man of the largest and finest understanding"; in eloquence Burke surpassed all orators, ancient and modern (X, 114, 339). Although he could find Burke capable on occasion of pettiness (XIV, 186), in general he overpraised him, no doubt partly because of the harmony of their political views, and because Burke illustrated his special theory of rhetoric. De Quincey was not an admirer of Godwin's novels; he subjected *Caleb Williams* to a most amusing—if highly inaccurate—travesty (XI, 326–35).

Some of De Quincey's most acute and valuable criticism deals with his English contemporaries. To the analysis of Wordsworth's poetry he devoted his most sustained formal criticism (XI, 294–322). His brief exposure to *The Prelude* in manuscript early in their acquaintance impressed him strongly, for he retained an astonishingly accurate recollection of the poem, and he saw its literary and historical importance (II, 279). In *The Excursion* he discovered two formal defects—its "undulatory" development and its occasional unpoetic colloquialism—and he ridiculed details of the plot and characterization with unsparing common sense. He also surprisingly took exception to the Solitary's view that the French Revolution had failed, calling it "childish impatience." He drew attention to Wordsworth's shorter poems as containing deeper truths than his philosophical poems, and he pointed out Wordsworth's great gift for revealing connections among things only dimly related before, thereby bringing to life truths which have lain dormant and indistinct in men's minds (XI, 315). He noticed Wordsworth's unique powers of observation and the unexampled depth of "his sympathy with what is *really* permanent in human feelings" (XI, 321). Most of De Quincey's attention to Wordsworth is devoted to his thought; he has little to say about his technique, although he praises him for the purity, accuracy, and propriety of his grammar and idiom (X, 127–28). Despite the admiration he expressed for Wordsworth's critical theory, he found fault with the famous preface to the second edition of *Lyri-*

cal Ballads as imprecise and injudicious, particularly in that it failed to make clear which poets it was stigmatizing as negative models. On the whole, De Quincey's estimate of Wordsworth, while one-sided and partial, is very clear-sighted and shrewd.

On Coleridge's works De Quincey wrote comparatively little specific criticism, apart from his exposures of Coleridge's borrowings. In general, he usually gave Coleridge credit for profound learning and penetration of mind; but he considered Coleridge's great gifts to have been partly invalidated by the effects of opium, and found him handicapped by deficiency in the power of teaching and communicating (X, 77). His German, De Quincey considered limited; his Greek, unequal to its early promise; his French, poor; and his Latin, though fair, inferior to Wordsworth's. On Coleridge's poetry De Quincey wrote little, apart from a brief and partly playful, though interesting, interpretation of "The Ancient Mariner" as a study of penitential sorrow for the violation of love, whose guardian spirit pursues the Mariner like an avenging angel or nemesis (XIII, 195–96). He spoke of Coleridge's poems as exquisite but unequal, and he suggested that his poetic fountain was choked up by opium (V, 207). De Quincey's ambivalent view of Coleridge is perhaps best summed up in his comparison of Herder with Coleridge: "the same all-grasping erudition, the same spirit of universal research, the same disfiguring superficiality and inaccuracy, the same indeterminateness of object, the same obscure and fanciful mysticism . . . , the same plethoric fulness of thought, the same fine sense of the beautiful, and (I think) the same incapacity for dealing with simple and austere grandeur" (IV, 381).

De Quincey recorded critical estimates, brief or extensive, of many others of his English contemporaries. Although he had as a boy found Scott's "Lady of the Lake" "disgusting," his few remarks on Scott are mainly favorable (*e.g.*, V, 70). He granted Southey immense erudition and "a combination of two striking qualities, viz. a peculiar command over the visually splendid, connected with a deep-toned grandeur of moral pathos"; but he considered him limited in subject matter and style, incapable of rising to splendid declamation or impassioned fervor (V, 238; II, 346). Of Lamb he wrote, "considered as a man of genius, he was not in the very first rank, simply because his range was a contracted one: within that range, he was perfect . . ." (III, 47). De Quincey was troubled by Lamb's stylistic incapacity for lofty and sustained flights and by his insensibility to music (V, 234–35); but he had to grant that "the essays of 'Elia' are as exquisite a gem amongst the jewellery of literature as any nation can show" (III, 37). De Quincey tended to overpraise his friend John Wilson ("Christopher North"), but he was capable of acknowledging Wilson's "general tendency to bend to the prevailing opinion of the world . . ." (V, 284).

De Quincey felt a strong personal, political, and intellectual aversion to Hazlitt. He pronounced him no thinker, finding his thought fractured and discontinuous. He considered Hazlitt's writing splenetic and peevish, his learning contemptible—"Hazlitt had read nothing" (V, 231). Yet De Quincey was able to rise above his prejudice to grant Hazlitt a teeming fertility of intellect and to conclude that all men must ultimately concur in admiration of him (XI, 341–54). De Quincey, who admired Landor's work, did what he could to rescue it from eclipse; but he criticized him for degrading religious notions, some culpable coarseness, and an outrageous theory of spelling (XI, 395–474).

Perhaps nowhere more than in his brief analysis of Shelley did De Quincey demonstrate his sporadic ability to set his rigid prejudices aside and to reach a perceptive and compassionate estimate. Shelley's religious and political views should have made him contemptible to De Quincey, but instead De Quincey saw, under Shelley's boyish rebelliousness, his utter sincerity, his incorruptible nobility of soul, and his striking genius (XI, 354–77). Keats, on the other hand, De Quincey misjudged woefully, dismissing him haughtily as a social nonentity and a political impostor. In *Endymion* Keats was guilty of false sentiment and effeminacy, and generally he was given to scandalous abuse of the English language. De Quincey tempered his assault with a few words of high praise for *Hyperion* and with the admission that Keats intermittently aroused deep admiration. He later regretted some of his hasty abuse (XI, 377–93; IV, 416).

He also sought to make amends for his savage attack on Carlyle for his translation of Goethe's *Wilhelm Meister*, which he had denounced as overrun with vulgarisms and Scotticisms (XI, 223 n.). But, even after the two had become friends, he was still able to object to Carlyle's proneness to denounce abuses for which he could suggest no remedies (IV, 300–301). Of most of the other emerging Victorian writers, De Quincey had little to say. He was slow to recognize Dickens because of his extravagance, his want of fidelity to life, and perhaps his vulgarity; but he conceded his good-natured human warmth. Thackeray he rejected as a cynic. Among the few American authors he noticed, he depreciated Emerson as a feeble copy of Carlyle; and he found his style offensive for its monotonously short and simple sentences, but he came to respect the man and his work. Hawthorne he and his family admired.

De Quincey's negative view of the French nation in general influenced his criticism of French literature. Since he regarded the French as wanting in depth and simplicity of feeling and as being far from virtuous in their public and domestic life, he found their sensibility artificial and sensual, and their literature vicious (IV, 383). He contended that France was the only literary nation which had produced no paramount book. He attributed what he considered the comparative poverty and atrophy of French literature in his own age to a tendency of the French to become too absorbed in their own manners and thus to fail to have an invigorating infusion of foreign influence (XI, 260). However, his moral prejudice against the French had apparently led him to neglect their literature; therefore, his judgments must be largely disallowed on the grounds of his comparative ignorance.

In comparisons between French and German literature, De Quincey tended always to favor the German; and, on the whole, his attitude toward the latter was much more positive. He called attention to the recent remarkable vitality and productivity of German literature, and he declared its contemporary output, apart from poetry, "by much the best in Europe . . ." (II, 85; XI, 261). He praised the Germans for the innocence and simplicity of their lives and for the high value they attached to intellectual pleasures (IV, 382). On the other hand, De Quincey found much to object to in German literature—so much, in fact, that his overall view seems predominantly negative. Characteristically, his opposition was based primarily upon stylistic considerations. He repeatedly asserted that the Germans were negligent of style, or that style was an inconceivable idea to the German mind. The principal fault of German style—and especially Kant's—was its tendency toward over-stuffed sentences, ones too long and too complex (II, 83–84; X, 159–62).

Chief among De Quincey's positive services to German literature were his appreciation, as has been noted, of Jean Paul Richter and his translations from Richter and from Lessing's *Laocoon*.
His work on Richter appeared in 1821—at the outset of De Quincey's career, just after the *Confessions*—and in 1824 (XI, 259–93).
He praised Richter for his twofold power over the pathetic and
the humorous; for his restless, wide-ranging intellect; and for the
overflowing opulence of his wit. Carlyle's later work on Richter
was much more thorough and superseded De Quincey's, but De
Quincey deserves the credit for first drawing the attention of the
English—including Carlyle—to Richter. In his annotated translation of thirteen of the twenty-nine sections of Lessing's *Laocoon*,
which appeared in 1826–27, De Quincey also did some important
pioneering.

His writings about most other German authors are less significant. His treatment of Goethe is outrageously insensitive and mis-
guided. He dismisses *Faust*—in a single sentence—as impene-
trably obscure, and *Wilhelm Meister* as both obscure and morally
repulsive; he calls *Werther* Goethe's best work, but nevertheless
predicts a well-deserved decline in Goethe's reputation (IV, 395–
421). In his early review of Carlyle's translation of *Wilhelm Meister*, he depreciates Goethe recklessly, denouncing the novel for
moral outrage, depraved taste, and capricious oddity, and he sub-
mits the work to a wickedly mocking burlesque (XI, 222–58). He
radically underestimates Goethe's knowledge, and he leaves his
magnificent achievement in lyric poetry unacknowledged. In fact,
De Quincey seems really not to have known very much about
Goethe. His treatments of Schiller and Herder are similarly thin
and unsatisfactory. Despite such aberrations, De Quincey's criticism, if it is approached cautiously and selectively, affords the
reader many valuable insights, confronts him with challenging
judgments, and offers him a good deal of lively entertainment.

CHAPTER 6

History, Semi-Fiction, and Fiction

I *History*

BECAUSE De Quincey devoted a great deal of his life to the study of history, a large number of his published writings are about historical topics. He distinguished three main types of historical writing: the narrative, the scenical, and the philosophic (V, 354–60). He himself wrote comparatively little straight narrative history; his interests led him chiefly to the scenical and to the philosophic. He was fascinated by broad theories of historical development, but he could also devote great intellectual energy to the analysis and resolution of minute, particular historical questions. He liked to explore the causes of historical events, large or small, and to appraise the consequences, especially in moral terms. Occasionally, historical topics launched him into soaring flights of eloquence and into the painting of magnificent panoramas.

The historical theories he found most congenial were alternation, dialectical development, and progress. He adopted the view of Paterculus and others that the human genius moves through alternating periods of activity and repose, creation and reflection; and he found the principle amply illustrated in the history of both Greece and England (X, 196–216). At the same time, he saw history in developmental terms, a somewhat surprising orientation for a conservative of his ilk. He described the process of historical development as an interplay between opposing forces, the ultimate course of tendency emerging from counterbalancing short-range movements or from compromise; he interpreted in this fashion the history of English political parties and the long-term results of the French Revolution.[1]

De Quincey's vision of historical development as progressive was probably influenced by Kant, whose "Idea of a Universal History on a Cosmopolitical Plan" he translated in 1824 (IX, 428–44).

He saw all of human history as a gradual advance toward a higher state: the West rising above the East; the Romans, above the Greeks; Christian civilization, above the pagan; and modern Protestant England, above the Catholic and Continental cultures. He confidently predicted for the future a great era of human expansion based on a revolution in political justice and on technological developments—if man moved forward morally at the same time. He foresaw a political and religious union of Europe (XI, 409; XIV, 285). He discovered symptoms of progressive development in the history of religion, government, language, literature, transportation, and communication.

The fact that De Quincey's historical writings were produced for the periodical press probably militated against any very sustained consecutive effort. His excursions into historical theory were brief, as were most of his specific historical investigations and narratives. He sometimes frankly professed to be treating only those passages of history which had been inadequately or mistakenly treated by others, and his journalistic purposes led him to seek the striking or novel and to treat it in popular terms.

His longest consecutive historical narrative is "The Caesars," which ran in six issues of *Blackwood's* in 1832–34 (VI, 225–420). His aims in writing it seem to have been mixed. He intended to write a series of accounts of the private lives of the Caesars, drawing his material from Suetonius and from the comparatively little-known Augustan historians. Unfortunately, he also undertook to trace the history of the emperors from Julius Caesar to Diocletian, adopting as his unifying theme the investiture of the imperial office with a sacred majesty and grandeur of power which survived until it was finally extinguished by the reforms and the Oriental decadence that Diocletian introduced. However, as De Quincey tells us, he was forced to write "The Caesars" without access to his books, which probably hampered him in fulfilling his broader aim, as did his native incapacity for developing and sustaining a large structure. He devotes a disproportionate amount of space to Julius Caesar and Augustus, less to Caligula and Nero, and then hurries superficially over the others. The work is written in a tone of sustained seriousness, with a strong moral bias, and with comparatively few digressions and lighter touches. Some of the anecdotal sections are highly entertaining, and there are moments of great eloquence. However, the interstices are packed with dry factual, analytical, and theoretical material drawn from the limited sources he had at hand. The end result is a work derivative, indeterminate in theme, and without structure, but informative and intermittently very readable.

De Quincey wrote several briefer papers dealing with various segments of ancient history. In a separate, closely argued paper on the Roman Empire, "The Philosophy of Roman History" (VI, 429–47), he theorized that the decline of the empire was continuous from the time it reached its greatest extent and lost the stimulus of strong external counter-pressure.

He also wrote an essay on Greece under the Romans (VII, 250–78), contending that the Eastern empire defended European civilization while it was maturing. In another essay, really an abstract from a French source, on the pagan oracles in the early Christian era (VII, 44–100), he defended the moral influence of the oracles and attacked the impression created by Church Fathers that the oracles soon died out in early Christian times. Christian history also engaged his interest; he developed an obsessive interest in the problem of the identity of the Essenes. At great length, and returning to the subject again and again, he argued that there was no such tribe as the Essenes and that they were really early Christians disguising their identity for self-defense. In the process of supporting this view, he was forced to make a villain out of Josephus for differing with him.

In other papers, De Quincey dealt with a variety of historical subjects: Charlemagne, Joan of Arc, secret societies, the evolution of the English Constitution, and religion in England in the past two centuries; and he did a very free translation of a long German essay on the history of the Rosicrucians and Freemasons. In papers on Ceylon and the opium question with China, he exposed his deeply rooted British imperialism. As a brief appendix to his essay on "The Revolution of Greece," he wrote a stirring account of the history of the Suliotes and their heroic struggle for independence and survival against the overwhelming pressure of the Turks (VII, 319–30).

De Quincey deserves more credit than he has usually received as a chronicler of his own times, for his works abound in vivid, entertaining pictures of contemporary England. The curious turnings of his long life acquainted him with many social levels and with varied scenes, including the estates of royalty and nobility, industrial cities and fashionable resorts, the villages and lanes of Wales and the Lake Country, and the teeming back streets of London and Edinburgh. He was always interested in manners, in questions of status, and in the changes time was working in the English scene. His sensitive, speculative, analytical, and whimsical cast of mind kept him a fascinated observer of life; and his gifts for character portrayal and scene-painting made him a skillful recorder of what he saw.

The most memorable products of his powers for reviving past scenes occur in "The English Mail-Coach," where the spectacular bustle and confusion of the coaches gathering in the city at nightfall, the excitement that greets them as they spread the latest news along their routes, and the fervent rivalries and sudden dangers of coach travel are all vividly recorded forever. Similar memorable scenes surprise the reader again and again in De Quincey's works, some of them historic, like the visit of representatives of the victorious Allies to London in 1814 (III, 60–71) and the final session of the Irish Parliament (I, 219–23); others simply and sharply reveal the manners and attitudes—the conditions of life—in De Quincey's England. He called attention to many subtle changes in daily life, such as the substitution of the word "employer" for "master" and "mistress," and the effect of the proliferation of books in forcing greater selectivity upon the reading public.

His great skill in the reportorial narration of actual events is especially clear in two of the most stirring passages he wrote—the account of the Williams murders of 1811 appended to "On Murder Considered as One of the Fine Arts" (XIII, 70–124) and the story of the deaths of George and Sarah Greene in a Lake Country blizzard while their six small children awaited them in their lonely cottage.[2] Both papers were based on written accounts by others—Dorothy Wordsworth for the former, contemporary newspapers for the latter—but De Quincey skillfully heightened the facts. In both he gradually builds suspense and then sustains it by delaying the climax, thus evoking the utmost horror and pathos from his materials. His imaginative reconstruction of the scenes in all their realistic detail greatly enhances the effects of these narratives. Another sample of De Quincey's skill in the narration of actual events is his moving account of a challenge to a duel mistakenly issued to a lawyer friend of his (III, 165–69).

II *Semi-Fiction*

De Quincey published eight works of fiction and two of semi-fiction (or historical fiction). Most of these were translations or adaptations from foreign works; only one or two were original. Especially worthy of attention are the two works of historical fiction, "The Revolt of the Tartars" (1837) and "The Spanish Military Nun" (1847), both of which were based on foreign originals.

"The Revolt of the Tartars," which De Quincey translated and adapted from a French version of a German work,[3] has generally been regarded as one of his finest pieces, perhaps the best narrative he ever wrote (VII, 368–426). It deals with a historical event, the revolt of a Tartar or Kalmuck nation against Russian rule in 1761; and the flight of the Tartars across Central Asia to the borders of China. This event, as it reached De Quincey in his source, was almost made to order for his imagination and style. The awesome solemnity of such a mass movement of people through such a remote and hostile setting, with all the suffering presumably involved, was like some of the scenes in his own most unforgettable dreams.

In handling this material, De Quincey was somewhat limited by the nature of his source; but he freely heightened and embellished the material to create the effect he wanted. He introduces his account with comparisons to other great migratory ordeals, and then gives a careful description of the intricate conspiracy which leads to the revolt. The Tartar nation involved had migrated less than a century before from China to the banks of the Volga, northwest of the Caspian Sea. But now, as a result of political intrigue and personal rivalries, they are persuaded to gather their flocks, pack their belongings, burn their villages, and flee back toward the East.

An arduous and perilous journey takes them two thousand miles across the deserts, rivers, and frozen steppes of Asia toward China, a horde of about six hundred thousand souls, including over two hundred and fifty thousand women and children. They encounter dreadful hardships and sufferings from heat, cold, famine, and disease, as well as ferocious attacks by the pursuing Russian armies and by hostile tribes. Most of their animals die, and they themselves perish in great numbers. After following their movements through imaginary scenery about half-way on their journey, into the midst of their misfortunes, De Quincey abruptly leaves them and shifts the point of view ahead to the Chinese witnesses of the catastrophic conclusion of their journey.

From the Emperor's hunting lodge on a mountainside overlooking Lake Tengis, one watches as the fleeing Tartars emerge out of an approaching desert dust-cloud. Now in the last stages of famine, thirst, and exhaustion, over half their number having perished, they are being pursued and slaughtered by savage Bashkirs. The Tartars rush into the lake itself to quench their thirst, there to drown or be butchered, until they are finally rescued by the Chinese. One of the most memorable scenes in De Quincey's writings, it is a worthy climax to the entrancing tale. The whole account has a hallucinatory, dreamlike quality; and the prose is swift and majestic. Out of his congenial source material, De Quincey wrought one of his masterpieces.

His other principal semi-fictional narrative, "The Spanish Military Nun" (XIII, 159–237), although it has often been admired and sometimes extravagantly overpraised, is less impressive. It is based closely, and without adequate acknowledgment, on a French summary of a story drawn from the memoirs of a seventeenth-century Spanish nun-adventuress named Catalina.[4] De Quincey's version takes the form of a mock-picaresque novelette, burlesquing the life story of the central character, whom he calls "Kate," "Kitty," and even "Pussy." Although he announces near the outset that he does not find her an interesting person, he refashioned her character completely and proceeded to recount her adventures, including a convent childhood in Spain, a voyage to South America, a shipwreck, a male disguise, a business career, some duels, a military career, a flight across the Andes, a murder over gambling, a rescue from the scaffold, a return to Spain and fame, and a final return to South America and a mysterious disappearance in Vera Cruz. While there are passages of amusing mockery, some entertaining stretches of fanciful narration, and some grand scene-painting, the whole tends to become tiresome because De Quincey makes little effort to maintain narrative illusion, continuity, or proportion; instead, he indulges in grotesque facetiousness, digressions, and mere spinning of words.

III *Fiction*

Few of De Quincey's works in pure fiction are of any interest today. His novel *Klosterheim* (1832), the only original [5] work he first published in book form, can still be read with some interest and amusement; but it suffers from serious weaknesses. Coleridge praised it warmly,[6] but De Quincey himself was not proud of it; he tried to dissuade Fields from republishing it in the American collected edition, and he omitted it from his own collected edition.

Klosterheim is a Gothic romance set in Germany during the Thirty Years' War. Early in the novel there is an extended description of the approach of a huge cavalcade from Vienna through dangerous forests to Klosterheim. This perilous mass movement De Quincey handles well, as in "The Revolt of the Tartars" and in some of his dream fantasies; he even adopts the same structural device he was to use in the former, interrupting his narrative account of the movements of the travelers and shifting his point of observation to the anxiously waiting citizens of Klosterheim, who watch from the walls as the cavalcade finally arrives in panic flight, under attack by the hostile forest outlaws.

From this point on, the story settles into the characteristic pattern of the Gothic novel, with diabolical intrigue, a mysterious masked figure, flight and pursuit down corridors and hidden passageways, ladies in distress, and a surprise ending. While some scenes are well handled, the plot structure is not well articulated; and, while the style is generally careful and elevated, it shows some signs of haste. In De Quincey's canon, *Klosterheim* must be regarded, as he apparently saw it, as a mere potboiler; but it can stand comparison with most of the novels of the Gothic movement, which had already faded by the time *Klosterheim* was published.

Only two other fictional works of De Quincey deserve more than passing mention. "The Household Wreck" (XII, 157–233), a sentimental romance which De Quincey published in 1838, not long after the death of his wife, is his only work of fiction based on contemporary life and the only one, apart from *Klosterheim*, believed to be original. The interest of the story derives mainly from the suspicion that it reflects De Quincey's anguish at the time of his wife's death; and the tale is perhaps tinged with resentment against those who, he may have felt, had treated her cruelly and unjustly, possibly including the Wordsworths. The story is prefaced with a solemn passage, which De Quincey specifically calls rhetorical, on the mutability and tragic suffering that afflict human life. The narrative which follows is introduced as an illustration based on fact. Told in the first person, it begins with an account of the narrator's happy marriage and rises to a climax in an apostrophe to his wife, who is described in tender, affectionate terms that may be thought to represent De Quincey's elegy on his wife Margaret. The story then relates the utter ruin of the family. The work has little merit or interest apart from the possible biographical reference.

Another story, published in the same year, "The Avenger" (XII, 234–85), tells of the systematic, bloody vengeance of a part-Jewish hero on those guilty of cruelty to his family; his revenge is complicated by his love for, and secret marriage to, the grand-daughter of one of his victims. The hero nurses his wife through her final illness, and then soon dies himself. Like "The Household Wreck," this story has been thought to reflect De Quincey's reaction to his wife's death; and it may also bear traces of the recurrent pariah or Wandering Jew theme of his dreams, as well as other psychological symbols of his inner conflicts.[7] However, it seems likely that "The Avenger" derives from some unknown German source; and, in any event, it is hardly an impressive work of art.

The remaining five works of fiction published by De Quincey— "The Fatal Marksman," "The Incognito," "The Dice," "The King of Hayti," and "Mr. Schnackenburger"—are translations (acknowledged or not) from inferior German romance, mystery, and farce, and are completely negligible.

A final estimate of De Quincey as a writer of fiction must find him very limited. Although he had a great gift for the depiction and caricature of actual persons, he had very little skill in the creation of fictional characters. He was capable of effective description, moments of passionate eloquence, and occasional delightful strokes of humor. But in the understanding and mastery of the techniques of fiction, such as the manipulation of point of view, the sustaining of narrative illusion and suspense, the uses of dialogue, and the organic unification of a work in terms of deeply significant theme, he was sadly lacking.

CHAPTER 7

Miscellaneous Works

A MONG De Quincey's multifarious publications are a number
which do not fit comfortably into any of the major categories
already considered. A few of these rank with his more interesting
products, while others, although their interest has faded with the
passage of time, must be mentioned in any comprehensive account of his life's work.

I *Humor*

His two humorous papers entitled "On Murder Considered as
One of the Fine Arts," published nearly thirteen years apart
(1827, 1839; XIII, 9–69), constitute one of his masterpieces and
illustrate a peculiar side of his strange genius better than any
other of his works. A brilliant *tour de force* in sustained irony, "On
Murder" is presented as a connoisseur's lecture in London before
a "Society for the Encouragement of Murder." Although avowing
his disapproval of murder, the speaker insists that one must acknowledge the existence of discrimination and taste in people's
reactions to different murders; and he therefore proceeds to dis-
cuss the subject in terms of its artistic values—"from our art, as
from all the other liberal arts when thoroughly mastered, the result is, to humanise the heart. . . ."

After giving a history of murder since Cain, he emphasizes the
period since the seventeenth century, "The Augustan Age of Murder," when the assassination of philosophers prevailed. He then
analyzes the art of murder, after the fashion of Aristotle's analysis
of tragedy in the *Poetics,* and discusses such elements as the
choice of victim and the method of murder ("Fie on these dealers
in poison, say I: can they not keep to the old honest way of cut-
ting throats, without introducing such abominable innovations
from Italy?"). In defending himself against the charge that his
remarks might encourage murder, the speaker reaffirms his oppo-

sition to it; "For, if once a man indulges himself in murder, very soon he comes to think little of robbing, and from robbing he comes next to drinking and Sabbath-breaking, and from that to incivility and procrastination. Once begin upon this downward path, you never know where you are to stop" (XIII, 56).

The work achieves multiple ironic effects, with its solemn mock-seriousness, its systematic parade of erudition, and its casual, detached treatment of gruesome, horrifying matters. In the contrast between its grisly subject and its cool, pragmatic tone, "On Murder" invites comparison to Swift's "A Modest Proposal." While not so Classic in unity and control as Swift's great piece, it contains strokes of wit as delightful and as horrible. De Quincey himself acknowledged the parallel in his "Postscript" of 1854 (XIII, 70–124), characteristically awarding himself the palm on the ground that his piece has a more universal appeal than Swift's because it is based on a more universal human tendency.

However, although De Quincey's irony is successfully sustained through about fifty pages of his two articles, the wit and humor are not uniformly sophisticated. In the first article there is a passage of crude and strained farce in the description of a fight between a novice murderer and a Munich baker, and the second article degenerates into extravagant and heavy-handed buffoonery concerning a gloomy murder-club member called "Toad-in-the-Hole." Nevertheless, in its peculiarly macabre way, "On Murder" remains one of De Quincey's most original and amusing works, a sort of final fruit of his long, avid, and increasingly humorous interest in sensational murders, which was reflected in the pages of *The Westmorland Gazette* under his editorship, as well as occasionally in his letters and other writings.

Another example of De Quincey's humorous writing is the little paper called "Sortilege and Astrology" (XIII, 251–69), which shows him in his mood of free, relaxed, self-mocking burlesque. This piece contains the amusing description of his ceremonial random selection of a piece for publication from his chaotic bath-tub file, as well as ridiculous anecdotes and playful satire on astrology.

II *Politics and Political Economy*

Politics and political economy engaged De Quincey's mind and his pen intermittently throughout his life. For many years he apparently wrote regular articles on passing political questions for

Blackwood's; these have never been collected and probably never will be. However, nine of his more important works on politics and political economy have been collected and republished, filling most of Volume IX in the standard edition; some of his newspaper writings on the same subject have recently become available;[1] and many passing excursions into these fields can be found in other De Quincey works.

Economics first attracted his attention during his university years, and he studied it further during his early residence in Grasmere. But, when Wilson sent him a copy of Ricardo's *Political Economy and Taxation* in 1818, it roused him, as has been noted, temporarily from deep narcosis and launched him into the study which was to become one of the obsessive enthusiasms of his life. At the outset of his career, he published two articles on Malthus, and his "Dialogues of Three Templars," mainly an exposition and defense of Ricardo's theory of value. He returned to the subject in mid-career, publishing other articles on Adam Smith's and Ricardo's theories; and he gathered some of these and reworked them for his book *The Logic of Political Economy* (1844). The interest survived into his last years, for in 1852 he published an article on the gold rush in California, in which he analyzed the possible effects of the recent discovery of gold on the value of that metal.

While De Quincey's knowledge of political economy was limited to a few of the leading theories of his time, he did develop some expertise. He studied Ricardo closely and became a skillful expositor and an enthusiastic, but not uncritical, partisan of his theories. He also studied Adam Smith, perhaps mainly to be able to argue for the superiority of some of Ricardo's views; and he made Malthus into a sort of *bête noire* for presuming to criticize Ricardo. De Quincey defends Ricardo's theories against Malthus' criticisms, and he counterattacks by assailing Malthus' own logic. De Quincey's writings on political economy offered nothing of remarkable originality, nor did they add up to a comprehensive treatment of the subject, being restricted to the definition of certain basic principles—such as value, rent, and profits—which has long been superseded.

The only interest these works have today is in the insight they offer into his powers of close logical analysis and argument, combined with imaginative resourcefulness in exposition. The deep and enduring impression which his university training in Aristotelian logic had made upon him is nowhere clearer than in the keen, lucid, subtle distinctions and arguments in his works on political economy. His recourse to tables and diagrams reminds one of his love of mathematical precision. At the same time, his wide-ranging ingenuity of illustration leads him at one point in *The Logic of Political Economy,* for example, to compare the exchange values of a rhinoceros, various kinds of horses, *Paradise Lost,* masterpieces of Italian painting, salmon, Croton oil, slaves, and land. These writings are imbued with a fervent, single-minded earnestness that De Quincey seldom exhibited elsewhere.

De Quincey's principal papers on politics and political theory have a little more enduring value. Two of them, written—incongruously—for *Tait's,* a liberal journal, proved to be too conservative to be digestible; and Tait, after publishing a rebuttal to the first, declined to publish the second, which only appeared posthumously (IX, 314–94). These are clear, coherent, vigorous polemical writings. De Quincey's political outlook is of considerable historical interest. Growing up in the era of the Napoleonic wars and in a comfortable bourgeois family, he apparently inherited unquestioningly the patriotic, conservative views of his mother and her friends; but he really gave little thought to politics until he met Wordsworth and Southey in 1807, when he was twenty-two. Their comparatively liberal and irreverent views shook him, and he was soon deeply involved with Wordsworth's ardent concern for the Peninsular Campaign. De Quincey's strong opposition to the French in this first political awakening probably contributed to his lifelong aversion to almost everything French, which only relaxed toward the end of his life.

His main bent remained conservative, sometimes extremely so; but curiously, his reactionary Toryism came to be tempered by the already mentioned progressivism. He developed the notion of progress through the adjustment of social antagonisms, which he found in Kant, into an all-embracing dialectical theory of political history, whereby political progress results from resolution of the tension and conflict between radical and conservative, democratic and aristocratic, revolutionary and reactionary forces. This concept enabled him ultimately to take a much more balanced view of the French Revolution than Wordsworth was able to do. De Quincey acknowledged that France was better and happier, her poor better off, for the Revolution (". . . it *has* succeeded."

XI, 312), but only because the opposition she had met had purged
the Revolution of its evils.[2] The hero of this outcome was Ed-
mund Burke, whose wise opposition had made possible the beneficial middle course. Burke became De Quincey's chief political
model.

De Quincey applied the same dialectical theory to the history of
the Whig and Tory parties in England, seeing them as mutually
dependent, and as gradually producing through their interplay
the English Constitution, "in its kind the noblest work of the human mind working in conjunction with time, and . . . Provi-
dence" (IX, 309). "England owes much of her grandeur to the
depth of the aristocratic element in her social composition, when
pulling against her strong democracy" (XIII, 274). He came to
regard all political change as evil in its process, though potentially
good in its results; and he saw in this paradox an analogy to the
means by which God produces good from the conflict with evil.
Political progress thus meshed in his mind with the providential
redemptive process at work in the world, with the result that he
looked forward with some confidence to the solution of political
problems, the union of Europe, and the reign of peace and brotherhood on earth. The Battle of Waterloo struck him as an apocalyptic event in this process.

Despite his theoretical progressivism, De Quincey remained a
deeply conservative Tory aristocrat in most of his practical opinions, respectful of royalty, rank, and ceremony, fearful and contemptuous of democracy. He ridiculed the Reform Bill: "To have
an eight-thousandth or a ten-thousandth share in the manufactur-
ing one or two legislators is too trivial an honour to be valued . . ." (IX, 345). He also opposed most other reform legisla-
tion of his later years, such as Catholic emancipation and the
secret ballot. He seems to have looked backward to some imaginary lost political paradise in the past.[3] However, he was capable
of ridiculing his own politics, calling himself "the most bigoted of
Tories" and "a specimen of the fossil Tory"; and he surprises his
reader occasionally with incongruously liberal views. He opposed
corporal punishment; he praised Milton and treated the popular
politics of the seventeenth century as patriotic; and, whenever he
touched on the sufferings of the poor, or such unfortunates as
prostitutes and female mine laborers, he showed himself deeply

compassionate and even capable of indignation (*e.g.*, VIII, 299 &
n.).

De Quincey's writings on international politics, apart from the
French Revolution, are better forgotten. His two papers on China
expose utter ignorance of Chinese culture and express blind, jin-
goistic imperialism. He justifies the wars by which England forced
the opium trade on the reluctant Chinese and exacted new concessions from China. De Quincey treats the Chinese as incurably
savage (XIV, 193). The only extenuation one can offer for these
bigoted papers is that De Quincey's son Horace had gone to
China, and had lost his life there. De Quincey also took a stand on
war, as on dueling, which is abhorrent to the modern conscience;
he treats it perversely and even flippantly as inevitable and in
some respects useful and beneficial (VIII, 369–97; XIV, 193). His
intent seems not to have been ironic.

III *Religion*

As for religion, another major preoccupation of De Quincey's
pen, his developmental view of history influenced his position. He
saw the Church of England as the latest product of an evolution-
ary process through which God's revelation was gradually becoming plainer to mankind. As Christianity was far superior to all
other religions, so the Church of England was superior to other
Christian institutions. While this view supported a narrow, insular
dogmatism in his attitudes on comparative religion, it nevertheless
enabled him to take a remarkably liberal stand in his later years in
the developing conflict between science and religion. He spoke out
strongly against the literal intent of Old Testament chronology,
and he repeatedly affirmed that there could be no real hostility
between the Bible and geology or the other developing sciences.
To De Quincey, scientific truth was no part of the purpose of the
Bible or of Christ's mission; and it would have been a distraction
from the spiritual and moral message which was the real burden
(VIII, 35–41; XIV, 312–24).

In addition to his obsessed writings on the Essenes, De Quincey
took part in other religious controversies of his day. He wrote an
essay on "Protestantism," defining and defending the fundamen-
tals of that faith, and rejecting bibliolatry and the doctrine of verbal inspiration as unnecessary adjuncts (VIII, 244–309). In an-

other essay he compared Christianity to various ancient religions in order to show that only Christianity had all the characteristics necessary to become an organ of political movement (VIII, 207–43). At the time of the "Disruption" of the Scottish Church in 1843, he published a rambling and somewhat ill-informed article on the subject for an English audience, tracing the history of religion in the British Isles during the past two centuries and contemptuously opposing the democratic tendency of the secessionists from the Church of Scotland (XIV, 219–62). In an essay on Judas Iscariot he supported the view that Judas did not intend to betray Christ, but only sought to force his hand into the assumption of an earthly kingdom (VIII, 177–206).

De Quincey's love of mystery—his lively sense of the unknown possibilities of experience—is strongly reflected in some of his writings on religion. In his essay "Miracles as Subjects of Testimony," he undertakes a systematic criticism of Hume on the credibility and communicability of miracles (VIII, 156–76); and, in an essay on "Modern Superstition," he takes the position that the very possibility of religion depends upon superstition because it is a disposition toward sympathy with the invisible which tends to evolve into religion as man advances (VIII, 404–51). Among his manuscripts after his death were found many other writings on biblical questions and various religious topics.

IV Philosophy

De Quincey also published some writings in the field of philosophy. During his early manhood he entertained grandiose ambitions to become the philosophical benefactor of mankind (E, 250), and throughout his life he referred to himself with rueful humor as a philosopher. It seems possible that he really had the intellectual capacity for significant philosophical achievements. His love of fine logical distinctions and searching logical analysis left its mark on many of his works. His strongest philosophical interest, probably because of the influence of Wordsworth, Coleridge, and Kant, was in psychology; and it conditioned many of his writings, especially those on critical theory and dreams. Nevertheless, despite his aptitude and interest, De Quincey's philosophical ambitions were thwarted by the weakness of his character, by his strong predisposition to a narrow and conservative religious commitment, and by his Romantic love of mystery and reliance upon feeling. He confessed himself "from my earliest years, a reverential believer in the doctrine of the Trinity, simply because I never attempted to bring all things within the mechanic understanding, and because, like Sir Thomas Browne, my mind almost demanded mysteries in so mysterious a system of relations as those which connect us with another world, . . . and because nature herself, mere physical nature, has mysteries no less profound . . ." (II, 154). His general philosophical position can be inferred from his scattered comments; but, apart from his critical writings, he left no significant original work on philosophy. Nevertheless, his views of other philosophers, his work on Kant, and his essays on various quasi-philosophical subjects have some historical interest.

De Quincey's aversion to Plato and his greater respect for Aristotle have already been noticed. He admired Bacon, although his few comments on Bacon are almost entirely unrelated to his philosophy. He included Hobbes among those he professed to hate, and he was very critical of Locke (in whose work he believed he had detected a fatal error when he was still a boy), mainly because he found Locke and his followers hostile "to all that is unfathomable by the mere discursive understanding" (III, 130). He barely mentioned Spinoza and Descartes, but he seems to have known Leibnitz better. He respected Hume because of his service to Kant, though he found his conclusions uncongenial. As for David Hartley, although De Quincey rejected much of the associational theory, he continued to admire Hartley's main work because of its elaborate theorizing and monumental architectural grace (II, 154).

De Quincey's treatment of Kant is peculiarly uneven.[4] He made large claims and promises for his own work on Kant, and he criticized the work of his predecessors severely. However, he never produced his projected definitive work; instead, he published translations of various minor works of Kant, the largely translated biographical sketch of Kant's last days, one critical essay mainly on Kant, and several briefer critical comments on Kant and his English translators.[5] De Quincey seems to have grasped accurately some of Kant's principal ideas, such as the categories, the forms of perception, and the impossibility of knowledge of the noumenal world, at least in terms of specific understanding; and he appreciated Kant's terminology. No doubt his writings on such matters were of some service in the dissemination of Kant's ideas in England.

On the other hand, De Quincey was apparently confused about some of Kant's doctrines, such as the distinction between "transcendent" and "transcendental"; he left considerable areas of Kant's thought out of account; and he derived utterly unfounded interpretations and impressions from Kant. The deep disillusionment and distress which De Quincey said that his early studies of Kant produced in him—he found Kant's philosophy completely destructive—seem to have resulted from a very incomplete apprehension of Kant's large aims and effects and from a really mistaken judgment of Kant's implications for religion. The strong appeal he felt in many of Kant's views was thus obstructed by his anxious belief that Kant was anti-Christian (II, 155–56). This religious reaction against Kant apparently affected much of De Quincey's subsequent treatment of Kant and his work. In addition to exaggerating the destructiveness of Kant's philosophy, he occasionally wrote contemptuously of Kant's style, assailed some of his ideas, impugned his veracity, and accused him of never having read a book. Nevertheless, the overall impression that De Quincey's treatment of Kant leaves, despite its unevenness, is one of deep respect for both the philosopher and the man.

Several of De Quincey's writings touch on other philosophical and quasi-philosophical questions. For example, in his essay "Casuistry," he defines casuistry as moral discrimination and then offers a series of illustrations of the sorts of problems with which it deals (VIII, 310–68). His essays on dueling, war, and suicide touch on philosophical issues, however perversely at times; and his analysis of superstition in his essay "Modern Superstition" is of some interest (III, 160–96; VIII, 369–451).

V Education

De Quincey published a series of papers on education early in his career, and he returned to the subject for brief comments at various points in subsequent years (X, 9–80; XIV, 9–45). Most of his views were remarkably advanced and progressive for his time, and they are generally sane and at times even wise. In the vagrant epistolary series called "Letters to a Young Man Whose Education Has Been Neglected" (1823; X, 9–80), he deals with educational theory and a number of specific educational questions, along with various other subjects. He seriously questions the value of the lecture system at Oxford. He declares the cornerstones of sound education to be logic, carefully selected languages, particular branches of metaphysics, and mathematics. He questions the value of language study as a discipline because, unlike the sciences, languages are not governed by universal law or system. Instead, they are arbitrary and conventional, and so they tend to deaden the intellect instead of leading it on to new syntheses; unless balanced by more valuable studies, language study "is the dry rot of the human mind." He particularly opposes the study of Greek on the grounds that the labor involved would not be adequately rewarded since most of the values of Greek literature survive in translation. Since he believes that all of Latin literature will probably never be translated, the study of that language is still indispensable. Among modern languages German is most worthy of study because the principal intellectual activity of the era is conducted in that language. De Quincey's questioning of the value of language study is especially remarkable because this was the area of his own greatest aptitudes and attainments.

In a paper published the following year, "Education of Boys in Large Numbers" (XIV, 9–45), a review of Matthew Davenport Hill's account of the Hazelwood School system, De Quincey expressed his hearty approval of the very advanced code of self-government practiced at that school, as well as its policies on the distribution of time, reward and punishment, motivation, and voluntary labor. He also opposed memorization as an educational tool: "Whosoever would show himself a great artist in the profound but as yet infant art of teaching should regard all arbitrary taxes upon the memory with the same superstition that a wise lawgiver should regard the punishment of death" (XIV, 31).

Subsequently, De Quincey touched on education in various papers devoted primarily to other subjects. Despite his doubts mentioned above concerning the general value of Classical studies, he made a systematic defense of them as a specialized study (IV, 172–76). His critical reservations on the education offered at Oxford are counterbalanced by an eloquent passage in his autobiography on the idea of a university and on the unique excellence of Oxford (II, 17–21).

VI *Other Subjects*

De Quincey's great natural aptitude for languages led him to take a lifelong interest in language as a subject of study. He maintained his early mastery of Greek by reading in that language daily throughout much of his life; he also had a fair mastery of Latin, German, and French, together with a smattering of Danish, Italian, and Hebrew. A tireless speculator on etymological and lexicographical questions, he was always pausing in his writings to comment, either directly or in footnotes, on the history or meaning of words. His unsleeping word consciousness—his precise, analytical, and historical sense of the words he is using—tends to foster a similar awareness in his reader. He also devoted a few articles primarily to linguistic matters. Among his earliest publications were an article on the traces of a Danish origin in the Lake-Country dialect (XIII, 373–83) and a note on Anglo-German dictionaries (X, 426–28).

His essay entitled "Language" (X, 246–63) is his most extensive theoretical treatment of the subject, but in "The English Language" (XIV, 146–61) and elsewhere he also touches on theoretical questions. His theory of language is remarkably liberal. He sees language as continuously developing, and he opposes the purists, pointing out that there is no abstract right or wrong in language because "The usage is the rule . . . ," [6] and because colloquial usages often gain general acceptance and greatly enrich the language (I, 196 n.). He predicts the gradual world domination of four languages—English, Spanish, Portuguese, and Russian—and the disappearance of non-literary languages (X, 33); and he also predicts the displacement of all other languages by English (II, 251).

Science was one subject on which De Quincey pretended to no authority; he found much of it distasteful (*E*, 330), and made a joke of his ignorance: "Grosser ignorance than my own in most sections of natural history is not easily imagined. I retreat in panic from a cross-examination upon such themes by a child of five years" (VIII, 298 n.). Nevertheless, a few times in his life he interested himself in scientific questions, and traces of his interests appear in his writings. He gives an amusing account of his and Wilson's theorizing and investigations on the comparative sizes of successive ocean waves (VII, 67 n.). His intimate Glasgow friend

Professor J. P. Nichol, the astronomer, drew his attention to astronomy, although the article he published on the subject characteristically concentrates on the mysteriousness and immensity of space, and the fantasies it inspires (VIII, 7–34). In the same article he returns to the question of the age of the earth, the subject of one of his earlier translations from Kant (XIV, 69–93). His writings on opium show a scientific understanding of the operation of that drug. Some of his psychological speculations and his efforts at precise recording of dreams approach a scientific attitude. He interested himself in the anesthetic properties of chloroform soon after their discovery in 1847; and he wrote a vigorous, informed answer to the religious objections to its use, one which his son Francis appended to his doctor's graduation thesis a little over a year later (XIV, 286–93).

De Quincey wrote a number of single essays on other miscellaneous subjects. These include his historical-critical essay on conversation (X, 265–88), which is mainly interesting for its remarks on Johnson, Burke, and Coleridge; his account of the conditions of travel in modern Greece (VII, 331–67); his comparison of French and English manners (XIV, 327–34); and minor works on a few other scattered subjects which he published as notes or articles or left in manuscript. And, finally, in this survey of De Quincey's almost incredibly varied life output, it should be mentioned that he has some claim to attention as a translator. Indeed, a very large part of his published canon consists of works translated, paraphrased, condensed, summarized, or "De-Quinceyfied" from foreign sources, with or without acknowledgment. His power to render materials of the most unequal merit—through such widely varying techniques of "translation"—into careful and eloquent English prose has seldom, if ever, been equaled.

CHAPTER 8

De Quincey's Style

D E QUINCEY'S own style broadly reflects his various theories of style. As has been seen, he viewed prose style both as an instrument and as an end in itself. Its functions as an instrument were in his view two: to enhance the intelligibility of a subject which is obscure and "to regenerate the normal power and impressiveness of a subject which has become dormant to the sensibilities" (X, 260–61). In subjective writing, he saw style and thought as inseparable. On the other hand, he also regarded style as an art in itself, capable of yielding an independent esthetic pleasure. These notions influenced his own stylistic practice.

I *Variety*

The quality of De Quincey's style which deserves primary emphasis is its variety. He saw clearly that style depends on subject, and the variety of his subjects is almost matched by that of his style. His preeminence in the mastery of certain elaborate, rhetorical effects has tended to obscure the great flexibility and adaptability of his style. He was as capable of crisp, functional exposition as he was of grandly orchestrated rhapsody; he could be gayly, mischievously playful as well as solemnly, passionately sublime. He could also adapt his style to the demands of countless intermediate levels of function and feeling. His prose can sing; it can saunter, march, or run; it can quiver with apprehension, melt with sympathy, or flash with anger. It erects great castles like an exhalation; it exfoliates layers of meaning like a plant. Extended reading of De Quincey leaves one as greatly impressed with the supple, ductile versatility of his style, as of his mind.

Nevertheless, for all this variety, there is, running through his work like an identifying thread, the unmistakeable strand of the man's individuality. There is a sense of great care and poise, of decorum and control, of sensitive fastidiousness in the manage-

ment of even the least effects; and, at the same time, there is the
ease and aplomb of the established virtuoso, who fingers his instrument with a confidence born of great natural gifts and long
study, which have made him the master of all it can perform. The
most characteristic level of the prose is dignified and stately, tending towards elaborateness and formality. De Quincey, always
concerned with clarity and coherence, is never harsh or crude,
never merely flamboyant or bombastic. Few if any writers have
labored more scrupulously and revised more painstakingly than
he. He is ever apologizing for his work because he has had to give
it to the printer's boy before he was satisfied with it, but the signs
of haste and carelessness are seldom discernible to sensibilities less
refined than his.

His greatest claim to stylistic preeminence and originality is in
the elaborate, rhetorical, musical effects of grandeur and magnifi-
cence, mystery and pathos. Here he was trying to break new
ground, to replace the fashionable, pallid correctness and ornate
pomposity of Gibbon and his generation with a fluent and graceful, rhythmic and melodic, eloquent and richly colorful medium
commensurate with man's deepest feelings and loftiest visions. It
has been suggested that De Quincey, together with Wilson and
Landor, accomplished a revolution in prose style comparable to
that of Wordsworth and Coleridge in poetry.[1] Certainly, the most
remarkable and memorable exercise of his powers is found in his
sustained flights toward the sublime, especially in his dream visions and meditations, but also here and there unexpectedly
throughout his works.

But these spectacular achievements should not blind one to his
mastery of other levels of style. The grace and lucidity of his expository, narrative, and descriptive writings on all sorts of subjects
deserve equal notice and respect. He could write as clean, unclut-
tered, and idiomatic prose as anyone in his century when he
wished. The range and propriety of his diction, his fine sense of
balance and parallel, his infinite care in transition, and his finely
discriminating ear for euphony seldom failed to render his prose
luminously clear, pleasantly graceful, and perfectly commensurate
to the demands of his subject.

The sources of De Quincey's style lay primarily in the great
seventeenth-century writers he most admired—Jeremy Taylor, Sir
Thomas Browne, and Milton. Although he took a very negative

view of the great eighteenth-century heirs of the English Cicero-
nian tradition—notably Johnson and Gibbon—and liked to think
of himself as reacting against them, he knew their work well and
was probably influenced by them. An earlier influence, which has
already been mentioned, was perhaps the sermons of Reverend
Hall, his tutor from age eight to eleven and a half; he was forced
to give close attention to these sermons in order to write the
weekly summary which Hall demanded of him. It also seems
quite possible that his close, admiring attention to the prose writings of Wordsworth and Coleridge during his formative years
may have conditioned his practice in some respects; and his adulation of Burke as a rhetorician suggests another possible formative influence. And, finally, his enthusiasm for the work of Jean
Paul Richter may have resulted in some stylistic debt. From each
of these varied models he may have drawn some qualities, but he
soon assimilated them fully since his own authentic voice was already formed in his earliest published writings.

II *Tone and Diction*

The tone of De Quincey's prose is subject to great variation;
although the dominant note is one of dignity, stateliness, and formality, it is often qualified by gentle irony, and he readily ascends
to passion or descends to banter. He often adopts the sophisticated journalist's tone of authoritative, patronizing condescension
and confident dogmatism, even on subjects about which his information is very sketchy; and, in his most polemical mood, he is
capable of fierce pugnacity and withering sarcasm. His belliger-
ence sometimes seems a transparent and half-humorous pose. On
the other hand, his whimsical love of nonsense so seldom sleeps
for long that some critics have asked in despair whether De Quincey is ever thoroughly serious about anything. Occasionally, his
jesting seems offensively inappropriate and tasteless; but this trait
is perhaps excusable as his effort to conform to the practices of
some of his journalistic peers. After all such vicissitudes have been
acknowledged, the residual tone that De Quincey's prose leaves
singing in the inner ear is that of a resourceful, courtly grace and
decorum, capable of sublimely soaring passion and of playful
humor.

De Quincey's vocabulary is immense. His interest in words, his
great natural gifts as a linguist, and his capacious memory gave

him a range of vocabulary exceeded only by that of Shakespeare
and Milton. A beautiful and impressive diction he held to be one
of the chief graces of style (VIII, 91); he used his own vast resources with the utmost discrimination and precision. He liked to
throw in unusual words, often pausing to comment on them in
passing. The ordinary reader of De Quincey encounters many unfamiliar words, especially nouns and adjectives, most of them of
Greek or Latin derivation. At times his diction approaches pedantry, especially in his frequent use of words and phrases from the
Classical languages in the original; but he disarms objections by
often resorting to mock-pedantry, playfully applying lofty and
learned language to commonplace or trivial subjects. For example, in speaking of Wordsworth's one experience of drunkenness at Cambridge, he comments wryly, ". . . he was not too far
gone to attend chapel decorously during the very acme of his ele-
vation" (II, 266); and elsewhere he threatens to take vengeance
on any reader who questions his omissions, "by mere dint of pan-
diculation, vulgarly called yawning . . ." (III, 299). He liked to
use unusual technical, colloquial, dialectical, and foreign words,
tagging them as such by remarking parenthetically, "to speak in
legal phrase," or "speaking Germanicé," "Yankeeishly," "transat-
lanticé," "nautically," or "astrologically." Several of his unusual
words he acknowledges as his own coinage: involutes (as a
noun), passiuncles, orchestric, infibulate, titubate, parvanimity.

It should not be thought from all this, however, that De Quincey's vocabulary is characteristically heavy, polysyllabic, Latinate
or pedantic. Although he specifically defended polysyllabic and
Latinate diction against Anglo-Saxon purists, his own practice was
governed by the rule of appropriateness to the subject; and sample
analyses have shown that the proportion of Latin to Anglo-Saxon
words is not remarkably high in his writing.[2] An impression of
polysyllabic Latinism may be created by the prominence he gives
some such words, through emphatic positioning and other means.
Actually, his diction in most of his work, while it is seldom for
long purely simple and unobtrusive, is on the other hand seldom
merely ponderous or pompous. Within the terms of his individual
manner, it is usually well fitted to its function. There are a number
of words and expressions which recur frequently enough in his
writings to seem somehow representative: "orbicular," "hieroglyphic," "thaumaturgic," "insulated," "systole and diastole,"

"polar opposition," "terraquious," "pariah," "suddenly." It has
been pointed out that in his impassioned prose there are recurrent
key words which reflect his preoccupations in those pieces, such as
"secrecy," "malice," "flight," "pursuit," "panic," "peril," "deliver-
ance," "serenity," and "sleep." [3] In summary, De Quincey's vocabulary is remarkably capacious, his use of it resourceful and
individual, precise and appropriate; his diction carries the stamp
of his dignified and gracious formality and his varied learning.

III   *The Art of Sentence Structure*

It is in the architecture of sentences that some of the greatest
virtuosity of De Quincey's style is to be found. The English sentence was a remarkably versatile instrument in his hands. He acknowledged that the sentence is subject to a complex art in itself
(X, 258), and he devoted infinite pains to the ordering and elabo-
ration of his own sentences. He was always aware of the sentence
as a unit of verbal music, and he arranged and developed it with
as close attention to its cadence as to the precision of its meaning.
He was quick to notice and deprecate limitations in the sentence
art of others, and he particularly ridiculed what he considered the
fatal flaw of German prose style—overstuffed sentences. He opposed inordinate length of sentences because he felt that one of
the two chief secrets of style is in the way sentences modify each
other; and, if they become too long, they lose this power of interplay (X, 259). He also objected to excessive reliance on periodic
structure as a vice of style, although he acknowledged that it is
the form "which a perfect eloquence instinctively seeks" (II, 246),
and he often used it himself.

De Quincey's sentences are seldom of inordinate length; in his
passages of prose poetry they are normally short. His more elaborate sentences are usually so well articulated that they escape
heaviness and obscurity. Short, crisp sentences are frequent; however, simple sentences are not the norm in De Quincey's writing.
He seldom fails to qualify the bare assertion; he delights in building up balanced pyramids of clauses or phrases and in suspending
parenthetical interpolations along the line; but he does so without
losing control or clarity. Some of these magnificent structures are
among the chief glories of his achievement.

Parallelism and parenthetical elements are the most prominent features of his sentence style, both often being boldly developed to the point of luxuriance, in what he called "the pomp of cadence, or sonorous ascent of clauses" (V, 235). Another characteristic trait is inversion, for emphasis and variety. He often begins sentences with emphatic transposed adverbs, followed by inverted subject and verb ("Here also danced the future wife . . . ," "Yet now did I hear . . . ," "Thus easily was healed . . ."). He also often transposes objects of verbs, especially when they are demonstrative or personal pronouns, to a position before subject and verb ("But two things I must add . . . ," "This practice, however, he discontinued . . . ," "*That* I have illustrated . . . ," "Him I led astray, him I beguiled . . ."). Another, occasional inversion is that of adjective and noun ("of expressions careless or ill chosen"). He makes frequent use of colons, semicolons, and dashes to keep the syntax of his sentences clear; and he manages internal transitions with great care.

The principal fault of his sentences tends to be an excess of qualification and parenthetical intrusion, sometimes diluting his thought to the point of tedium or distracting the reader with irrelevancies.[4] He can overstuff sentences as badly as the Germans he condemned for it. Some of his excessive elaborations and his intrusions are humorous, but others are merely tedious and tasteless. In his later years this tendency toward fine-drawn overelaboration and longueur grew worse and adversely affected some of his final revisions of his works.

But even more than in individual sentences, the secret of De Quincey's style lies in the relation between sentences—as he himself pointed out, the two chief factors of style are transition and the mutual modification of successive sentences. The musical phrasing of his prose reaches beyond the individual sentence and embraces extended series of sentences in carefully developed patterns. His parallelisms and antitheses often continue through several successive sentences, or through long antiphonies of questions and answers, even triple and quadruple patterns of repetition, sometimes building incrementally toward a passionate climax (*e.g.*, I, 48–49). He was intensely aware of the flow or interplay between successive sentences, both in meaning and in music, over a long arc. He was scrupulous almost to a fault about transitions between sentences, keeping his connections perfectly clear and perfectly appropriate at all times. It has been estimated that as much as a quarter or a third of his writing on any page is likely to consist of forward and backward connections.[5] He was also pre-ternaturally alert to eliminate any harsh or crude sound patterns in a wide context. At the pinnacles of feeling he often bursts into rhetorical questions, exclamations, or apostrophe ("O, just, subtle, and all-conquering opium!" III, 395). Thus De Quincey's prose tends to be organized into long, multi-sentenced groundswells of meaning and music, which at stormier moments can rise into tidal waves.

This kind of sequential patterning results in some splendid paragraphs. However, the paragraph does not seem to have been a unit of composition to which he habitually devoted careful attention. Sometimes a unit of his rhetoric soars out over several paragraphs, but often it spends itself in less than a paragraph, or begins and ends in mid-paragraph. His irrepressible powers of association interrupted the flow of his thought and sent him off on tangents too readily to permit him to fashion his movement consistently to the pattern of the paragraph. His paragraphs tend, therefore, to be long and to lack form.

IV Architectonics

The total structures of De Quincey's writings are not usually controlled, symmetrical, or economical. He was comparatively uninterested in larger considerations of architectonics. Like his contemporaries, the great English Romantic poets, he disliked submitting his creative impulse to the restraint of a preconceived form. He preferred to give the associative, analogical powers of his mind free rein and to follow wherever they led. As a result, the characteristic structure of his works is expansive, elaborative, and discursive. His rhetoric is often that of amplification; his narration frequently takes longer than the events it recounts.

De Quincey seldom begins by announcing an overall theme. Instead, he usually starts with a peripheral or tangential consideration and then follows a train of chance associations which may lead him either into more central concerns or entirely off the subject. The dam of his erudition keeps springing leaks, and suddenly he has embarked on an account of the etymology of a word he has used, on an extended literary analogy, or on a brief historical dissertation. A strong impulse to teach his audience seems to motivate these excursions. At other times the interpolations are personal anecdotes, or eloquent apostrophes. This excursiveness generally gives the impression of an extremely active mind, seeing qualifications and analogies, and exploring ramifications; occasionally, however, it seems mere verbal flourishing, a tiresome and vagrant word-spinning to fill space and to avoid really coming to grips with a subject. Sometimes he includes digressions within digressions, and adds further associations by way of footnotes, and even footnotes on footnotes. Single digressions often continue for twenty or twenty-five pages, and the supposed subject of the essay is dwarfed or obliterated in the process. When he does announce a systematic plan in advance, he often fails to carry it out in the sequel.

De Quincey was well aware of his own digressiveness. He often indicates his digressions and apologizes for them. He attributes them to the native characteristics of his own mind, "having the advantage of a prodigious memory, and the far greater advantage of a logical instinct for feeling in a moment the secret analogies or parallelisms that connected things else apparently remote . . ." (III, 332). But he was not always apologetic; several times he defended his freely digressive structure on artistic grounds: "Well, but this (you say) is a digression. Why, true; and a digression is often the cream of the article" (*PW*, II, 22); ". . . those wandering musical variations upon the theme, . . . by the eternal interest attached to the *subjects* of these digressions, no matter what were the execution, spread a glory over incidents that for themselves would be—less than nothing." [6] It certainly is true that many of the finest things De Quincey wrote are found in digressions, including such narrative vignettes as his accounts of the seducer of Buttermere (II, 174–84), the drowning woman's life recall (III, 434–36), and the forsaken bride who secluded herself for twenty years (I, 207). The free play he gave to his associative, digressive impulses seems to foreshadow the stream-of-consciousness techniques of Joyce and Woolf; it also seems to relate to his own theoretical support of the elaborate style and his definition of rhetoric as a sort of mind-play. At a few points he even seems to be treating digression with the same self-mocking humor Byron uses in *Don Juan*, for De Quincey no sooner apologizes for one digression than he launches into another.

While there is much to be said in explanation and extenuation of De Quincey's vagrant, associative, digressive structure, one must finally acknowledge that, at its worst, it constitutes his most serious weakness as a writer because it is often utterly destructive of unity and continuity. Many of the digressions are too distractingly irrelevant to their contexts, and many seem merely fussy and pedantic gratuitous information. Their extent is sometimes so great as to overwhelm the supposed subject, and the interruption of the flow of thought can be infuriating. On those rare occasions when he creates the impression that he is merely multiplying words to fill space, he tempts his reader to close the book. Almost any reader will come to feel that he could work some real improvements in many of De Quincey's writings by a little of the judicious editing and rearrangement which the author himself failed to apply.

De Quincey's writings are not, however, invariably diluted with digressions. In a few works, and particularly some in which he was translating or paraphrasing fairly closely from someone else's original, he managed to produce well-knit, unified wholes. And, even when he was digressive, he was not necessarily diffuse since he still usually wrote with pungency and power. As has been noted, one of his greatest skills was in scene-painting; and sometimes successive grand pictures are kaleidoscopically articulated, each being elaborately developed in itself, then abruptly terminated and succeeded by another. There is comparatively little description of nature as such in his work; his natural scenes tend to be vague. His best description deals with man and his feelings, about which he is most precise.

V   *Sound Patterns and Images*

But certainly one of the most important considerations in any study of De Quincey's style is his management of sound and especially of rhythm. His lifelong love of music tuned his ear to the nicest discrimination, and much evidence supports the view that he was as painstaking in the arrangement and modulation of the sound patterns of his prose—and especially of the passages of "impassioned prose"—as he was in fashioning any other of its features. Many hints suggest the hypersensitivity of his ear. He had a horror of crude or excessive alliteration, and usually used such devices only in their subtlest and most subdued forms. He recorded his distaste for such coarsely repetitive sounds as occur in the name "John Donne" or the title *Burke's Works* (II, 313). He once substituted nine words in order to avoid the expression "master-builder" because he could not bear to have two successive trochees ending with the *er* sound.[7] He was always careful to avoid such harsh juxtapositions and crude repetitions of sound.

Nevertheless, through skillful voweling and subtle onomatopoeia, consonance, and such, he usually kept the sound of his prose remarkably in tune with its purpose. Close analysis of those passages in his works which can be called "prose poetry" seems to reveal that their peculiar sonorousness may result in part from a predominance of voiced elements and of semi-vowels.[8] Study of the revisions he made in some of his musical compositions, such as the "Dream-Fugue" in "The English Mail-Coach," when preparing them for republication in the collected edition, reveals the most fastidious manipulation of the sound patterns. The intense concern he felt for the musical movement of such passages probably resulted from the sense he had of some mysterious relationship between "rhythmus," dreams, and passion, and from his conviction that the sustained, rhythmic style is superior to all others. In short, he believed he was attempting an unprecedented achievement in the highest art of which prose is capable.

The secrets of De Quincey's rhythmic art have as yet been only slightly unraveled. Saintsbury held that the rhythm of ninety-five per cent of De Quincey's prose, however carefully controlled it may be, is standard, and that only in the impassioned prose, or prose-poems, such as the "Dream-Fugue" and "Levana and our Ladies of Sorrow," did he create remarkably new rhythmic effects.[9] Efforts at scansion of extended passages reveal comparatively little. The rhythm is highly varied; he seems usually to have avoided regular poetic meter. The rhythmic coefficients seem to be phrases, clauses, and whole sentences, often with incremental variations imparting a sense of rising or falling, or of forward motion, over a long arc of several such elements.

While similar types of metrical feet sometimes recur enough in close context to bring brief passages to the brink of poetic meter, the variations are usually sufficient—and normally the rhythms are subtle and complex enough—to distinguish the movement from ordinary verse meters. Likewise, one can find numerous examples of the three main types of Latin *cursus* and of the native English cadences.[10] However, such analytical devices fail to reveal the governing principles of the rhythms one's ear detects; the

movement is too intricate, varied and elusive, although it can
never be missed. Perhaps it is best not to try to reduce these
rhythms to precise mechanical formula, but to recognize them instead as subtly varied, broadly patterned, and beautifully conso-
nant with their function.

De Quincey's imagery bears out the impression that his prose is
more auditorily than visually oriented. His images are often very
clear and exact, sometimes even to the point of fussiness. They are
also sometimes surprisingly far-flung. Images drawn from music
are very common. Among visual images, those having to do with
motion are most common. Since he so frequently describes objects
or persons in motion, the visual outlines tend to be vague and
blurred. There is also often a suggestion of movement on the part
of the writer or speaker himself, as if there were a turning of the
head or a raising or lowering of the eyes, accompanied by such
exclamations as "Lo!" "Behold!" and "Alas!" [11] Of colors, he is most
likely to mention such rich ones as gold, crimson, and purple. His
similes and metaphors draw most often on animal life, travel
books, literary characters, and technical subjects, in addition to
music and motion.[12] He also makes a great deal of use of personifi-
cation. Finally, literary allusion and quotation are a very common
feature of his writings. His use of foreign words, phrases, and
quotations, especially from the Classical languages and without
translation, creates a problem for the modern reader.

CHAPTER 9

Conclusion

I *Recapitulation: Leading Characteristics*

IT MUST always be remembered that nearly all of De Quincey's writing was done for the periodical press of the early nineteenth century. The young field of periodical journalism was burgeoning under keenly competitive conditions in his day. The journalistic possibilities of sensationalism and combativeness were still being explored. It was widely felt that a magazine article, to be successful, must "have a character"; that is, it must take firm and sometimes novel stances, must be livened with wit or leavened with humor, and must have a personal flavor.

It was to this world that De Quincey brought his teeming intellect and fastidious taste. Certainly he was more learned, and a more serious artist, than most of his colleagues. It became his role to help open a new medium of popular culture, the magazine article on a learned subject, tailored to capture and hold the interest of the general reader. Drawing on the fund of his habitual reading on topics of current scholarly concern and on all sorts of curious, out-of-the-way subjects, he undertook to condense, popularize, and even sensationalize such materials for the magazine consumer. He had anxious editors and a little-known public to keep happy, with few precedents to guide his judgment. The pressures on him to produce were insistent, both from his employers and from his own acute consciousness of his desperate financial needs.

Many of the emergent characteristics of his writing surely resulted from his efforts to adapt himself to the prevailing conditions of this established and developing business. Many of the passages which now strike the reader as tasteless banter, irresponsible polemic, personal calumny, pretentious pseudo-scholarship, or downright plagiarism reflect established practices among *Blackwood's, Tait's,* and their competitors; or they show the pathetic recourses to which the conditions of journalistic work in his time could drive a man of De Quincey's makeup and circumstances. At times he was reduced to pandering directly to ephemeral public tastes. Nevertheless, it must also be remembered that, without these external compulsions, De Quincey might have written very little; and they certainly are also partly responsible for some of the admirable qualities of his work, such as its painstaking clarity. All considered, the wonder is not that his writings contain so many flaws, but that, in spite of being produced under such limiting circumstances, they are so uniformly well written and contain so much of enduring power and delight.

While he embarked on his career as a journalist out of financial need, and with some reluctance, condescension, and even contempt for the trade, as time wore on and it became apparent that this work was to be his for life, he came to take it very seriously indeed, developing a deep sense of responsibility to teach his readers and to cast some new light on whatever he touched. He wrote slowly and carefully, revising and refining endlessly whenever he could. In middle and later life he occasionally betrayed a hope and a faith that some of the works of the major periodicals of his day, to which he had given much of the best of his life's work, would achieve immortality.

Anyone who reads extensively in De Quincey's works is certain to be impressed with the extraordinary range of his interests and knowledge. The central concern of his long life was the love of learning and mind-play. As he himself put it, "from my birth I was made an intellectual creature; and intellectual in the highest sense my pursuits and pleasures have been, even from my schoolboy days" (III, 211). Endowed with one of the superior intellects of his time, he delighted in its exercise. His restless curiosity led him down most of the highways, and into countless obscure byways, of human knowledge. The unlikeliest-seeming subjects could arouse him to extraordinary expenditures of intellectual energy and enthusiasm. He could quickly master the essentials of widely disparate intellectual disciplines, and he enjoyed the mental gymnastics involved in drawing hair-fine logical distinctions, pursuing theoretical chains of causation, and formulating and defending bold generalizations.

It is true that De Quincey often contented himself with brief and superficial encounters with subjects that attracted his attention, contributing little or nothing original to them, but merely condensing or refurbishing the work of others for public consumption. However, the simple fact that he was reading in so many different fields and could summon the energy, under the stimulus of poverty, to harvest so much from them in his careful and graceful prose writings is in itself impressive. His most distinguishing characteristic is an omnivorous love of ideas, which is often contagious to his readers. Following in his traces through the many volumes of his varied works, one is always aware of an unusual mind at work. His retentive memory gave him a vast fund of information to draw on, and his special gift for seeing connections and analogies kept it all at his fingertips. Many of the subjects which engaged his interest are still interesting today; and, on some of the more ephemeral subjects he dealt with, there is still some fascination in observing the way his mercurial mind operated.

The psychological bent of his interests comes as close as anything else to constituting a central focus for his diverse works. His friend John Wilson had seen this in him as early as 1830, when he quoted his "English Opium-Eater," a character modeled on De Quincey in *Noctes Ambrosianae,* as saying, "My chief, almost my sole study, is of the laws of mind, as I behold them in operation in myself, and in the species." [1] De Quincey tended, whenever possible, to adopt a psychological perspective on his subject. He shared the interest of many of his contemporaries in the analysis and description of mental powers. Like Wordsworth and Coleridge, he was committed to a depreciation of the unaided understanding, and to an adumbration and exaltation of the subliminal and transcendent powers of the mind. His critical theory and practice were conceived primarily in psychological terms.

Perhaps above all else De Quincey was interested in the dark thresholds of the human mind—in fancies, dreams, visions, and all the mysterious intimations of man's inner life. He believed that some of man's most important powers are to be found in dreams, in the occult, and in the "understanding heart." His intense interest in dreams, visions, reveries, artistic inspirations, human eccentricity, madness, and all the effects of opium was no idle curiosity; instead, it was an expression of his conviction that at the dim periphery of mental life could be found the best clues to reality and value. Perhaps even more clearly than Wordsworth and

Coleridge he developed a theory of the unconscious mind which anticipated later formulations; and, as has been noted, he constructed an elaborate theory of dreams to support his conviction of their supernal significance. He also developed a prose instrument commensurate as none before to the re-creation of the strange, intense, and mobile world of dreams and fantasies, with their weird distortions of time, space, and sequence. In the literary projection of that world he broke new ground and left works of unique power.

Much has always been made of the curious combination in De Quincey of the dreamer and the logician. It is true that his youthful training in logic left permanent traces on his work. The careful lucidity of his prose, the dialectical keenness of his analysis, and the enthusiasm he shows for casuistry and logical posers—all bear witness to this characteristic. His sense of logical discipline often conditioned his treatment of his subject. It led him to some fresh insights and sound judgments which might otherwise have been impossible to him; and it occasionally restrained his vagrant, passionate, and fanciful impulses in salutary ways.

However, De Quincey's powers and accomplishments as a logician must not be overestimated. The most characteristic movements of his mind were nonlogical—the sudden leap of free association, the release and fascinated observation of pure feeling and fancy, and the love of everything curious and mysterious. His applications of logic—often superficial, half-playful, or perverse—are as likely to lead him into tiresomeness or absurdity as to guide him to truths. The essential De Quincey is not the logician but the fastidious artist of precise, elaborate, and sometimes eloquent prose; the man of curious intellect, ready humor, and sympathetic interest in everything human; and the uniquely active dreamer and fantast with a lay psychologist's interest in his own dreams and fantasies.

His works, whatever other faults they may have, are seldom devoid of human interest. He was no dry-as-dust pedant withering his years away in a garret. Family life, the pressure of affairs, and his pedestrian habits kept drawing him out of his study. His observations and analysis of the human life around him were extraordinarily sharp; his human sympathies, wide. His imagination could also project him into the situations of the characters—real and imaginary, from all periods—whom he encountered in his reading. His delight in human eccentricities and in amusing and revealing gossip and anecdote combined with his bold and sometimes mischievous candor to fill his works with a uniquely living panorama of a social era and its intellectual concerns.

And the most interesting presence in this scene is finally his own. De Quincey probably never fully realized that his own true subject—and what was to be his chief claim on the regard of future readers—was himself. From his first important published work, the *Confessions,* through the autobiographical reminiscences of his middle period, to the remarkable dream fantasies recorded in his sixties, De Quincey wrote a great deal about himself—more than Rousseau. The self-portrait that gradually emerges from his writings—directly from the autobiographical works and indirectly from the tenor of his other works—is his most engaging and durable creation. The comedies and tragedies of his childhood; the mysterious upheavals of his youth; his long encounter with opium; the tumult and glory of his dream visions; his relations with the strange and famous people he came to know; his turbulent family and professional life; and his lively and erratic responses to a lifetime of reading and observation—all this he recorded, some with unexampled frankness and some with curious reticence, some with mocking humor and some with melodramatic pathos. The record is scattered and fragmentary, but it adds up to one of the most absorbing human portraits that English literature affords.

Despite his intermittent polemical asperity and occasionally heartless-seeming exposures of human frailties, De Quincey's dominant attitude finally seems to be a kind, compassionate tolerance that is based on a rueful recognition of life's mystery and harshness, and man's pathetic fallibility. In his broad and affectionate tolerance of life, if in little else, he might be said to resemble Chaucer. This acceptance is the deepest and most endearing level of his humor. His sympathy with poverty and suffering, with everyone wretched or injured, was quick. He sought to bring everything human—however eccentric, perverse, or ostracized—back within the pale of his readers' consciousness and concern. Conversely, he sought to deflate the inhumanly pompous or pretentious with dexterous applications of his prickly wit.

His humor appears in much more than the gentle underlying amusement at the *comédie humaine* and the taste for eccentrics. It also takes the forms of scholarly anecdote and inkhorn wit,

learned caricature and mock-heroic, adroit stabs of satire, off-beat
drollery reminiscent of Burton or Sterne, grave whimsy and gentle
irony, puns, gay *jeux d'esprit*, burlesque, and extravagant foolery.
He often drew upon Joe Miller's jests (*e.g.*, VI, 140), and he
openly confessed his incorrigible love of nonsense (XIV, 304). He
took an irreverent delight in exposing the ridiculous in solemn or
pretentious persons, and he could often find grounds for laughter
in subjects customarily treated with gravity. The most disarming
characteristic of his humor is that its favorite target is himself.

A balanced estimate of De Quincey's work must also take account of its flaws and limitations. The weaknesses of his character
and the harassed circumstances in which he did much of his writing left their marks on his work. His scholarship is erratic and
unreliable; he is often inaccurate in fact and quotation; he is given
to hasty, extreme, and aberrant judgments; he sometimes stub-
bornly pushes questionable theses much too far; and his outlook is
often insular and prejudiced. He is repeatedly guilty of plagiarism, or something approaching it.

The absence of formal restraint and control is the most notice-
able fault of De Quincey's manner. Most of his writings lack unity
and proportion, and much that they include seems irrelevant or
inconsistent, while their coverage of their supposed subjects
often seems incomplete. At his worst, he is guilty of aimless wandering, chattering prolixity, and tedious verboseness that weary
and anger his reader.

His tone occasionally becomes offensively inappropriate. Even
when he is ill-informed or in error, he often adopts a condescending, patronizing tone, glibly dogmatic or pedantic, pretending to
much more knowledge and authority than he really has, but disarming his reader by his cocksure arrogance, bluffing with confident assertion. His often laudable independence of outlook can be
carried to the point of truculence, impudent effrontery, and tasteless flippancy. His candid revelations about his friends and acquaintances sometimes overstep the bounds of good taste, and approach calloused malice. His humor can be forced, tiresome, or
grotesquely incongruous with its context. At the opposite extreme,
his tone sometimes offends by an excessively solemn sanctimoni-
ousness or an effusive sentimentality.

De Quincey often had a great deal of insight into his own
weaknesses, criticizing and ridiculing himself for them, although

he seems to have been powerless to correct them. The characteristic flaws of his writings are often the by-products of their excellences, or they can be attributed to the conditions under which he was forced to write. The extent to which they may seem to undercut his solid virtues, and to invalidate sectors of his work, varies from reader to reader. But, when all necessary concessions have been made, a substantial body of unique, varied, and artful prose remains to challenge, inform, and delight.

II *Reputation and Influence*

De Quincey's reputation has been subject to various distortions and vicissitudes; nevertheless, his work has occasionally exerted important influences on other writers. The passing of some of the journalistic fashions he served has inevitably diminished some of his earlier eminence. Various misconceptions of the man and the writer, some of which he fostered himself, have long placed him in a false light. However, in recent decades a succession of scholarly studies of his life, his thought, his criticism, his sources, and the effects that opium had on him have begun to dispel the myths that have always clung to him; and his reputation is being reconstituted on firmer ground.

For the most persistent misconception of De Quincey—that of "the Opium-Eater"—he was himself partly responsible. In that guise he first burst upon the public consciousness with the publication of the *Confessions* at the outset of his active career. Nothing he ever published afterwards created a comparable sensation. There were at least seven English and four American editions during his lifetime, and a French version was published by Alfred de Musset in 1828. Certainly some of this interest was aroused by the title of the work and by its suggestion, however inaccurate, of lurid revelations about forbidden pleasures.

De Quincey was shrewd and needy enough to exploit this notoriety. He held forth the promise of revelations to come; he adopted "the English Opium-Eater" as a *nom de plume;* and he returned to the subject of opium and its effects at later stages of his career. While he did not attribute his famous dream visions exclusively to opium, he let them seem to have resulted in part from the effects of the drug. Since much of his writing on other subjects was anonymous, he became known primarily as a writer on the effects of narcotic addiction, and as one whose own erratic and fanciful writings best illustrated those effects. Thus developed the myth of the drug-soaked genius, whose soaring imagination, magniloquent style, and weird imagery were all the products of opium intoxication.

After De Quincey's death, the *Confessions* continued to govern his reputation; it went through countless editions, with only occasional intervals of a few years, and was often translated. Since there was little systematic study of narcotics until long after his death, De Quincey's account assumed an authoritative status and actually dominated the scientific and public views of the effects of opium for several generations. No doubt it continues to influence the folklore about the drug even today. As a result, the general public and many critics have often assumed that opium is sufficient to account for everything noteworthy about De Quincey.

De Quincey's ecstatic celebration of the pleasures and medicinal virtues of opium, his defense of the drug against various misconceptions, and the brevity and cursoriness of his treatment of the pains of opium did have one unfortunate side effect—that of encouraging many of his readers to try it for themselves, with the frequent result of addiction. Among those known to have been so influenced are the poet Francis Thompson and the writer William Blair.[2] Patrick Branwell Brontë may also have been partly led to opium by De Quincey.[3] Medical records show many other traces of De Quincey's influence on addicts.[4] As the evils of addiction became better known a generation or two after the publication of the *Confessions,* and as the Victorian moral bias consequently turned the force of disapproval on the use of opium, De Quincey came in for reprobation as a dissolute voluptuary whose work was tainted by the poison of the drug and of the alcohol in which he dissolved it. The fact that De Quincey came to be admired in rebellious avant-garde circles in France and subsequently in England probably enhanced this moral obloquy. The fear of De Quincey's works as insidiously corrupting survived into the twentieth century.[5]

This long domination of De Quincey's reputation by the myth of "the Opium-Eater" caused a distorted conception of the man and his work. It tended to obscure the fact that the vast majority of his works had nothing to do with opium and were virtually untouched by the opium habit. Protests were voiced as early as the turn of the century, but only recently has growing scientific knowledge of the effects of opium begun really to dispel the myth. It is now recognized that opium does not cause dreams or give them a special character, that it gives pleasure only to psychopaths, that many of the ills opium was thought to cure were actually withdrawal symptoms of the drug itself, and that it does not intrinsically alter human character. As a result, a leading scholar of the literary effects of opium has said of De Quincey: "Neither his character nor the direction of his life can have been greatly altered by drugs." [6] This new assessment of the effects of opium on De Quincey has done much to restore balance to the critical evaluation of his works.

In the meantime, other conditions had affected De Quincey's reputation in very different ways. His gossipy and revealing articles on his famous friends and acquaintances in *Tait's* in the 1830's and 1840's were signed and appear to have created a strong impression among the literary circles that saw them. However, the mixed feelings they generally aroused probably kept them from greatly enhancing De Quincey's reputation. Since the last thirty years of his life were spent almost exclusively in Scotland, he gradually dropped out of public awareness in England; and his solitary, elusive way of life in Edinburgh also obscured him from public notice there, with the result that he was largely forgotten by the time of his death. In short, it appears that De Quincey was generally underestimated by his contemporaries; and what reputation he had was based on a very limited knowledge of his work. However, the publication of the collected editions toward the end of his life reawakened interest in his work; both the American and the Edinburgh editions were reissued several times, as was also the standard edition of Masson, which first appeared in 1889–90.

After the collected editions began to appear, the impressive range of De Quincey's work first became fully known; and another distorting image which he had to some extent cultivated during his lifetime—that of the scholar of universal knowledge, or the "polyhistor"—gained wide currency. De Quincey had felt no scruples against pretending to a great deal more knowledge than he really had on some of the subjects he wrote about. He was skillful at concocting articles out of translations and condensations of works he had encountered in his erratic reading, and he often published these without adequate acknowledgment of his debt. On the contrary, his versions were commonly presented in a con-

fident, even condescending tone which suggested that they were
mere trifling by-products of a profound and capacious scholarship
which was in full command of the subject; and he often promised
fuller treatment in subsequent works, which, however, usually
never appeared. He knew how to create an illusion of scholarly
authority, precision, and originality; but often he really knew little
or nothing more about his subject than he had learned from the
work or two he was drawing on.

Nevertheless, the ruse worked, and his magazine-reading public, and most of the later readers of his works in the collected
editions and elsewhere, accepted reverentially the image he
projected of the polyhistor—Classicist, philosopher, critical theoretician, and historian—precise and profound in his scholarship,
informed and original in his criticism and philosophy. Not until
recent times have qualified scholars examined his scholarship—his
thought, his criticism, and the relation of his writings to their
sources—closely enough to discover his limitations. It has now
been revealed that he was frequently careless of factual accuracy,
his thought was generally derivative and often muddled, and he
was heavily dependent on limited sources—with or without acknowledgment—for as much as sixty per cent of his published
work.[7] The myth of the polyhistor has largely been dispelled.

Victorian criticism in general treated De Quincey in accordance
with the spirit of the age. Most of the early critics tended to emphasize and praise his wit and humor as a principal merit, which
suggests that it was largely in tune with the age when he wrote it.
However, there were a few dissenting voices; and gradually, as
tastes in humor changed, a chorus of critics found his humor shallow, forced, and tasteless.

De Quincey's style also had an important influence on his reputation. The development of taste in literary style in Victorian England brought his reputation as a stylist to a pinnacle in the era of
Ruskin's prominence. Subsequently, however, as plainer, more
utilitarian prose displaced the elaborate style, a reaction set in;
and De Quincey came to be viewed as too florid and rhetorical,
artificial and hollow. Among Victorian authors on whom De
Quincey is known—or has been thought—to have exerted influence are Carlyle, the Brontës, Dickens, Ruskin, Thomson, Steven-
son, Wilde, and Shaw. John Stuart Mill praised his writings on
political economy and some of his examples. More recently, D. H.

Lawrence found De Quincey endlessly fascinating; and George Saintsbury, Virginia Woolf, and Dylan Thomas acknowledged his influence. De Quincey's merits as a stylist have been partially restored to the credit they deserve.

On the other hand, there was always some strong, vocal opposition to De Quincey. Some critics found him wanting in moral ballast and seriousness of purpose. In 1868 J. H. Stirling, who assailed De Quincey's treatment of Kant, raised serious doubts about the value and substance of his work in general.[8] In 1874 and subsequently, Leslie Stephen published very influential and unsympathetic judgments. Stephen, who found him a "sluggard" and "effeminate," charged him with "an utter want of moral strength." [9] Henley's damning epithet "Thomas De Sawdust" is well known. By the end of the century De Quincey's fortunes seem to have sunk to a low ebb, from which they have only partially recovered in the last thirty years.

In the meantime, curiously, De Quincey sometimes had a greater impact abroad than in England. It was in America that the idea of a collected edition of his works was first conceived. Apparently for a time De Quincey was all the rage among some American readers. He received adoring letters from American admirers, children were named after him, and American travelers sought him out in Edinburgh. Hawthorne, who was a close and admiring reader of his works, found him much more justly appreciated in America than in England.[10] It has been suggested that the works of Poe and Melville may bear traces of his influence.

De Quincey seems to have had an especially important influence on French Romantic literature. In 1828, when Alfred de Musset was only eighteen, he published his *L'Anglais Mangeur d'Opium,* a very free translation or adaptation of De Quincey's *Confessions;* among other basic changes, it converted the protagonist into a coarse sensualist. Although de Musset's version was not widely known, it exerted a strong influence in French creative circles. It was the inspiration for Berlioz' *Symphonie Fantastique* and may have influenced Gerard de Nerval's *La Rêve et la Vie.* It was read and admired by Balzac and left clear traces on several of his works, perhaps also conditioning his artistic outlook in important ways.[11] Gautier and other French Romantics probably knew the de Musset edition and were influenced by it. Indeed, the whole movement of visionary poetry in French Romanticism may have received added impetus. It has also been suggested that Flaubert felt the influence of De Quincey.[12]

But De Quincey's most important influence in France was on Baudelaire,[13] who became a passionate admirer of De Quincey for the rest of his life. Baudelaire read the *Confessions* in the original English, and he apparently also knew de Musset's version. His discovery of De Quincey came in his early manhood, and his reading probably encouraged him in his own experiments with opium and hashish. But more importantly, it affected his whole emotional and esthetic orientation—his penchant for the dreamy and melancholy, his mysterious feeling for eternity in time, his preoccupation with the miseries and psychological curiosities of city life, and his style. Many of his works bear specific or general traces of De Quincey's influence. In *Les Paradis Artificiels Opium et Haschisch* (1860), he included a translation of the *Confessions*— "ce merveilleux livre"—and some of the *Suspiria*, skillfully abridged and interspersed with his own comments, showing a remarkable sympathetic responsiveness and critical discrimination. Since French Symbolism and Surrealism derived in part from writers influenced by De Quincey, and since twentieth-century English and American literature was deeply influenced by these French movements, it is possible to argue that De Quincey's greatest surviving effects on his own literary tradition have been created, indirectly, through the French.

There have been other translations of the *Confessions* and of others of De Quincey's works as well into French. German and Italian versions of the *Confessions* appeared in the 1880's. It has even been suggested that De Quincey's influence may have reached Russia and left traces in the works of Gogol and Dostoyevsky.

The question of De Quincey's place in literary history has occasioned some doubts. His time of birth relates him to the middle generation of English Romantic writers: he was a close contemporary of Leigh Hunt, John Wilson, Thomas Love Peacock, and Lord Byron. However, in certain respects he has seemed not to fit comfortably into the Romantic Age in which he lived. His love of precise and systematic logic, his political and religious conservatism, his lack of concern with theories about Nature, and his absorption in Classical studies seem to set him apart from most of the leading Romantics and to relate him to seventeenth- and eighteenth-century intellectual climates. On the other hand, the traces of decadent Romanticism, moralistic criticism, bourgeois domestic genre-painting, John-Bull jingoism, and decorous reserve relate him to the Victorian Age, which embraced the latter and more productive part of his life.[14]

However, a comprehensive survey of De Quincey's characteristics shows that his closest affinity is still with the Romantics, despite his divergences. The ultimate recourse of his thought is to feeling, and the sense of mystery dominates his impulse toward precise and ordered knowledge. He shared the psychological interest of the Romantics and their preoccupation with the occult and transcendent powers of the human mind. He had a strong intuition of timelessness, and he explored its relation to the worlds of dreams and fantasy. He reveled in the weird, the strange, and the exotic. He valued solitude and self-knowledge highly; and he felt a passionate concern for children, abandoned and bereft women, and outcasts. He took an optimistic view of human nature and held out utopian hopes for the future. In his criticism he placed a greater stress on thought and feeling in art than on form. All these factors relate him to his contemporary Romantics, and in their company he should be allowed to remain.

III *De Quincey Today*

Although before the 1930's De Quincey was subject to little close scholarly study and his reputation was beclouded by myths, since that time the record has largely been set straight in a series of careful critical investigations and evaluations. The principal facts of his life have been ascertained and interpreted in a succession of excellent biographies; his philosophical and critical thought has been analyzed and assessed; and the uses he made of his source material have been clarified. The result has been the emergence of a different and more authentic understanding of De Quincey and a sounder appraisal of his literary stature.

One point upon which most of the leading students of De Quincey in recent years are agreed is that nothing simple or obvious about De Quincey is true. He was a complex, subtle, and elusive man who interposed varied masks between himself and his reader. The people who met him or sought him out and recorded their impressions, seldom penetrated far beyond the outer defenses of his shyness and reticence. Thus De Quincey will always remain to some extent a mysterious stranger. Likewise, his works are so extremely varied and uneven that they resist reduction to formula. But a few major shifts and clarifications of judgment have gradually brought him into truer focus.

It is now recognized that opium is of minor importance to his achievement. Little or nothing that he wrote was much affected by his addiction, and his account of the operation of the drug, fascinating though it remains, has been superseded by more scientific studies and must be qualified by an awareness that much which De Quincey attributes to opium is really due to the prior and independent condition of his own mind and character.

Another major change has taken place in the comparative valuation of the different classes of De Quincey's works. A majority of his published writings have now come to be viewed as more or less skillful pieces of journalistic patchwork—condensations, redactions, and translations based on whatever limited materials were available at the time. He was much less capable of independent scholarly and creative production than he has long seemed to have been. Instead, he was most freely productive when he had someone else's work to provide him with a stimulus or a framework. He deserves some credit as a translator, and as an adapter of other men's scholarship to journalistic presentation. Some of his more thorough assimilations and thoughtful transformations of source materials are among his finest works and merit consideration as original works of art. On the other hand, he sometimes did violence to his borrowed materials in an effort to make them seem novel and original. He also occasionally worked hastily or from inadequate sources, with inferior results, and he sometimes merely copied or translated directly, without acknowledging the extent of his indebtedness. In sum, in that large sector of his work in which he was drawing upon source materials, he appears no longer as a deeply learned scholar-essayist but as a gifted and eccentric gentleman-scholar turned opportunistic journalist, generating sporadic and uneven magazine articles from the fruits of his past studies and his current reading.

One hesitates to dismiss any group of De Quincey's writings lightly, with a pat generalization, because many of the rifts in his duller, thinner, or more derivative writings are loaded with true De Quinceyan ore. Suddenly his prose takes the wings of passion or fancy, or he launches out into a curious anecdote or an absorbing digression, which seems amply to repay one's patience. Nevertheless, a few general judgments seem warranted.

De Quincey's philosophical and historical writings now appear less important than they were formerly thought to be. While he performed some service to the English-speaking world by calling attention to the recent developments in German philosophy and by educating the magazine-reading public to the history of philosophy and to emergent ideas, his philosophical scholarship was sketchy; and he contributed little or nothing of importance that was new to the development of philosophy. His historical writings are largely derivative and often biased, but some of them remain interesting for their special emphasis or for magnificent scene-paintings. Several of his finest passages are to be found in reportorial chronicling of recent events and current scenes.

As a critic, De Quincey has undergone some diminution of prestige. His theoretical efforts do not prove to be thoroughly clear and consistent, nor are his ideas systematic or original. However, he threw some new light on past and current doctrines; and his position is historically significant. In practical criticism he is often more effective, capable of illuminating and original insights, remarkable summations, and independent judgments. But he cannot always be relied upon because he is erratic and prejudiced.

In semi-fictional narrative he achieved a few fine successes, but his pure fiction is largely translation from inferior originals and is almost totally negligible. Most of his works on politics, economics, education, science, and religion were mainly topical and ephemeral; they retain some historical interest, and in occasional passages of general reflection or stirring eloquence they still live as literature; but, in general, they have lost their relevance.

It is finally on his most original writings that De Quincey's enduring appeal and his claims to greatness must chiefly depend. Despite the occasional solid virtues and brilliant flashes of his derivative works, the one-third or two-fifths of his published writings which arose out of his recollections of his own experience and his firsthand observations of other people contain the highest percentage of what is living literature in De Quincey's canon. His autobiographical sketches, including the *Confessions* and many of the *Suspiria,* his London and Lake reminiscences, his various accounts of persons he knew, and the many passages of autobiography and self-revelation which are scattered widely among his

works—these are the true grain which has best survived the winnowing of time and scholarship. Unfortunately, even these works
remain fragmented as well as flawed with distracting or tiresome
digressions. Nevertheless, the De Quincey who emerges from
them is a fascinating human being—a man of restless intellectual
curiosity and energy, of keenly discriminating logical faculty, of
soaring imagination, of elfin and wayward humor, and of infi-
nitely painstaking artistry. Somehow, after extended reading of
his works, one develops a sense of intimacy with him, and perhaps
even respect and affection for him despite all his faults. At the
very least, one must acknowledge the sporadic power and the historical significance of his genius.

Like his great Romantic contemporaries, he was able to shift
the values of ordinary experience, to charge familiar things with
fresh emphasis. He could dissolve the events of his childhood in
dreamy mistiness and compassionate irony. He could bring individual characters or mass movements to life in brilliantly elaborated sketches and panoramas. And he developed a prose instrument commensurate with the weird and gorgeous pageantry of the
subconscious mind, opening up unsuspected poetic possibilities in
a prose style ideally suited for the purpose. One thing the reader
of De Quincey can be sure to find almost anywhere, on any page
of his writings, is excellent prose; for in the sensitive grasp and
artful manipulation of the English language De Quincey has had
few peers among prose writers.

In conclusion, it seems clear that De Quincey deserves an hon-
ored place in the second or third rank of English Romantic authors. A full appreciation of his work requires a love of mind-play
for its own sake and a responsiveness to the more stately, elaborate, and elevated effects possible to English prose. He is best in
individual passages scattered unpredictably throughout his works.
He should preferably be read in a leisurely, browsing manner
which seeks out and savors these passages. Perhaps the hurried
pressures of contemporary life, and the impatience with any prose
that aspires above the simple, colloquial, and utilitarian, militate
against the enjoyment of writers like De Quincey. Perhaps also he
left too few works which are unflawed by digressions, verboseness, or minor lapses of taste ever to win the unqualified admiration his better moments seem to demand.

No doubt there will always be patient, thoughtful readers who can meet De Quincey on his own ground. His works offer enough varied rewards of insight and delight to ensure him a continuing audience of such readers. For a wider public, the best hope for De Quincey—although it seems heresy to suggest it in this age of scrupulous fidelity to authentic texts—lies in new selective editions in which the best of his work is preserved and in which the more dispensable digressions and dross are excised—in short, volumes which supply some of the editorial discretion, the sense of formal restraint, and the artistic economy which one unfortunately seeks in vain in this otherwise marvelously gifted and enjoyable writer.

Notes and References

Chapter One

1. There is a curious confusion in the evidence on the relative ages and the order of birth of De Quincey and his sisters. It is customary among De Quincey's biographers to speak of him as the second son and fifth child of his parents, following his own account (I, 29 n.). The eldest child was his first brother, William, probably born in 1781 or early 1782. He was baptized March 1, 1782; and it was customary in that period for a child to be baptized within a month of birth. (However, De Quincey calls him "older than myself by more than five years," an age which would place his birth some months before the marriage of the parents, which took place in November, 1780. De Quincey is not a reliable witness on dates and ages.)

Next, we are told, came three sisters, Elizabeth, Jane, and Mary, in that order, followed by Thomas. De Quincey speaks of Jane as two years his senior (I, 33); however, the family memorial gravestone in St. Anne's Churchyard, Manchester, gives her dates as 1786–1790, which leads some scholars (Masson and Sackville-West) to assume that De Quincey was mistaken and that Jane was actually his younger sister. If so, this would make him the fourth child, a fact which they fail to notice. The fact that Jane was baptized a year after Thomas, on September 18, 1786, seems to confirm this order.

Horace A. Eaton (*Thomas De Quincey* [New York, 1936], hereafter referred to as *E* in the text), a principal authority on the facts of De Quincey's life, is extremely confused and confusing on this matter. He gives two different dates for Jane's death, 1786 (8) and 1790 (13), and also quotes the gravestone birth date without noticing that this would make her younger than Thomas (17 n.). Further obscuring the issue, he says (13 & n.) that Jane was eleven months older than Thomas, "Not 'about two years older' as he wrote," here apparently confusing Jane with Mary, who De Quincey said was eleven months his senior (III, 310). Eaton treats Mary as older than Thomas on p. 8, but calls her younger on pp. 35 and 36. Further complicating the evidence, W. C. B. Eatwell calls Jane the eldest sister, and Elizabeth the second sister (in A. H. Japp, *Thomas De Quincey* [London, 1877], II, 311), but this must be an error.

2. De Quincey's tombstone incorrectly assigns his birth to Greenhay, which had not yet been built at the time.

3. Here and throughout, such parenthetical references are to *The Collected Writings of Thomas De Quincey*, ed. David Masson (Edinburgh, 1889–90), 14 vols.

4. *De Quincey Memorials*, ed. A. H. Japp (London, 1891), I, 10.

5. Thomas spelled the "De" both with a capital and with a small letter, but custom has established the capital letter as the standard spelling.

6. De Quincey says (I, 114) that William died during his sixteenth year. Presuming that William was born in 1781 or 1782, this would place his death about 1797, when Thomas was eleven or twelve. Edward Sackville-West (*Thomas De Quincey: His Life and Work* [New Haven, Conn., 1936], 13 n.) says William probably died at age eighteen; but he does not present evidence.

7. Printed in Eaton, pp. 35–36. De Quincey's letters have never been published in a collected edition. Many of them can be found in the principal biographies, and in partial collections, listed in the bibliography below. While he was not a regular or a distinguished letter writer, many of his letters are important; and some are delightful.

8. Reproduced by Masson in *The Collected Writings*, XIV, 368.

9. *A Diary of Thomas De Quincey: 1803*, ed. Horace A. Eaton (London, 1927), p. 219 n. (Hereafter referred to as *Diary*.)

10. This curious episode has proved unconvincing to one of De Quincey's biographers, Sackville-West, who presents elaborate, if finally inconclusive, arguments to support his hypothesis that De Quincey failed to return the draft and that his later fear of the consequences was what made him endure his sufferings in London, instead of returning home. One of his seven arguments seems to be based on a misinterpretation of De Quincey's statement (III, 319) that he had to pay one hundred and fifty pounds on coming of age; Sackville-West says (pp. 39–40) that De Quincey had to pay this amount "on account of the affair," referring to the affair of the forty-guinea note; but it seems clear that De Quincey is saying that amount was charged against his inheritance by his guardians to defray the expenses of his sister's pursuit of him through the Lake Country.

11. De Quincey's accounts of this period in the two versions of the *Confessions* are inconsistent. In the original version (1821), he says he was houseless for the first two months in London; in the revised version (1856), he says he took lodgings for the first seven or eight weeks and then moved into Mr. Brunell's house (III, 353). The latter version

seems more plausible. Perhaps there was an interval of outdoor living between the two lodgings.

12. *Memorials,* I, 90–91.

13. It is not known how this reconciliation was effected.

14. In *Memorials,* I, 92, Japp says De Quincey did not go directly home from London but first went to Everton. However, Eaton (87) and De Quincey himself (III, 374) have him going to the Priory first.

15. *Diary,* p. 181; reproduced in Eaton, p. 91.

16. Reproduced in Eaton, pp. 95–96, and by John E. Jordan, in *De Quincey to Wordsworth: A Biography of a Relationship* (Berkeley, California, 1962), pp. 28–29.

17. Jordan, *De Quincey to Wordsworth,* pp. 40–41.

18. The most authoritative and up-to-date work on opium and its effects on writers, including De Quincey and Coleridge, is Elizabeth Schneider's *Coleridge, Opium and "Kubla Khan"* (Chicago, 1953), on which I draw extensively, here and below, in discussions of De Quincey and opium.

19. Dorothy Wordsworth to Lady Beaumont, December 6, 1807, *The Letters of William and Dorothy Wordsworth: The Middle Years,* ed. E. de Selincourt (Oxford, 1937), I, 159.

20. Jordan, *De Quincey to Wordsworth,* p. 53.

21. Curiously, De Quincey gave two different accounts of his first meeting with Wilson: the one mentioned here (V. 262–63), and another recorded by Emerson, as follows. Once when De Quincey was traveling in Wales and stopped at an inn, he learned that a gentleman lay there sick and sore with wounds, because he had prankishly paid attention to a country girl and had been waylaid and beaten by her lover and his friends. De Quincey sent up his card and made Wilson's acquaintance. *Journals of Ralph Waldo Emerson,* ed. E. W. Emerson and W. E. Forbes (Boston and New York, 1912), VII, 397.

22. *Henry Crabb Robinson on Books and Their Writers,* ed. E. J. Morley (London, 1938), I, 104.

23. C. H. Hendricks, "Thomas De Quincey, Symptomatologist," *Publications of the Modern Language Association,* LX (1945), 828–40.

24. W. C. B. Eatwell, "A Medical View of Mr. De Quincey's Case," in Japp, *Thomas De Quincey,* II. App. I.

25. George M. Gould, "De Quincey," *Biographic Clinics* (Philadelphia, 1903), I, 17–40. Both Gould and Eatwell overstate their cases.

26. These implications of the dreams in the *Confessions* are worked out in detail by Dr. Wilhelm Stekel, *Die Träume der Dichter* (Wiesbaden, 1912), pp. 236–44.

27. R. S. De Ropp, *Drugs and the Mind* (New York, 1961), p. 145.

28. J. Scott Duckers, "The De Quincey Family," *Times Literary Supplement*, CMLXXIX (Oct. 21, 1920), 684.

29. M. H. Abrams, *The Milk of Paradise* (Cambridge, Mass., 1934), p. 67 n., says it was about equal to a pint of whisky a day; but Jeannette Marks, *Genius and Disaster: Studies in Drugs and Genius* (New York, 1926), pp. 174–76, says a quart to a quart and a half. But the effects of opium and alcohol may tend to counteract each other, one being initially a stimulant and the other almost entirely a depressant. Schneider, p. 308 n.

30. *The Life and Letters of John Gibson Lockhart*, ed. A. Lang (London, 1898), I, 97–98.

31. *Robinson on Books*, I, 187.

32. See Jordan, *De Quincey to Wordsworth*, p. 319.

33. See John E. Wells, "Wordsworth and De Quincey in Westmorland Politics, 1818," *Publications of the Modern Language Association*, LV (1940), 1080–1128.

34. "The Incognito," *Knight's Quarterly Magazine*, V (July, 1824). Knight's attribution to De Quincey of the translation, and the note on the author, of Tieck's "The Love Charm," published by Knight in the single issue of his temporarily revived magazine in autumn, 1825, and reprinted by Masson (XII, 563–67), has been challenged by H. K. Galinsky in "Is Thomas De Quincey Author of 'The Love Charm'?" *Modern Language Notes*, LII (1937), 389–94.

35. See Kenneth Forward, "Libellous Attack on De Quincey," *Publications of the Modern Language Association*, LII (1937), 244–60.

36. *Passages of a Working Life*, quoted by Japp, *Thomas De Quincey*, I, 262.

37. Printed in Eaton, pp. 307–308.

38. An account of this connection appears in *New Essays by De Quincey*, ed. Stuart M. Tave (Princeton, New Jersey, 1966), pp. 3–22.

39. Wilson's daughter's account of this episode is reproduced in Eaton, pp. 324–25.

40. Thomas Carlyle, *Reminiscences*, ed. J. A. Froude (New York, 1881), p. 203.

41. De Quincey's legal difficulties in Edinburgh are described in detail by Kenneth Forward, in "De Quincey's *Cessio Bonorum*," *Publications of the Modern Language Association*, LIV (1939), 511–25, from which most of the information in this paragraph is drawn.

42. The date usually given—1835—has been corrected by C. O. Parsons, "The Woes of Thomas De Quincey," *Review of English Studies*, X (1934), 190–99.

43. *Journals of Emerson*, VII, 390 ff.

44. Printed by Japp, *Thomas De Quincey*, II, 295–301.

Chapter Two

1. De Quincey's classification is adopted by H. S. Salt, *De Quincey* (London, 1904).

2. See Sackville-West, p. 190.

3. Schneider, p. 77.

4. "De Quincey's Autobiography," *The Common Reader,* Second Series (London, 1959), pp. 132–39.

5. The most authoritative comparison of the two versions is that of Ian Jack, *Publications of the Modern Language Association,* LXXII (1957), 122–46.

6. Japp, *Thomas De Quincey,* II, 110.

7. In the latter paragraphs of the original "Introductory Notice" to *Suspiria,* not included in the revised version printed by Masson (XIII, 333–40).

8. *Ibid.*

Chapter Three

1. *Posthumous Works of Thomas De Quincey,* ed. A. H. Japp (London, 1891), I, 4–5. (Hereafter referred to as *PW.*)

2. *Ibid.,* I, 4–28.

3. *PW,* I, 16; see also pp. 26–28.

4. See Stekel, *loc. cit.*

5. (XIII, 369) By "the present Confessions" De Quincey means the *Suspiria,* not *The Confessions of an English Opium-Eater.*

6. George Saintsbury, *A History of English Prose Rhythm* (London 1912), p. 318.

7. This passage (XIII, 288) was much longer in the original version; Masson provides the original form in a note (XIII, 289–92). The comparison to ballet is Mario Praz's, *The Hero in Eclipse* (Oxford, 1956), p. 82.

8. The fugal structure is analyzed in detail by Calvin S. Brown, Jr., *The Musical Quarterly,* XXIV (1938), 341–50.

Chapter Four

1. Jordan counts over 200 allusions to Wordsworth in De Quincey's writings. *De Quincey to Wordsworth,* p. 357.

2. Japp, *Thomas De Quincey,* II, App. V.

3. Carlyle, *Reminiscences,* p. 518.

4. Japp, *Thomas De Quincey,* I, 301.

5. Albert Goldman, *The Mine and the Mint* (Carbondale and Edwardsville, Illinois, 1965), p. 33.

6. *Ibid.,* p. 35.

Chapter Five

1. John E. Jordan, *Thomas De Quincey, Literary Critic* (Berkeley, California, 1952), pp. 5–7 (source for the factual information throughout this paragraph).

2. Oliver Elton, "Thomas De Quincey," in *A Survey of English Literature, 1780–1830*, (London, 1912), II, 332.

3. George Saintsbury, *A History of Criticism and Literary Taste in Europe* (New York, 1904), p. 412.

4. René Wellek, "De Quincey's Status in the History of Ideas," *Philological Quarterly*, XXIII (1944), 268.

5. Wellek shows that De Quincey found precedents for most of the following views in English and German criticism. *Ibid.*, pp. 248–72.

6. *Robinson on Books*, I, 162.

7. Jordan, *De Quincey, Literary Critic*, p. 4.

8. *Robinson on Books*, I, 195.

9. René Wellek, *A History of Modern Criticism: 1750–1950* (New Haven, Conn., and London, 1965), III, 115.

10. A. H. Japp, "Some Unconscious Confessions of De Quincey," *Gentleman's Magazine*, CCLXI (1886), 128.

Chapter Six

1. (IX, 313–94); "Lessons of the French Revolution,—An Unpublished Paper," *The Independent*, LXXVII (January 15, 1914), 28–29.

2. In "Early Memorials of Grasmere," (XIII, 125–44).

3. Goldman, pp. 114–27.

4. *Ibid.*, pp. 127–40.

5. I.e., no source has yet been found, although there may well have been one. See *ibid.*, pp. 155–57.

6. Mrs. Margaret Wilson Oliphant, *Annals of a Publishing House: William Blackwood and His Sons* (Edinburgh and London, 1897), I, 419–21.

7. Brooks Wright, "The Cave of Trophonius: Myth and Reality in De Quincey," *Nineteenth-Century Fiction*, VIII (1953–54), 290–99.

Chapter Seven

1. Tave, ed., *New Essays*.

2. "Lessons of the French Revolution."

3. An interesting summary of De Quincey's political outlook has been made by Stuart M. Tave in *New Essays*, pp. 17–22.

4. The basic treatment of De Quincey's relation to Kant is in René Wellek's *Kant in England 1793–1838* (Princeton, 1931); it should be read in the light of Sigmund K. Proctor's treatment in *Thomas De*

Quincey's Theory of Literature (Ann Arbor, 1943), Chapt. II, and Wellek's rejoinder in *Philological Quarterly*, XIII (1944), 248–72.

5. "Kant on National Character, in Relation to the Sense of the Sublime and Beautiful," "Kant's Abstract of Swedenborgianism," "Kant on the Age of the Earth" (XIV, 46–93); "Idea of a Universal History on a Cosmopolitical Plan" (IX, 428–44); "German Studies and Kant in Particular" (II, 81–109); "The Last Days of Immanuel Kant" (IV, 323–79); "Kant in His Miscellaneous Essays" (VIII, 84–126); "On the English Notices of Kant" (X, 64–80); see also II, 155–56; X, 262 n.

6. *PW*, I, 216; and see also vol. II, ch. XIV.

Chapter Eight

1. Malcolm Elwin, *De Quincey* (London, 1935), p. 63.

2. A. S. Cook, "Native and Foreign Words in De Quincey," *Modern Language Notes*, I (February, 1886), 15–16.

3. Lane Cooper, *The Prose Poetry of Thomas De Quincey* (Leipzig, 1902), pp. 58–59.

4. William Minto, *A Manual of English Prose Literature* (Boston, 1889), p. 53.

5. M. B. Anderson, "The Style of De Quincey," *The Dial*, XII (August, 1891), 99–100.

6. From the last sentence of the original "Introductory Notice" to *Suspiria*, not in Masson.

7. H. M. Paull, "De Quincey and Style," *Fortnightly Review*, N.S., CXII (1922), 152–62.

8. Cooper, pp. 18, 77.

9. Saintsbury, *Prose Rhythm*, pp. 301–21.

10. Saintsbury (*ibid.*) scans selected passages from the *Suspiria* and elsewhere; Shozo Kobayashi, *Rhythm in the Prose of Thomas De Quincey* (Tokyo, 1956), scans the entire "Dream-Fugue" and classifies the feet and cadences, but his decisions often seem debatable, and his results inconclusive.

11. Cooper, p. 78.

12. Minto, pp. 55–58.

Chapter Nine

1. *The Works of Professor Wilson*, ed. Ferrier (Edinburgh and London, 1855), II, 398.

2. See Abrams, p. 22, and *"An Opium-Eater in America" and "The Fratricide's Death,"* ed. R. C. Bald (Aurora, New York, n.d.), p. 24.

3. *Memorials*, II, 210.

4. Charles E. Terry and Mildred Pellens, *The Opium Problem* (New York, 1925), pp. 59–60, 94.

5. *E.g.*, Marks, *Genius and Disaster*, pp. 28, 169.

6. Schneider, p. 72.

7. See "V.R.," "De Quincey: Some Objections and Corrections," *Notes and Queries*, CLXXVI (1939), 417–18; CLXXVII (1939), 3–6, 42–45, 189–91; CLXXIX (1940), 204–207, 417–20, 434–36; Wellek's "De Quincey's Status in the History of Ideas" and *A History of Modern Criticism*, III, 110–20; Jordan's *Thomas De Quincey, Literary Critic;* and Goldman's *The Mine and the Mint*, p. 159 & *passim*.

8. "De Quincey and Coleridge upon Kant," *Jerrold, Tennyson and Macaulay with Other Critical Essays* (Edinburgh, 1868), pp. 172–88.

9. *Hours in a Library* (London and New York, 1874), I, 322–65; and *Dictionary of National Biography* (1888), XIV, 385–91.

10. Japp, *Thomas De Quincey*, II, 146–47.

11. A strong statement of the influence of De Quincey on Balzac and Gautier may be found in Randolph Hughes' "Vers la Contrée du Rêve: Balzac, Gautier, et Baudelaire, Disciples de Quincey [*sic*]," *Mercure de France*, CCXCIII (August 1, 1939), 545–93.

12. The principal works tracing De Quincey's influence on French literature are described by John E. Jordan, in *The English Romantic Poets and Essayists*, ed. C. W. Houtchens and L. H. Houtchens (New York, 1957), pp. 344–46.

13. G. T. Clapton, *Baudelaire et De Quincey* (Paris, 1931).

14. See Praz, pp. 75–86.

Selected Bibliography

PRIMARY SOURCES

Eaton, H. A., ed. *A Diary of Thomas De Quincey: 1803*. London: Noel Douglas, 1927. An interesting diary and notebook De Quincey kept for a few months just after his escapade in Wales and London.

Hogg, James, ed. *The Uncollected Writings of Thomas De Quincey*. London: James Hogg, 1890. 2 vols. Contains a few works not included in Masson.

Japp, A. H., ed. *The Posthumous Works of Thomas De Quincey*. London: William Heinemann, 1891. 2 vols. Contains a few essays and many interesting fragments drawn from MSS., and not included in Masson.

Masson, David, ed. *The Collected Writings of Thomas De Quincey*. London: A. & C. Black, 1889–90. 14 vols. The standard edition, several times reprinted. Contains much information about De Quincey and his works. Appendices list his principal publications chronologically, the contents of two other collected editions, and the principal works omitted in this edition.

Tave, Stuart M., ed. *New Essays by De Quincey*. Princeton, New Jersey: Princeton University Press, 1966. Contains a selection of De Quincey's principal contributions to two Edinburgh newspapers in 1827–28. The most considerable sampling of De Quincey's hitherto uncollected political writings.

SECONDARY SOURCES

Abrams, Meyer H. *The Milk of Paradise*. Cambridge, Mass.: Harvard University Press, 1934. Includes a study of De Quincey and opium.

Axon, W. E. A. "The Canon of De Quincey's Writings," *Transactions of the Royal Society of Literature*, Second Series, XXXII, Part I (1913), pp. 1–44. Supplements Green's bibliography.

Bonner, William H. *De Quincey at Work: As Seen in One Hundred and Thirty New and Newly Edited Letters.* Buffalo, New York: Airport Publishers, 1936. Collection of letters of De Quincey and his family, mostly from 1851 to 1860.

Chew, Samuel C. *A Literary History of England.* Ed. A. C. Baugh. New York: Appleton-Century-Crofts, 1948. Sound general appraisal.

Clapton, G. T. *Baudelaire et De Quincey.* Paris: Société d'Édition "Les Belles Lettres," 1931. Study of the influence of De Quincey on Baudelaire.

Cooper, Lane. *The Prose Poetry of Thomas De Quincey.* Leipzig, dissertation, 1902. A treatment of the classification of De Quincey's works, the relation of opium to his writing, and the stylistic characteristics of the "impassioned prose," the last a little over-restrictive and arbitrary.

Dowden, E. "How De Quincey Worked," *Saturday Review,* LXXIX (1895), 246–48. Close study of the revisions of "The English Mail-Coach."

Eaton, Horace A. *Thomas De Quincey: A Biography.* New York: Oxford University Press, 1936. The fullest biography in terms of factual material. Contains many letters and documents. Unfortunately not very reliable on dates.

Elton, Oliver. "Thomas De Quincey," in *A Survey of English Literature: 1780–1830.* London: Edward Arnold, 1912. Vol. II, pp. 312–33. Excellent critical appraisal; finds key to style of "impassioned prose" in verbal balance.

Elwin, Malcolm. *De Quincey.* London: Duckworth, 1935. Good brief biographical summary, but presses dogmatically the view that De Quincey consciously cultivated a dual personality.

Goldman, Albert. *The Mine and the Mint.* Carbondale and Edwardsville, Illinois: Southern Illinois University Press, 1965. Fullest treatment of the relation of De Quincey's writings to their sources, showing him to be more the journalist than the "polyhistor." Works mainly from De Quincey's own hints.

Green, J. A. "Notes on the Portraits of Thomas De Quincey," *Manchester Quarterly,* XXXII (1913), 177–84. Chronological description of the principal surviving likenesses of De Quincey.

———. *Thomas De Quincey: A Bibliography Based upon the De Quincey Collection in the Moss Side Library.* Manchester Public Free Libraries, 1908. A descriptive list of 796 De Quincey items, including magazine articles, books, collected editions, manuscripts, selected editions, biography and criticism, scrap books, and portraits. Supplemented by W. E. A. Axon, listed above.

Hogg, James, ed. *De Quincey and His Friends.* London: Sampson

Low, Marston and Co., 1895. Contains contemporary records of
De Quincey by Colin Rae-Brown, Richard F. Cotton, W. C. B.
Eatwell, J. R. Findlay, James Hogg, Francis Jacox, Richard
Woodhouse, and others. Convenient, but not wholly trustworthy.

Hughes, Randolph. "Vers la Contrée du Rêve: Balzac, Gautier, et
Baudelaire, Disciples de Quincey [sic]," *Mercure de France,*
CCXCIII (August 1, 1939), 545–93. Strong statement of the
case for De Quincey's influence on French literature.

"Impassioned Prose," *Times Literary Supplement* (September 16,
1926), 601–602. Best brief treatment of De Quincey's style in his
prose poetry.

Jack, Ian. "De Quincey Revises His Confessions," *Publications of the
Modern Language Association,* LXXII (1957), 122–46. Detailed
comparison of the 1822 and 1856 editions.

Japp, A. H. (H. A. Page, pseud.). *Thomas De Quincey: His Life and
Writings.* London: J. Hogg & Co., 1877. 2 vols. The "official" biography, untrustworthy and badly organized; contains much interesting and valuable information.

———, ed. *De Quincey Memorials.* London: William Heinemann,
1891. 2 vols. Collection of letters to De Quincey from family and
friends, letters and notes from De Quincey to others, and other
documents of and information about the De Quinceys' circle. Important but not wholly trustworthy.

———. "Some Unconscious Confessions of De Quincey," *Gentleman's
Magazine,* CCLXI (1886), 117–35. Interesting extracts from unpublished manuscripts, with some observations on De Quincey's
procedures.

Jordan, John E. "Thomas De Quincey," in *The English Romantic Poets
and Essayists: A Review of Research and Criticism,* ed. C. W.
Houtchens and L. H. Houtchens. New York: Modern Language
Association, 1957. pp. 299–347. Very extensive critical biblio-
graphical survey, full of useful information and balanced judgments, covering all major items up to date of publication. The
most valuable single tool for study of De Quincey.

———. *Thomas De Quincey, Literary Critic: His Method and
Achievement.* Berkeley: University of California Press, 1952. Systematic and exhaustive examination and appraisal of De Quincey's practical criticism. Appendix lists *loci critici.*

———. *De Quincey to Wordsworth: A Biography of a Relationship,
with the Letters of Thomas De Quincey to the Wordsworth Family.* Berkeley and Los Angeles: University of California Press,
1962. Thorough treatment of the relationship between the two
writers, with sixty letters of De Quincey to Wordsworth and his
family.

Kobayashi, Shozo. *Rhythm in the Prose of Thomas De Quincey.* Tokyo: Dainippon Printing Co., 1956. Consists mainly of a compilation of quotations from works on English prose rhythm and on rhythm in De Quincey, followed by a detailed, elaborate scansion of the third section of "The English Mail-Coach" that is of dubious accuracy and utility. Reaches no significant conclusions.

Landreth, P. "Emerson's Meeting with De Quincey," *Blackwood's Edinburgh Magazine,* CLV (1894), 480–91.

Lee, Vernon. "Studies in Literary Psychology: I. The Syntax of De Quincey," *Contemporary Review,* LXXXIV (1903), 713–23. Analysis and largely unfavorable judgment of De Quincey's style, tracing some of its characteristics to psychological sources.

Masson, David. *De Quincey.* English Men of Letters. New York and London: Harper & Brothers, 1901. Based on Japp's *Thomas De Quincey,* but more orderly and concise.

Metcalf, John C. *De Quincey: A Portrait.* Cambridge, Mass.: Harvard University Press, 1940. Enjoyable and valuable general, appreciative biographical introduction. No notes.

Minto, William. "Thomas De Quincey." *A Manual of English Prose Literature.* Boston: Ginn & Co., 1889. Excellent, and still the most complete, analysis of De Quincey's style. Needs some correction in the light of later work.

Musgrove, Sydney, ed. *Unpublished Letters of Thomas De Quincey and Elizabeth Barrett Browning.* Auckland, N. Z.: Auckland University College Bulletin No. 44, 1954. From originals in the Auckland Public Library.

O'Rourke, Ann Agnes. "A Critical Survey of Recent Writings about Thomas De Quincey." Unpublished M.A. thesis, University of Illinois, 1945. An extensive survey of De Quincey's reputation, and of scholarly and biographical studies of De Quincey, especially 1930–1945.

Page, H. A. (See Japp, A. H.)

Patterson, C. I., Jr. "The Romantic Critics' Conception of the Novel: Hazlitt, Coleridge, and De Quincey." Micro-filmed dissertation, University of Illinois, 1950. Shows De Quincey's view of the novel to be more complex and respectful than it was previously considered.

Pollitt, Charles. *De Quincey's Editorship of the Westermorland Gazette.* Kendal: Atkinson & Pollitt, 1890. Contains samples of De Quincey's contributions.

Poulet, Georges. "Timelessness and Romanticism," *Journal of the History of Ideas,* XV (1954), 3–22. Romantic apprehension of a human timelessness, as illustrated in De Quincey, Baudelaire, and others.

Powell, A. E. (Mrs. E. R. Dodd). "De Quincey." *The Romantic Theory of Poetry*. New York: Longmans, Green and Co., 1926. Perceptive and valuable study of De Quincey, though it overstresses his expressionism.

Praz, Mario. *The Hero in Eclipse in Victorian Fiction*. Trans., Angus Davidson. London: Oxford University Press, 1956. Treats De Quincey as a transitional figure between Romanticism and the Victorian Age.

Proctor, Sigmund K. *Thomas De Quincey's Theory of Literature*. Ann Arbor: University of Michigan Press, 1943. Studies De Quincey's relation to the history of philosophy and critical theory. Valuable, but needs correction in the light of Wellek's "De Quincey's Status in the History of Ideas," and Jordan's *Thomas De Quincey, Literary Critic*, qq.v.

["R"] "V. R." "De Quincey: Some Objections and Corrections," *Notes and Queries*, CLXXVI (1939), 417–18; CLXXVII (1939), 3–6, 42–45, 189–91; CLXXIX (1940), 204–207, 417–20, 434–36. Critical attack on De Quincey, stressing particularly his factual inaccuracy.

Robinson, Henry Crabb. *Henry Crabb Robinson on Books and Their Writers*. Ed. Edith J. Morley. London: J. M. Dent & Sons, Ltd., 1938. 3 vols. Contains many interesting comments on De Quincey, some written originally in cipher, based on observation and on remarks of Wordsworth and others.

Sackville-West, Edward. *Thomas De Quincey: His Life and Work*. New Haven, Conn.: Yale University Press, 1936. Best critical biography, although the author overemphasizes a few highly speculative solutions to biographical problems.

Saintsbury, George. *A History of Criticism and Literary Taste in Europe*. New York: Dodd, Mead, & Co., 1904. Vol. III. Early and fairly well-balanced judgment of De Quincey as a critic.

————. *A History of English Prose Rhythm*. London: Macmillan & Co., 1912. Restricts De Quincey's rhythmic prose to a small percentage of his work, and finds its governing principle in variety and in avoidance of poetic metrification.

Salt, Henry S. *De Quincey*. London: G. Bell & Sons, 1904. Critical survey of the works, following De Quincey's own classification. Stresses the dreamer and mystic; valuable though superficial.

Schneider, Elisabeth. *Coleridge, Opium and "Kubla Khan."* Chicago, Illinois: University of Chicago Press, 1953. Best study of the relation of opium to the works and reputation of Coleridge and De Quincey.

Sehrt, E. T. *Geschichtliches und religiöses Denken bei Thomas De Quincey*. Berlin: Neue Deutsche Forschungen, Bd. 103, 1936.

Contains the best assessment of De Quincey's historical thought.

Stekel, Wilhelm. *Die Träume der Dichter*. Wiesbaden: J. F. Bergmann, 1912. Contains a psychoanalytic interpretation of some of De Quincey's dream visions in the light of his autobiography.

Stephen, Leslie. "De Quincey." *Hours in a Library*. New York: Scribner, Armstrong & Co., 1875. Unsympathetic criticism, which makes some sound points, and has been very influential.

Wellek, René. "De Quincey's Status in the History of Ideas," *Philological Quarterly*, XXIII (1944), 248–72. (Reprinted in *Confrontations* [Princeton, N. J.: Princeton University Press, 1965], pp. 114–52.) Soundest, most authoritative evaluation of De Quincey as a philosopher and critical theorist.

————. *A History of Modern Criticism: 1750–1950*. New Haven, Conn. and London: Yale University Press, 1965. Vol. III. An unsparing estimate of De Quincey as a critic.

————. *Immanuel Kant in England 1793–1838*. Princeton, N. J.: Princeton University Press, 1931. Careful evaluation of De Quincey's treatment of Kant.

Wells, John E. "Wordsworth and De Quincey in Westmorland Politics, 1818," *Publications of the Modern Language Association*, LV (1940), 1080–1128. Contains De Quincey's "Close Comments upon a Straggling Speech," his first independent published work.

Woolf, Virginia. "De Quincey's Autobiography." *The Common Reader*. Second Series. London: The Hogarth Press, 1959. Best evaluation of De Quincey as an autobiographer.

Index

73992

828.7
L991

DATE DUE

GAYLORD			PRINTED IN U.S.A.